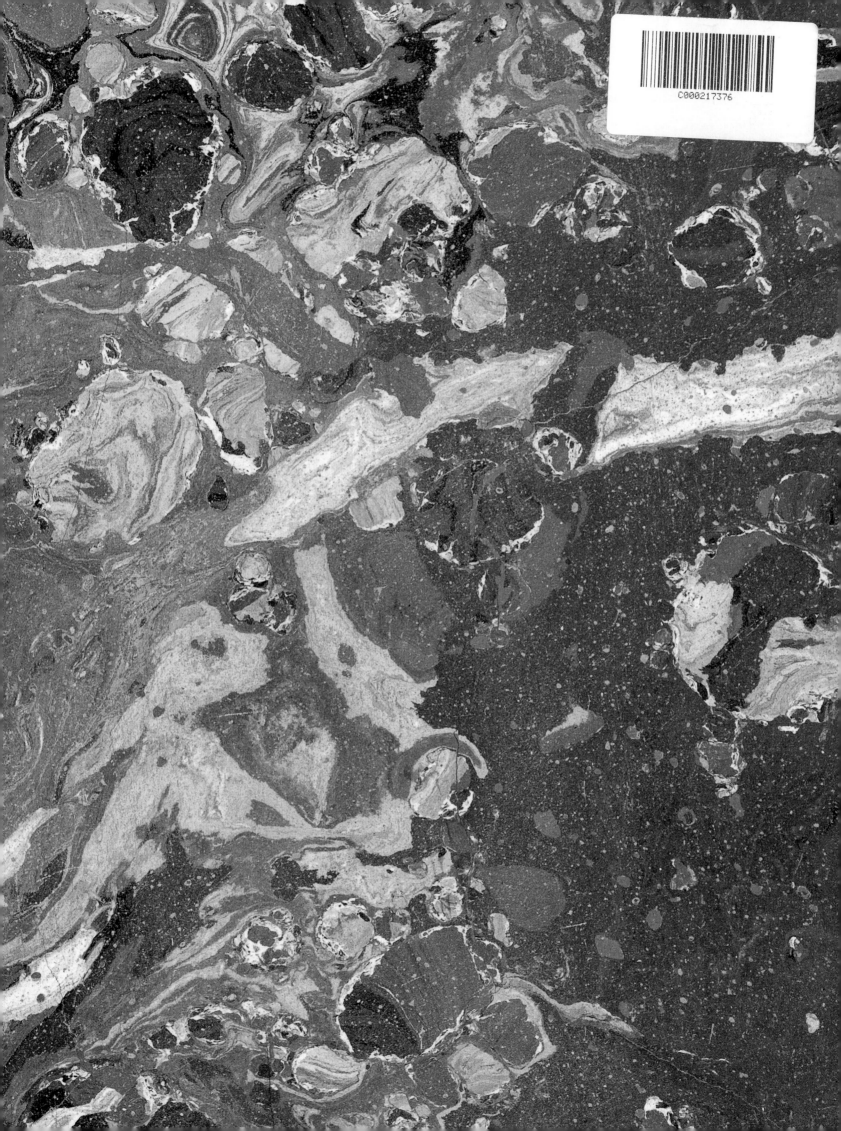

TREASURES OF THE
HABSBURGS

TREASURES OF THE
HABSBURGS

The Kunstkammer at the Kunsthistorisches Museum, Vienna

Edited by Sabine Haag and Franz Kirchweger

With contributions by Franz Kirchweger,
Claudia Kryza-Gersch, Paulus Rainer, Konrad Schlegel
and Katja Schmitz-von Ledebur

With more than 300 colour illustrations

 Thames & Hudson

Illustration captions:

page 1 View of Room XXVII of the Kunstkammer (Kunsthistorisches Museum, upper floor), with ceiling painting showing the coats of arms of the ancient Austrian Hereditary Lands, as well as the Kingdoms of Bohemia and Hungary. Karl Krahl (design) and Franz Schönbrunner (execution), 1888.

page 4 Collection of objects from the Kunstkammer, including the celestial globe of 1584 (p. 216).

page 8 Collection of objects from the Natural History Museum and Kunstkammer, including a bezoar in a gold mount (p. 165).

pages 10–11 *Patrons of the Arts in the House of Habsburg*, ceiling painting in Room XIX (Golden Room) of the Kunsthistorisches Museum, detail: Emperor Maximilian I, Emperor Charles V and Archduke Ferdinand II. Julius Victor Berger, 1890/91.

pages 50–51 Collection of ornamental goblets. Friedrich Hillebrand, Nuremberg, *c.* 1595/1600. Kunsthistorisches Museum, Kunstkammer, inv. nos. KK 1058, KK 1065, KK 1071, KK 1072, KK 1075, KK 1078, KK 1086, KK 1090, KK 1131, KK 1136.

Editors:
Dr Sabine Haag
General Director, Director of the Collection of Sculpture and Decorative Arts /
Secular and Ecclesiastical Treasury of the Kunsthistorisches Museum, Vienna

Dr Franz Kirchweger, Curator of the Collection of Sculpture and Decorative Arts /
Secular and Ecclesiastical Treasury

Object descriptions:
Franz Kirchweger (FKi), Claudia Kryza-Gersch (CKG), Paulus Rainer (PR),
Konrad Schlegel (KS), Katja Schmitz-von Ledebur (KSvL)

Translations from German:
John Winbigler and Douglas Deitemyer

Proofreading:
Elisabeth Herrmann

Graphic design:
Alexander Rendi, assisted by Eugen Lejeune

Art direction KHM:
Stefan Zeisler

Photo credits:
Unless otherwise specified © Kunsthistorisches Museum
Director of photography: Stefan Zeisler
Photographs: Christian Mendez
Photo processing: Michael Eder, Thomas Ritter

This edition first published in the United Kingdom in 2013 by
Thames & Hudson Ltd, 181A High Holborn, London WC1V 7QX

Original edition © 2012 Kunsthistorisches Museum, Vienna,
and Christian Brandstätter Verlag, Vienna
This edition © 2013 Thames & Hudson Ltd, London

British Library Cataloguing-in-Publication Data
A catalogue record for this book is available from the British Library

ISBN 978-0-500-51680-5

Printed in Austria

To find out about all our publications, please visit **www.thamesandhudson.com**. There you can subscribe to our e-newsletter, browse or download our current catalogue, and buy any titles that are in print.

Contents

Preface

The magnificent holdings of Vienna's Kunstkammer, also known as the Collection of Sculpture and Decorative Arts, make it one of the most important collections of its kind in the world. Today its richness and diversity can still in large part be traced back to the treasuries and art cabinets of the late Middle Ages, the Renaissance and the Baroque, which were assembled and passed on by several prominent collectors from the House of Habsburg. The power of this family, which was one of the most politically influential dynasties in Europe with far-reaching contacts and profound financial resources, was also reflected in the artistic quality and diversity of the collected objects. This aspiration continues to shape the extraordinary quality of the Kunstkammer's holdings even today.

The manifold objects from various Habsburg art collections of the 16th and 17th centuries, in which spectacular products of nature were presented on equal footing with extraordinary testimonies to human creativity, were distributed among the newly founded specialized imperial collections over the course of the 18th and 19th centuries; unfortunately, a number of objects were also irretrievably lost in the process. Visitors to the Vienna Kunstkammer, housed in a 19th-century museum building, will search in vain for what over the centuries became the symbolic epitome of a *Kunst- und Wunderkammer* or cabinet of curiosities: stuffed animals hanging from the ceiling and display cases packed full of exotic objects and bizarre oddities. What the Kunstkammer does offer, however, is a rich abundance of unparalleled examples of the goldsmith's and gemcutter's art, a wealth of magnificent bronze statuettes, objects of ivory, wood and amber, as well as mechanical masterpieces that owe their very creation solely to the principle and the spirit of the princely cabinet of arts and marvels.

The outward appearance of these objects – which in many cases was influenced by the particular interests, tastes and demands of the individual collectors, such as Archduke Ferdinand II (1529–95) and Emperor Rudolf II (1552–1612) – makes special demands on the viewer, as the materials the objects are made from and the artistic techniques used in their execution are often no longer familiar to us or even deemed worthy of appreciation. The presentation of the exhibits and the accompanying commentaries in Vienna's redesigned Kunstkammer are aimed at helping visitors better explore and grasp the complex and fascinating world of the historical *Kunstkammer* of the Habsburg princes. This book, featuring lavish full views and close-up images of the objects as well as descriptions of around a hundred and fifty of the collection's masterpieces, is part of the endeavour by everyone involved in this major project to make the Kunstkammer's holdings as accessible as possible to the general public.

The editors would like to express their gratitude to the many colleagues who have made this publication possible. Special thanks are due to the curators of the Kunstkammer: at a time in which the reorganization of the collection confronted them with even more challenges than usual, they did a masterful job of distilling their wealth of knowledge about the objects into the concise form of the descriptions the reader will find here. A large measure of the credit for the design of this volume is due to the great commitment of the Kunsthistorisches Museum's art director, Stefan Zeisler. Dr Elisabeth Herrmann also demonstrated untiring dedication in her exemplary editing and proofreading of the texts.

Not least, everyone involved in this endeavour would like to thank Christian Brandstätter Verlag for its cooperation in this project. We hope it finds a place on the bookshelves of a large number of art enthusiasts who – like us – are able to let themselves be delighted, moved and inspired by the countless magnificent facets of the masterpieces of Vienna's Kunstkammer presented here.

Dr Sabine Haag
General Director of the Vienna Kunstkammer/
Secular and Ecclesiastical Treasury

Dr Franz Kirchweger
Curator of the Vienna Kunstkammer/
Secular and Ecclesiastical Treasury

The Treasures of the House of Habsburg and the Kunstkammer:
The History and the Holdings

Franz Kirchweger

The Kunsthistorisches Museum and Kunstkammer: Museum Collecting in the 19th and 20th Centuries

In May 1890 Julius Victor Berger, a professor at the Vienna Academy of Fine Arts, received a commission for a ceiling painting in the largest exhibition room on the upper ground floor of Vienna's newly erected Kunsthistorisches Hofmuseum, the Imperial and Royal Court Museum of Art History. The commission provided very specific guidelines regarding design and content: 'This ceiling painting must be a historical representation of the most outstanding patrons and friends of art from the Austrian ruling family, namely, Emperor Maximilian I, Emperor Charles V, Archduke Ferdinand of Tyrol, Emperor Rudolf II, the Archdukes Albert VII and Leopold William and Emperor Charles VI. Each portrait...is to be accompanied by one or more secondary and explanatory figures – artists and scholars – to represent the period in which the ruler lived; the background may feature individual artworks, perhaps buildings, characteristic of the period.' Berger adhered closely to this description (pp. 10–11). Many of the artists portrayed alongside the rulers are depicted bearing and presenting artworks from the holdings of the imperial collections that were exhibited from 1891 on the museum's upper ground floor, some of them in the room where the ceiling painting itself was located, known as the Golden Room [2]. It was filled with large glass cabinets, both freestanding and wall-mounted, containing vessels and art objects of gold, silver and precious stones, such as rock crystal, jasper, agate and lapis lazuli. The *Saliera* (p. 124), the golden salt cellar that Benvenuto Cellini had created between 1540 and 1543 for King Francis I of France, was the only object to be placed on a stand of its own, which was designed by Karl von Hasenauer, the architect responsible for the interior design of the building. The *Saliera*

1 *Patrons of the Arts in the House of Habsburg.* Ceiling painting in Room XIX (Golden Room) of the Kunsthistorisches Museum, detail: Benvenuto Cellini with the *Saliera*. Julius Victor Berger, 1890/91.

can also be seen in the ceiling painting: Cellini himself is shown holding it on his lap [1]. The Florentine goldsmith and sculptor is depicted in the group around Emperor Charles V, although the emperor never actually commissioned anything from the artist.

Cellini's salt cellar, at that time already one of the most famous and valuable objects in the museum, was the focus of the exhibition that was known as the 'Collection of Art-Industrial Objects of the Middle Ages and Modern Times'. The ceiling painting in the Golden Room emphatically illustrated the link between this collection and the various historical collectors of the House of Habsburg.

In the decades before and during the construction of the Kunsthistorisches Museum, the holdings of the imperial family were examined in search of potential objects for the new collection, including those in the Treasury, in

Franzensburg Castle at Laxenburg and in the Coin and Antiquities Cabinet as well as the Ambras Castle collection, which had been brought to Vienna in 1806. Many of the objects selected for display in the rooms of the museum when it opened in 1891 were thus given a common context for the first time.

Decisions about organizing the objects displayed in the nine rooms on the upper ground floor were made primarily on the basis of medium and technique, although all of the medieval artworks were displayed in a single room. Clocks, automata and scientific instruments were displayed in one of the smaller rooms, as was ornamental furniture. Works in gold and precious stones, objects in glass, enamel and clay, pieces carved from ivory, horn, amber and wood as well as small- and large-format sculptures of marble and bronze were the respective focuses of the other rooms.

Following the expulsion of the House of Habsburg-Lorraine from Austria in 1919, the newly founded republic took possession of the former imperial art collections. Understandably, the new political age rejected the original agenda of the Kunsthistorisches Museum, which had brought together the 'private collections' of the imperial family to create a monument to the patronage of the dynasty. Demands were heard for a radical reorganization of the museum's holdings with no regard to historical

development and structure. Economic hardship prevented these ideas from being fulfilled, but the end of the Austrian monarchy brought about numerous changes nonetheless.

The Collection of Art-Industrial Objects was not only renamed the Collection of Sculpture and Decorative Arts but also increased considerably in size. In 1921 the tapestry collection, consisting of some 900 large-scale wall hangings that were formerly used to decorate the various Habsburg residences, was incorporated into the wider collection. The holdings of the Treasury, which until the end of the monarchy had been separately administered, were also added to the collections, but those objects remained in their original rooms in the Hofburg Palace. Extensive additions were made to the holdings of Italian sculpture of the Middle Ages and Renaissance when those sections of the Este Art Collection were brought to Vienna after they were inherited by the heir to the imperial throne, Archduke Francis Ferdinand of the House of Austria-Este.

The Collection of Arms and Armour was also displayed on the upper ground floor until 1934, when it was moved to the Neue Burg. The vacated rooms were then occupied by the Collection of Sculpture and Decorative Arts, which opened a year later with an exhibition that included newly acquired objects displayed in twenty rooms. For the first time, the holdings were organized according to artistic and historical eras as well as according to the collectors

2 'The Collection of Art-Industrial Objects of the Middle Ages and Modern Times'. Room XIX (Golden Room) with the original display of 1891: view of a glass cabinet and Benvenuto Cellini's *Saliera*.

3 The Collections of Sculpture and Decorative Arts, redisplay of 1935, Room XIII, 'Charles V and the Italian High and Late Renaissance': view with Cellini's *Saliera* in the foreground and tapestries.

of the House of Habsburg and their respective eras and collections [3]. In the period between the two world wars, the museum curators used a strategy of purchase, sale and exchange to acquire cultural assets that might otherwise have been sold abroad, such as the Wilten Chalice (p. 56), and to expand and complete the holdings of the collection in general.

As early as 1920–21, plans were proposed to divide the Collection of Sculpture and Decorative Arts into a *Kunstkammer* and a sculpture collection under separate names. Numerous objects of porcelain, fired clay and glass subsequently entered the collections of the Austrian Museum of Applied Arts, despite their provenance in the collections of Rudolf II in Prague. Manuscripts, some of which had come from Ambras Castle, were moved to the Austrian National Library in 1936. Conversely, many sculptures were added to the collection, but most of these were moved to the Austrian Gallery in 1952–53. During this period, as was previously the case in 1936, the Collection of Sculpture and Decorative Arts sent various objects from its holdings for permanent display by the Kunsthistorisches Museum at Ambras Castle near Innsbruck. Other works were moved back to Ambras from Vienna in 1977 when a *Kunstkammer* was set up in the historical 16th-century style.

The various venues where the prospective objects for the Kunsthistorisches Museum's new Collection of Art-Industrial Objects were held in the second half of the 19th century had themselves been the result of reorganization and rearranging that had permanently changed the structures of the Habsburg collections from the 16th and 17th centuries. Since the early 18th century, the historical holdings, including natural or ethnographic objects, paintings and antiques, coins and medals, prints and books, had been kept and displayed together as a matter of course but increasingly had been separated and reassembled as individual groups in special cabinets. From there, they were taken in the second half of the 19th century to the various collections of the two new court museums (natural history and art history, respectively). These two buildings thus represented a logical conclusion to the separation of two areas – nature and art – whose juxtaposition, togetherness and entwinement had been so important to the concept of the historical *Kunstkammer* of the early modern age. Since that time, the immense diversity and range of the holdings of the former Habsburg collections has existed only as the sum of individually preserved parts, now scattered across the collections of the various museums.

That situation applies in particular to the holdings from the Collection of Art-Industrial Objects and the Collection of Sculpture and Decorative Arts, which in 1990 were given the new German name 'Kunstkammer' (the Collection of Sculpture and Decorative Arts became the English name for both collections). *Kunstkammer* was a name general used historically for art collections of the early modern age, including those of the Habsburg dynasty. As a result of the developments described here, the collection today cannot convey the complex meaning of a historical *Kunstkammer*, neither in a general sense nor from a specifically Habsburg point of view. Key groups of objects, however, mostly handed down from collectors and patrons of the House of Habsburg – such as the small bronzes, statuettes and lathe-turned works in ivory, vessels and cameos cut from precious stones – still lend the collection a character that is completely in keeping with important elements of the historical collections that preceded it. It is no accident that the programmatic ceiling painting in the Golden Room has a key role to play in providing a fitting context for these holdings.

From the family treasure of the Middle Ages to the imperial collections of the 19th century

There is documentary evidence dating from the mid-16th century for the presence of a collection called a *Kunstkammer* in Vienna. In 1554 Leopold Heyperger, the chamberlain of Ferdinand I (1503–64), recorded the receipt of various objects that had been brought to Vienna from Graz and placed in the 'Kunsst Camer'. In 1537 Ferdinand I had issued an instruction to the officials at court that expressly mentioned, along with items of material value, 'antiques, instruments and artworks' as a group and also cited artistic worth as a criterion for assessing value. This point of view marks a turning point in art history and the beginning of the Vienna Kunstkammer.

The Habsburg treasures before 1530

The first treasures of the House of Habsburg had of course been collected long before Ferdinand issued his instruction. By the time of Ferdinand I, the House of Habsburg had been ruling the Austrian hereditary lands for more than 250 years. From the beginning, the dynasty had sought to assemble all the things it needed in connection with its rule: material and symbolic treasures, insignia and jewelry, ornamental dishes and textiles, coins and other forms of precious metal as well as relics and documents. From the time of Duke Albert II (1298–1358), such holdings are documented as having been in Vienna's Hofburg Palace, and there is also evidence of efforts to assemble a 'house treasury'. The first concrete evidence that jewelry

Den grösten schatz hat er allein
Von silber gold vnnd edel stein
Von perlein gut auch köstlich gwat
Als nie keinm fürsten ward bekannt
Dauon zu gotes dienst vnnd eer
Vil geben hat vnd gibt noch mer

4 'Vault with Items from the Treasury of Emperor Maximilian I', from *The Triumphal Arch of Emperor Maximilian I*. Albrecht Altdorfer, *c.* 1515. Woodcut.

and silver dishes were kept in the sacristy of the Court Chapel dates from the year 1407.

In the second half of the 15th century, as a result of territorial partitioning between the various Habsburg lines, the Hofburg Palace lost its significance as a repository of Habsburg treasures. With great skill and persistence, Emperor Frederick III (1415–93) pursued his goal of reuniting in his own collection as many as possible of the precious items that had previously been divided among the different family lines. At his death, the extensive treasures were housed in Linz, Graz and Nuremberg, among other places. He must have been very reluctant to share this information with his family because his son Maximilian I (1459–1519) attempted with the help of a cleric to pry the locations of the secret treasures from his father during the latter's deathbed confession.

Maximilian I followed his father's example in keeping his treasures in various secret locations. On Maximilian's death in 1519, his heirs, Charles V (1500–58) and the latter's brother Ferdinand I, also had to comb the residences in Innsbruck, Graz, Vienna and Wiener Neustadt to determine the exact locations of his treasures.

Part of the *Triumphal Arch*, one of the great commemorative works commissioned by Maximilian I, includes a depiction of his treasury [4]. Treasure rooms with heavy vaulting, thick walls and barred windows, such as the one seen in this woodcut, existed in various places. Contrary to the depiction of the woodcut, however, the emperor's treasures were not strewn about on tables; generally they were kept in closed or even sealed chests that provided additional security and made it possible to remove them quickly in times of crisis.

Inventories and other sources that could tell us more about the Habsburg treasures of the 14th and 15th centuries have survived only in isolated instances. There is clear evidence, however, for the existence of both a secular and an ecclesiastical treasury. While the former contained insignia, jewelry, precious stones, ornamental dishes, coins and ceremonial garments, the latter held liturgical implements, devotional images, reliquaries and paraments. In the second half of the 15th century, the holdings were expanded, not only in quantity but also as regards the types of objects represented, indicating that the primary goal was no longer ostentation or amassing treasure as a reserve that could quickly be turned to money. In addition to the usual items, the treasury inventories began to list scientific instruments, coins, pagan weaponry and natural objects of an exotic or magical character, such as ostrich eggs, 'tongue stones' (see p. 72), 'toadstones' and coral.

In the course of dividing up Maximilian's estate among his heirs and the subsequent melting down of the precious metals and adaptation and reuse of objects in a different form, the Habsburg 'medieval family treasure' was almost entirely lost. The oldest extant piece still in the Vienna collection that can clearly be dated to that source is a sapphire ring from around 1400. Several objects can be traced back to the ownership of Emperor Frederick III because they are marked with his famous mystical monogram 'AEIOU'. These include an ornamental vase with lavish enamel decoration (p. 75).

At the death of Maximilian I, his castle in Wiener Neustadt alone housed forty chests of treasure. None of their incredibly rich and abundant content has been preserved, or at least cannot be identified as such today. It is likely that the magnificent goblet with his coat of arms inside the lid (p. 82) was part of that hoard, but there is no definite proof.

Written records referring to such objects as ostrich eggs and coral indicate the presence of new categories of holdings in the treasuries of the 15th century, and these were subsequently to become increasingly important. Taking the artistic sense and interests of King Charles V of France (1337–80) and his brother John, Duke of Berry

5 *Archduchess Margaret of Austria as a Widow.*
Netherlandish, after 1506. Oil on wood. Vienna,
Kunsthistorisches Museum, Picture Gallery,
inv. no. GG 5615.

(1340–1416) as a model, 15th-century collectors – especially at Italian courts such as that of the Medici family in Florence but also in Mantua, Ferrara and Rome – became interested in collecting a wide range of objects that were considered precious not only from a material but also from a conceptual point of view. That principle was reflected in encyclopaedic collections as understood in the early modern age, although it did not yet apply to the treasures amassed and shut away in closed treasuries by the emperors Frederick III and Maximilian I. It was Margaret of Austria (1480–1530) [5], the daughter of Maximilian I and Mary of Burgundy, who first provided the connection with the ideas emerging from France and Italy that foresaw the acquisition of precious objects less as a means of material security and superficial ostentation than for their potential to provide insight, edification and artistic enjoyment in the special rooms in which they were displayed.

Following the premature death of her brother Philip the Handsome, whose marriage to Joanna of Castile had initiated the rule of the Habsburgs in Spain, Margaret was appointed regent of the Habsburg Netherlands by her father, Maximilian I, in 1507. She built a residence in Mechelen across from the old court of the dukes of Burgundy, and it became a focal point for artists and humanist scholars. In its west wing, she housed her collection, made up of antique and contemporary artworks, portraits and religious showpieces as well as unusual natural objects, exotic items from the New World and an extensive library. Margaret gave personal tours of her collection to prominent visitors and travelling artists, including Albrecht Dürer. Several works by her court sculptor, Conrat Meit of Worms, including a medallion with a lifelike portrait of the archduchess (p. 108), are now in the Vienna collections, where they reflect Margaret's role as a patron and collector.

6 *Emperor Ferdinand I*. Attributed to Johann Bocksberger, Salzburg, mid-16th century. Oil on canvas. Vienna, Kunsthistorisches Museum, Picture Gallery, inv. no. GG 4386.

The Vienna Kunstkammer at the time of Ferdinand I and Maximilian II

Ferdinand I [6], who in 1521 assumed rule over the Austrian hereditary lands and moved to Vienna in 1530, had been familiar with his aunt's collection in Mechelen since his youth. Without a doubt his acquaintance with Margaret made a lasting mark on his view of the artistic

value of his possessions, as reflected in the instruction he issued in 1537 and in the founding of a *Kunstkammer* to house his collection.

Apparently owing to a lack of space, the Vienna Kunstkammer was originally not located in the Hofburg Palace but in a townhouse. From a note in 1558 mentioning the *'erpauung einer khunstkhamer'* ('building of a *Kunstkammer*') on the Hofburg site, we may give Ferdinand I credit for having created 'the first museum building in Germany' (G. Kugler). The lack of precise sources makes it difficult to arrive at a clear picture of the objects kept in the Kunstkammer at that time. There is documentary evidence that Ferdinand I acquired portraits and armour, coins and finds from antiquity. The chamberlain's receipt mentioned earlier indicates that a variety of objects entered the collection in 1554, including a glass cup, a board game, manuscripts, an ostrich egg and a spoon made of serpentine. For the first time the famous Agate Bowl and the *Ainkhürn* ('Unicorn Horn') are mentioned as being in the possession of Ferdinand I. After his death, his heirs made them part of the 'inalienable heritage' of the House of Habsburg.

The great diversity of the holdings is illustrated by the Mexican featherwork, which Ferdinand I received in 1524 as a gift from his brother Charles V [7]. In today's collection, the magnificent gameboard made by Hans Kels the Elder (p. 119) demonstrates the high quality with regard to form and content that was typical of the objects Ferdinand I collected. In his will of 1554, he left to his eldest son and successor, Maximilian II (1527–76), the imperial regalia along with his coin collection, expressly noting that his heir was to treasure and preserve it not so much for its material value but because of its age, diversity and systematic order.

Following the death of Ferdinand I in 1564, his three sons divided not only his treasures among themselves but also the Austrian hereditary lands. Maximilian II, who in 1562 had been elected king and thus successor to his father as emperor of the Holy Roman Empire, became ruler over Upper and Lower Austria with Vienna as his capital while Archduke Charles II (1540–90) ruled Inner Austria, and Archduke Ferdinand II (1529–1595) became the sovereign of Tyrol and the region known as the Vorlande or Further Austria, the Austrian provinces west of the Arlberg Pass. Thus the year 1564 saw the creation of two other independent and sovereign Habsburg residences and courts in addition to Vienna: at Graz and Innsbruck.

Unfortunately, little concrete evidence exists about the composition of the collection that Emperor Maximilian II (1527–76) [8] kept at various places in Vienna, including the Hofburg and the old mint. There is evidence that he

7 Feather fan. Mexican, early
16th century. Vienna, Museum of
Ethnology, inv. no. vo 43.381.

8 *Emperor Maximilian II.* Nicolas Neufchatel, *c.* 1566.
Oil on canvas. Vienna, Kunsthistorisches Museum,
Picture Gallery, inv. no. GG 374.

purchased paintings, sculptures and antiquities with the
help of the art dealer and antiquarian Jacopo da Strada
as well as exotic rarities. The rarer they were, the better
('*quanta rariora tanta meliora*'), he told his ambassador
to Madrid, Adam von Dietrichstein, who was commissioned to acquire appropriate objects for the collection.
A recently published inventory of Maximilian's holdings
in 1568 lists insignia and jewelry, coins and handstones,
clocks and scientific instruments, vessels of rock crystal
and silver and also includes such rarities as shells, tiger
skins and the hides of 'Indian goats'. The emperor personally guided prominent visitors through his collection. In
1572 he presented 'paintings and other things' to the elector Augustus of Saxony, including a portrait of a lawyer
by Giuseppe Arcimboldo, composed of books and documents. In 1574 Henry of Valois viewed 'many lovely and
unique things' in the Hofburg Palace, including paintings,
clocks and a wide variety of instruments.

Such accounts confirm that the Vienna holdings of
Maximilian II had a fundamentally encyclopaedic character. Their significance and the high esteem they enjoyed
in the 16th century is revealed by accounts such as that of

Giampaolo Lomazzo, who mentioned the emperor's outstanding 'museum worthy of being remembered forever'
in a work published in 1590 that expressed his appreciation for the painter Arcimboldo. Even clearer and more
to the point are the words of praise in a treatise published
in 1565 by Samuel Quiccheberg, *Inscriptiones vel tituli
Theatri amplissimi*. This work is significant as being the
first to outline a theoretical basis for organizing a museum
or collection. The author, who worked in Munich for Duke
Albert V of Bavaria, lists a series of exemplary collectors,
and he places the Habsburg emperor Maximilian II at
the top of the list. In his service, Quiccheberg notes, were
many artists, dealers and researchers working to expand
the treasures of his forefathers with ancient monuments,
paintings and other beautiful things that he kept carefully
preserved in his 'archive of wisdom'.

The inclusion of the collection of Maximilian II in this
treatise and its citation as 'by far the best example' creates a
direct connection to the concept of the ideal universal museum that Quiccheberg describes in his treatise as a visible
and accessible encyclopaedia of 'all earthly existence'. His
classification system was divided into five different classes
and multiple subgroups that included paintings, sculptures and decorative objects, ancient and foreign coins,
medals and weights as well as preserved animals, fruits
and seeds, metals and minerals, clocks, musical instruments and tools. As the theoretician Gabriel Kaltemarckt
so succinctly put it in 1587, such a *'Theatrum'* should primarily be an aid to the gaining of knowledge and insight
but should also serve as a place of introspection, moral refreshment and inspiration for budding artists. In practice,
aspects of entertainment and ostentation were surely also
involved, as evidenced by the tours of his collection that
the emperor conducted for his prominent visitors.

Because most historical collections have long since
been broken up and scattered, any specific influence that
the theoretical concepts formulated by Quiccheberg and
Kaltemarckt had on the detailed composition of princely
collections is difficult to pinpoint, but it must have been
relatively minor. They do provide, however, a basic impression of the multifaceted relationships and ideas that
characterized scholarly discussion in the 16th century
concerning the complex structures of princely collections.
They also provide an explanation for the understanding of
such encyclopaedic collections as a reflection of the entire
cosmos and the sum of existing knowledge of the world, as
a *'Theatrum mundi'* and an 'archive of wisdom'. The mi-
crocosm of the Kunstkammer collection was intended to
reflect the macrocosm, the objects in it supplying graphic
and symbolic evidence of the rulers' claims to sovereignty
over the world.

In its most significant details, Maximilian II's collection must have been in keeping with contemporary ideas concerning the ideal universal museum. That it can no longer be fully appreciated today is primarily due to the lack of comprehensive written sources on the holdings of the time and the difficulty of assigning extant works unambiguously to his collection. After Maximilian's death, its major holdings must have entered the possession and collection of his son Rudolf II, but this cannot always be documented. One such case is the two ornamental vessels made by the Milanese lapidary Gasparo Miseroni (p. 150), although there is documentary evidence that Maximilian II purchased similar pieces from him. They are specifically mentioned for the first time, however, in the Prague collection of Rudolf II, as are a large portrait medallion of wax (p. 142) created by the northern Italian sculptor Antonio Abondio, who worked as a portraitist in the service of Maximilian II, and various works in bronze by Giambologna (pp. 208–211), which Maximilian may have received as gifts from the Medici family.

In the case of the large, almost three-metre-high silver fountain in the 'shape of an imperial crown', there is clear documentation that Emperor Maximilian II commissioned it in around 1568 from the Nuremberg goldsmith Wenzel Jamnitzer, who completed the work under Rudolf II and delivered it to Prague. Sadly, the only surviving elements of this monumental work created to glorify the House of Habsburg are four supporting figures of gilt bronze (p. 144). The previously mentioned inventory of 1568 lists objects found in the rooms occupied by Maximilian in Vienna's Hofburg Palace. Among them are the Agate Bowl and the *Ainkhürn*. Other pieces that can potentially be identified as having been in that collection are a golden ceremonial sword with elaborate enamel decoration.

It is thus rather difficult to appreciate and understand the high status that Samuel Quiccheberg attributed to the collection of Maximilian II, which remains in the shadows cast by two Habsburg collections that were far better documented in the 16th and early 17th centuries. Today they remain the most important and characteristic examples of their kind: the collections of Maximilian II's brother Archduke Ferdinand II and that of Maximilian's son and successor, Emperor Rudolf II.

The youngest of the three sons of Ferdinand I, Archduke Charles II (1540–90), also installed a collection at his capital, Graz, and filled it with instruments, clocks and exotic objects. With regard to the size and quality of the holdings, however, that collection is inferior to those of his brothers and of his nephew in Prague. Charles II was particularly interested in tapestries and owned an astonishing 127 of them.

The collection of Archduke Ferdinand II at Ambras Castle

Archduke Ferdinand II (1529–95) [9] was named governor of Bohemia in 1547 by his father, Ferdinand I, and became ruler of Tyrol and other Further Austrian possessions on his father's death in 1564. During his time in Bohemia, the archduke had already begun amassing an impressive collection of suits of armour, which were valued as testimonies to their former owners and to the historic events at which they were worn. Later Ferdinand was to have a register of this 'armoury of heroes' compiled, the *Armamentarium heroicum*, which was published several years after his death as the first illustrated, specialized catalogue of a museum collection. As governor of Tyrol, Ferdinand gave Ambras Castle, situated above the capital city of Innsbruck, to his wife, Philippine Welser, with whom he had entered into a morganatic marriage in 1557. In the course of the renovation and expansion of the complex, he had four buildings, constituting the so-called Lower Castle, constructed to the south-west of the original structure. In 1572 the Library, the Antiquarium and the Small Armoury were installed in the Granary. Adjoining this was the actual museum wing, which housed additional parts of the armour and weapons collection, and – in a large, eight-axis hall with tall windows on both sides – the *Kunst- und Wunderkammer* (Chamber of Art and Curiosities). A drawing from about 1590 showing Ambras Castle from the east bears a written reference to the 'Bibliotheca' and 'Musaeum' as part of the castle complex [10].

Numerous sources shed light on Archduke Ferdinand II's great enthusiasm as a collector during his time in Tyrol and the objects he acquired. Thanks to the comprehensive inventory of the Chamber of Art and Curiosities compiled after his death in 1596, in this case we possess quite precise information about the size, structure and arrangement of the collection. According to this document, eighteen floor-to-ceiling display cases stood along the room's main axis as well as two smaller cases on the shorter walls. The hall was also equipped with tables, on which objects taken from the cases could be placed, and bench seats. In general, the exhibits in the cases were ordered according to a simple principle: objects of the same material, such as silver, iron or alabaster, were displayed together in the same case, regardless of their age, origins or importance. The cases themselves were furnished with linen drapes, and the insides were painted different colours, apparently with the intention of providing each group of objects with an appropriate background. This can be considered the first example of a collection whose presentation was consciously designed with its viewers in mind.

9 *Archduke Ferdinand II Wearing the 'Eagle Armour'.*
Francesco Terzio (?), *c.* 1556/57. Oil on canvas. Vienna,
Kunsthistorisches Museum, Picture Gallery, inv. no. GG 8063.

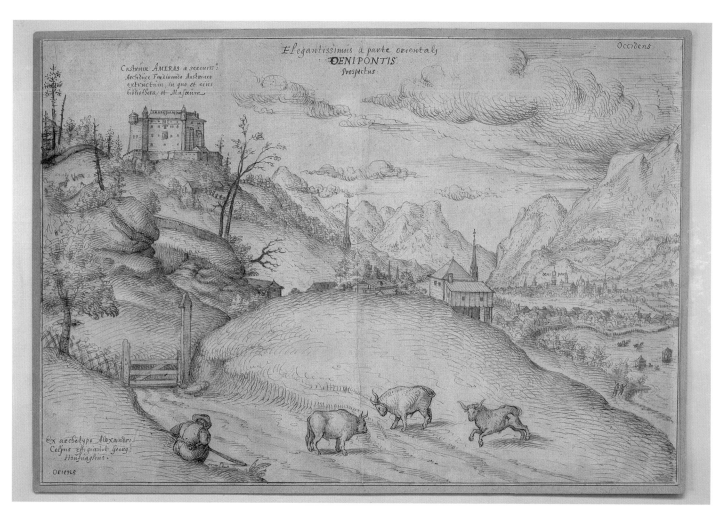

10 *View of Ambras Castle.* Joris Hoefnagel, 1582–91.
Pen-and-ink drawing. Vienna, Kunsthistorisches
Museum, Kunstkammer, inv. no. KK 5351.

The first case, whose interior was painted blue, contained the particularly precious vessels of gold and rock crystal; the second held silver objects, among them several specimens, apparently inherited, from the 15th century, as well as numerous natural objects set in precious metal mounts. Each of the next three cases was devoted to a special group: handstones (see p. 186); musical instruments; and clocks, scientific instruments and automata. These were followed by two cases separately displaying objects of stone and iron, while a third held valuable manuscripts and works of graphic art. After the case of early Mexican featherwork came two cases with objects of alabaster and glass, respectively. In the twelfth case were a number of works with colourful, multipartite scenes made of carved coral stems [11] as well as mussel and snail shells. Groups of small bronzes, porcelain, ornate cabinets, and weapons and wooden objects filled the following four cases. The seventeenth case was the so-called 'variety case', bringing together a diverse mixture of specimens ranging from natural objects and curiosities to exotic rarities and playing cards. The smaller cases positioned on the shorter walls held, among other things, works of ivory and mother-of-pearl as well as intricate objects of lathe-turned wood or ivory that today are unique in the world.

Stuffed animals hung from the room's ceiling and the walls were densely covered with paintings. The enormous number of both large- and small-scale portraits in the Ambras collection as well as the scores of suits of armour and weapons, which were arranged in themed groups in five halls of the museum wing, are testament to Ferdinand's great interest in concrete evidence of important and remarkable people. Portraits of family members, princes, warlords and heroes from all over the world had their place next to likenesses of giants, dwarfs and hairy men [12]. The Library contained some 3,500 titles in the form of manuscripts and prints. The walls of this room were hung with paintings and portraits as well, and minerals and medals were stored in large cases. In two small rooms adjoining the Library, hunting weapons were displayed, along with antiquities and later sculptures.

11 Coral Cabinet. Southern German and Genoa (?), 2nd half of 16th century. Wood, pearls,
mother-of-pearl, coral, plaster, mirror glass, velvet, gold braid, glass, bronze, lapis lazuli.
Kunsthistorisches Museum, Ambras Castle Collections, inv. no. AM PA 961.

In its documented holdings, many sections of which have been preserved in their entirety, the Ambras collection represents the ideal of an encyclopaedic collection in the spirit of the 16th-century *Kunstkammer*. It encompasses all of the groups considered essential for a cabinet of curiosities: artworks as products of man *(artificialia)*, products of nature *(naturalia)*, clocks and scientific instruments *(scientifica)*, mementoes *(memorabilia)*, curiosities and unusual objects *(mirabilia)* as well as products of foreign and unknown cultures. In order to expand his collection, Ferdinand employed agents, utilized diplomatic contacts and took advantage of connections through his sons to acquire desirable objects. He received numerous items as gifts, while he purchased others from estates, such as that of Count Ulrich IX of Montfort-Tettnang, who died in 1574 (p. 166), or commissioned them directly from artists or artisans.

In the case of glass products, Ferdinand even founded his own court glassworks in Innsbruck, where glassblowers from Murano, whom the city of Venice permitted him to bring to Innsbruck to work for a certain length of time, turned his ideas into reality, creating small figures (pp. 188–89), pictures and jewelry of coloured glass. The archduke was also a glassblower himself, and one simple glass beaker with a particularly precious gold setting studded with gems is believed to have blown by Ferdinand personally. Indeed, contemporary reports commonly made reference to the archduke using all types of tools, including a lathe, for manual tasks.

After the death of his wife, Philippine Welser, in 1580, Archduke Ferdinand convinced his two sons from this marriage to cede their hereditary share of Ambras Castle to him. In 1582 the fifty-three-year-old Ferdinand married his sixteen-year-old niece Anne Catherine Gonzaga. This marriage resulted in three daughters; Ferdinand was thus denied a male heir who might have succeeded him. In 1594, the archduke designated his younger son from his first marriage, Charles, Margrave of Burgau (1560–1618), as the heir to his collection. Charles was charged with keeping the holdings intact and in good condition 'in honourable memory' of his father, but in fact he showed little interest in the costly upkeep of Ambras Castle and the collection. He soon entered into negotiations to sell the castle to his late father's nephew, Emperor Rudolf II (1552–1612), who was determined to preserve the Ambras collection – which was famous even at that time, attracting many art-loving travellers – for himself and for the House of Habsburg. In 1606 he purchased the castle and the collection for 170,000 florins, although the holdings of the *Kunst- und Wunderkammer* alone were estimated to be worth some 100,000 florins. Aside from the removal

12 *Madleine Gonzalez, Daughter of the Hairy Man of Tenerife.* Southern German, *c.* 1580. Oil on canvas. Vienna, Kunsthistorisches Museum, Picture Gallery, inv. no. GG 8331.

of the two objects that were undeniably heirlooms, the Agate Bowl and the *Ainkhürn*, the collection remained at its original location, just as Archduke Ferdinand II had left it. In 1665 Emperor Leopold I had some of the most valuable manuscripts removed, and in 1713 coins and medals were transferred from Ambras to Vienna for Charles VI, but not until 1806, in the wake of political events and the ceding of Tyrol to the Kingdom of Bavaria, was it considered necessary to evacuate the entire holdings, as private imperial property, to Vienna for safekeeping.

Soon after their arrival in the imperial capital, the large groups of natural objects that could be assigned to the fields of zoology, botany and mineralogy, as well as the ethnographic objects, were for the most part removed from the Ambras holdings and passed on to the relevant natural science collections. Similarly, over the course of the 19th and 20th centuries, the armour and weapons as well as the paintings and manuscripts were incorporated into the corresponding specialized collections. Despite these changes

13 View of the current display of Archduke
Ferdinand II's Chamber of Art and Curiosities in
the Granary of Ambras Castle, near Innsbruck.

and losses, the holdings now distributed among the collections at Ambras Castle and the Vienna Kunstkammer still provide us with a fairly good impression of the diversity and range that this princely 16th-century 'cabinet of art' once possessed.

Ambras Castle, whose current Chamber of Art and Curiosities [13] is a modern adaptation of the way that the objects were historically displayed, today places its focus on the more bizarre and curious aspects of the collection: works made of coral, iron – such as the famous Prisoner's Chair – glass, papier mâché, lathe-turned objects of wood and ivory, as well as humorous drinking vessels, exotica and unusual items of clothing. In contrast, as early as the 19th century, the objects that were selected to be moved from the Ambras collection to Vienna's Kunsthistorisches Museum were chosen for their 'artistic value'. These specimens range from a splendid ostrich-egg goblet, tortoiseshell vessels, snail shells and elaborate cabinets to bronze statuettes, vessels of precious metals and rock crystal,

handstones, and glass and ceramic objects, which must have been particular favourites of Archduke Ferdinand II (pp. 166–92).

The Ambras collection was also the source of various medieval works that can today be found in the Vienna Kunstkammer, such as a Venetian gameboard, the famous decks of playing cards – including the *Hofämterspiel* and the *Hofjagdspiel* (p. 70) – the *Musterbuch* (see p. 66) and several splendid goblets owned by Frederick III (p. 75) and Maximilian I (p. 82). The first display case in Ambras Castle's *Kunstkammer* contained particularly precious mementoes: the gifts Archduke Ferdinand II received in 1570 from King Charles IX of France when Ferdinand served as proxy for the French king at the latter's wedding to Archduchess Elizabeth of Austria, daughter of Emperor Maximilian II. All four of these magnificent objects, whose immense value caused quite a sensation at the time, have been preserved, including Benvenuto Cellini's *Saliera* (see pp. 124–34).

14 *Emperor Rudolf II*. Hans von Aachen, Prague, *c.* 1600/3. Oil on canvas.
Vienna, Kunsthistorisches Museum, Picture Gallery, inv. no. GG 1124.

Emperor Rudolf II's *Kunstkammer* in Prague

Emperor Rudolf II (1552–1612) [14] was unquestionably the most important and passionate collector in the history of the House of Habsburg. He spent his youth at the Spanish court of his uncle, King Philip II (1527–98), whose rich and varied collection must have greatly shaped the young archduke's ability to understand and judge art. On his way back to Vienna from Spain, Rudolf visited his uncle Archduke Ferdinand II in Innsbruck and became acquainted with his *Kunstkammer* there. After the death in 1576 of his father, Maximilian II, whose inheritance and estate Rudolf had to share with his five brothers, the young archduke succeeded him as Holy Roman Emperor. Rudolf's awareness of his new rank found one of its manifestations in his activity as a collector, which was characterized by his unconditional demand for objects of unrivalled quality, exclusivity and rarity.

Unlike the collection of Archduke Ferdinand II at Ambras Castle, much of which survived the centuries nearly unscathed, Rudolf II's *Kunstkammer* suffered heavy losses as early as the 17th century through plundering and destruction. Nevertheless, numerous documents and an exhaustive inventory from the period between 1607 and 1611 once again provide us with a basic idea of the size and arrangement of the collection. The former splendour and impact of this collection – despite the great losses it suffered – is also amply demonstrated today by the holdings preserved in Vienna.

In 1583 Emperor Rudolf II moved the Habsburg court from Vienna to Prague, where he converted the royal castle in Hradčany into an imperial residence and in the process also created a suitable space for his treasures. The result was a total of nine rooms in two two-storey wings south and north of what was then known as the Mathematical Tower. The paintings, hung close together in three rows, were displayed on the second level of both wings, while the library and Rudolf's *Kunstkammer* were spread out over various rooms on the lower level. The so-called Front Art Chamber was located in two vaulted rooms south of the tower, and the Grand Art Chamber was installed north of the tower in a hall that was around 30 metres (98 feet) long and furnished with a flat roof, now known as the Spanish Hall. The Front Art Chamber contained a total of seventeen numbered display cases, while the Grand Art Chamber was furnished with twenty; some were open, others had doors, and they were each equipped with from three to six compartments. In the Grand Art Chamber, the cases were used to store larger objects, especially bronze statuettes, and between them hung stag's antlers. Numerous freestanding artworks were displayed on a long table in the middle of the room. Smaller tables, chests and cabinets, each of which held a large number of objects, stood between and beneath the windows.

Between 1607 and 1611 the imperial antiquarian Daniel Fröschl compiled an inventory of the holdings contained in the Grand Art Chamber, consisting of some 2,800 entries. The order of the entries, unlike that of the Ambras inventory of 1596, did not reflect the contemporary arrangement of the objects in the cases but instead followed a methodical system. Fröschl recorded the holdings and simultaneously placed them in an ideal order. Only his notes in the margins refer to the actual organization and location of the objects.

The inventory begins with an overview of the natural objects, then of the art objects and finally of the clocks and scientific instruments. By far the largest group recorded in the inventory was that of the products of nature. These included entire stuffed animals, skins, horns and teeth, coral and shells, minerals of various types (including silver ore, handstones and gems), fossils, and botanical objects such as woods, fruits and seeds. The list of art objects records specimens made of a wide variety of materials: gold, silver, rock crystal, agate, jasper, ivory, amber, wax, wood, stone and bronze; also mentioned are textiles, ceramics, porcelain, featherwork of non-European provenance, weapons, coins, medals, cameos, furniture, and works of graphic art, complete with printing plates. The final major group is composed of clocks and various instruments for making astronomical and geometric calculations. The presentation of this group of objects is continued in the Front Art Chamber, along with cameos and antique sculptures of stone and bronze. However, no inventory is known to exist of this section of the collection or of the some 3,000 paintings (according to contemporary accounts), the tapestries, the splendid weapons, the jewels or the insignia of the emperor.

In order to expand his collection, Rudolf II employed agents, artists and diplomats to purchase works of art, natural objects and exotic rarities while on their missions and journeys and send them back to him in Prague. The imperial envoy in Madrid, Count Hans Khevenhüller, was an especially prolific acquirer of important objects and artworks of the type favoured by the emperor. The persistent efforts by Rudolf II to obtain works by Albrecht Dürer are well documented. As early as 1585, he succeeded in purchasing the *Adoration of the Trinity* from the chapel of the Zwölfbrüderhaus in Nuremberg. After the conclusion of many years of negotiations concerning the acquisition of the estate of the cardinal and former state secretary to Emperor Charles V, Antoine Perrenot de Granvelle, not only did many more Dürer works find

15 The *Venus* of Cardinal Granvelle. Venice or Padua, *c.* 1500. Bronze, silver.
Vienna, Kunsthistorisches Museum, Kunstkammer, inv. no. KK 7343.

16 The *Gemma Augustea*. Roman, AD 9–12. Double-layered sardonyx, gold setting (17th century). Vienna, Kunsthistorisches Museum, Collection of Greek and Roman Antiquities, inv. no. ANSA IXa 79.

their way to Prague but also the bronze bust of Charles V (p. 112), which shortly thereafter was to serve as the direct model for the bust of Rudolf II (p. 195), and a small bronze statue of Venus with feet of silver, which at the time was thought to be a work of classical antiquity [15]. The emperor's great interest in classical objects in general is documented by the large number of important ancient cameos he acquired for his collection. Among them is the famous *Gemma Augustea* [16], whose connection to Caesar Augustus, the first Roman emperor, must have had tremendous significance for Rudolf. Like all Holy Roman

17 Crown of Emperor Rudolf II, later Crown of the Austrian Empire. Jan Vermeyen (attributed),
Prague, dated 1602. Gold, enamel, diamonds, rubies, spinels, pearls, sapphire, velvet. Vienna,
Kunsthistorisches Museum, Secular Treasury, inv. no. SK WS XIa 1.

emperors, Rudolf used Augustus as part of his name; he also adopted Capricorn as his astrological sign because it was the favourite sign of Caesar Augustus.

The emperor constantly expanded his collection not only through acquisitions of this kind but also through the countless commissions that he awarded directly to artists and craftsmen, many of whom were brought to Prague by the emperor to work for him. Painters including Giuseppe Arcimboldo, Hans von Aachen, Bartholomaeus Spranger and Joseph Heintz as well as sculptors and woodcarvers like Adriaen de Vries, Alessandro Abondio and Nikolaus Pfaff were employed in Rudolf's service. The goldsmiths Paulus van Vianen, Jan Vermeyen, Anton Schweinberger and Georg Lencker also worked at the Prague court, as did the instrument maker Erasmus Habermehl, the clockmaker Jost Bürgi and the lapidary artists Ottavio Miseroni, Caspar Lehmann and Giovanni Castrucci. Occasionally even artists who remained outside the city of Prague worked almost exclusively for Rudolf II and his collection, such as the Milanese lapidary artist Alessandro Masnago. In this way the emperor was able to attain the degree of exclusivity that he demanded for his collection. The vigour with which he pursued this ambition is vividly illustrated by the account that has been passed down regarding the celestial globe (p. 216) that Rudolf purchased from the Augsburg merchant Georg Roll. The story has it that Roll had sold Rudolf's brother Archduke Ernest a similar globe but at a significantly higher price, which led Rudolf to suspect that he had been given an inferior globe. The enraged emperor had Roll thrown into prison and swapped his globe for that of his brother.

As a result of the close collaboration between the various court artists and their direct focus on the artistic tastes of the emperor, a formal language became established in the art of the period around 1600, which scholars refer to as 'Rudolfine art'. This style is especially evident in cabinet pieces such as the famous ewer made from a coco de mer (p. 201), which represents a masterpiece of the highest order created jointly by sculptor, woodcarver and goldsmith. Another example of masters of different disciplines frequently working together in the service of the emperor is that of the lapidary artist Ottavio Miseroni, who was enormously skilled in taking extremely hard and brittle gemstones and carving vessels from them that appeared to be modelled from wax, and the jeweller and goldsmith Jan Vermeyen, who in many cases provided the exquisite settings for Miseroni's works (pp. 196, 232). Further testimony to the extraordinary level of the art produced at the Prague court in around 1600 is the crown of Rudolf II, attributed to Jan Vermeyen, which is a perfect symbiosis of insignia and artwork, truly fit for an emperor [17].

The holdings preserved today in the Vienna Kunstkammer offer many more examples of artistic achievements that demonstrate the extraordinary quality of Rudolf II's collection (see pp. 195–236).

The interplay of nature and art in the princely collections of the late 16th and early 17th centuries

By far the largest group of the Prague inventory of 1607–11 was that of natural objects in their original, unworked forms. Viewed partly as curiosities and partly as objects for study, these specimens were considered at the time to be extraordinary visual aids for understanding the world and divine creation. Assigned to this group were also the natural objects that had been worked and mounted, such as the coco de mer ewer (p. 201) and the monumental rhinoceros-horn goblet with lid, featuring the tusks of an African warthog (p. 203). Complex showpieces of this kind demonstrate in a particularly vivid manner their artists' understanding that 'many things belong neither completely to nature nor completely to art; rather, they are part of both', as Vincenzo Borghini said in 1570 with regard to his decorative programme for Francesco I de' Medici's *studiolo* in Florence's Palazzo Vecchio.

There is plenty of available evidence that even Emperor Maximilian II had a great personal interest in the natural sciences. He had his gardens stocked with rare plants and animals, some of which were the first of their kind to be brought to Central Europe, and sought the scientific knowledge of such renowned scholars as the botanists Charles de l'Écluse (Carolus Clusius) and Augier Ghislain de Busbecq. In Prague, his son and successor as emperor, Rudolf II, maintained botanical gardens and menageries with species so rare that Italian scholars, among them the famous Ulisse Aldrovandi in Bologna, entreated the Prague court to supply them with pictures of the exotic animals and plants for research purposes. Two impressive testimonies to the great interest in meticulously documenting the appearance of natural objects are the codex known as the *Museum of Emperor Rudolf II* and a bound set of depictions of plants and animals, both of which are today found in the Austrian National Library in Vienna. The latter set includes watercolours by the court painters Giuseppe Arcimboldo, Hans Hoffmann and Dirck de Quade van Ravesteyn. Among the illustrations are depictions of a blackbuck antelope [18], one of the species of ruminants whose intestines produce the so-called bezoar stone (p. 199), and of a mummified wild boar's head with ingrown tusks [19], which – according to the inventory of 1607–11 – was once part of Rudolf's Prague collection. The *Museum* also contains the image of an unusually large

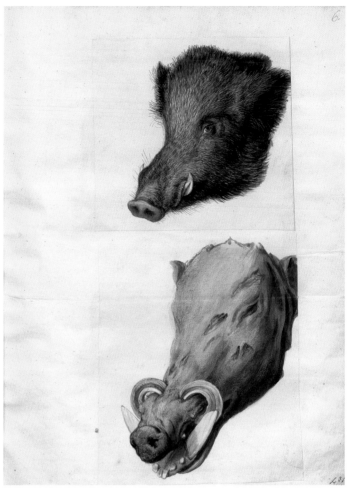

18 Blackbuck *(Antilope cervicapra)*. Miniature from the *Museum of Emperor Rudolf II*, Prague, after 1570. Gouache on parchment. Vienna, Austrian National Library, Department of Manuscripts, Autographs and Closed Collections, Cod. Min. 129, fol. 21r.

19 'Studies of Two Wild Boar Heads, One of Them with Ingrown Tusks'. Prague, *c.* 1600. Watercolour. Vienna, Austrian National Library, Department of Manuscripts, Autographs and Closed Collections, Cod. Min. 42, fol. 6r.

rhinoceros horn decorated with bands of gold filigree decoration [20], which the inventory describes as 'from Asino Indico' and assigns to the group of horns. Today it can be found in the Vienna Kunstkammer [21].

In view of the great attraction held by the exotic and the rare in nature and art during the era of the princely *Kunstkammer*, it is not surprising that, among the many natural objects recorded in the inventories of the collections in Prague and at Ambras Castle, the non-European species far outweigh any others. Examples of more local fauna and flora were featured in these collections primarily in the form of horns and antlers of native animal species, particularly when they were considered exceptional because of their size or deformities. Likewise, indigenous plants were generally only represented if they exhibited some peculiarity worthy of special note, such as fossilization or malformation, or were regarded as a part of a natural phenomenon, such as grain that was said to have fallen to earth like rain.

The list of objects from the animal kingdom found in the inventory of Rudolf II's collection comprises entire skeletons and stuffed specimens of mammals, birds, reptiles and fish, as well as individual body parts such as heads, teeth, beaks, shells, skins and horns of various kinds. While a number of these natural objects remained an enigma to the compiler of the inventory, Daniel Fröschl, who described them as 'peculiar', there is evidence that he took great pains to accurately identify the specimens, referring to authorities of the natural sciences such as Carolus Clusius and Conrad Gessner. The inventory even mentions scientific studies conducted on objects in the Prague collection, such as the case of a starfish that was dissected and two anatomized frogs. The plant world is represented in Fröschl's register with entries on foreign nuts, seeds, beans and spices. Many of the exotic natural-history objects – such as rhinoceros horns, coconuts, coco de mer nuts, nautilus shells, ostrich eggs, tortoise shells and bezoar stones – were given an artistic treatment and mount

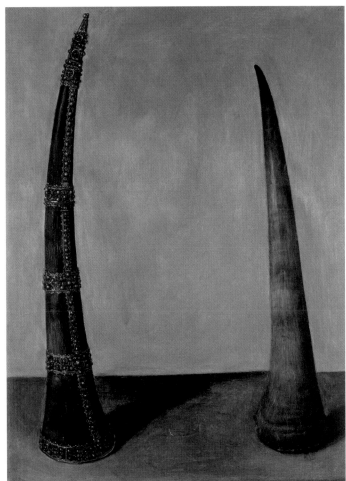

20 *Two Rhinoceros Horns.* Miniature from the *Museum of Emperor Rudolf II*, Prague, after 1570. Gouache on parchment. Vienna, Austrian National Library, Department of Manuscripts, Autographs and Closed Collections, Cod. Min. 129, fol. 12.

21 Rhinoceros horn with gold filigree decoration. Goa or Lisbon, *c.* 1580. Vienna, Kunsthistorisches Museum, Kunstkammer, inv. no. KK 3702.

or combined with other materials to create a grand show-piece that was purely decorative (pp. 164–68). In some cases, an entire animal, such as a bird of paradise or a fish, could be transformed into a remarkable cross between a stuffed specimen and a work of art by enamelling its beak or gilding its fins.

The creativity of the artist and the imagination of the beholder were given free rein in allowing and encouraging nature and art to interact in a playful way. Stones with striking patterns and colours, for example, were used by artists as the basis for sculptures or other images, ornate compositions were created from handstones (p. 186) and unusual scenes were crafted using coral [11]. Held in particularly high esteem in the 16th century was the

22 Mineral specimen with emeralds from Colombia. Tyrol (?), 2nd half of 16th century. Emerald, gilded copper. Vienna, Museum of Natural History, Department of Mineralogy and Petrography, inv. no. C 3281.

technique of natural casting; that is, making moulds of animals and plants directly from life. This method was used to make bronze or silver casts of plants and small animals such as snakes, lizards, toads or beetles (p. 182). Numerous entries in the inventory of the Prague and Ambras collections refer to small silver casts of animals and plants both as independent objects and as components of larger works. In order to further enhance their naturalistic appearance, these casts were sometimes also painted (p. 202). Plaster casts also found their way into princely art collections, taking forms ranging from the coats of arms of sovereign princes and other high-ranking dignitaries to deer's feet, pig's heads, fish, lizards, crabs, snakes, frogs and turtles. Rulers themselves were even involved in making casts of natural creatures. An inventory

taken of the Munich *Kunstkammer* in 1598 mentions a box containing sea plants, fish, crabs, snakes and lizards and states that Emperor Maximilian II 'formed imitations in plaster' of these objects with his own hands. This box was presumably similar to the famous 'quivering box' that is preserved today in the Ambras collection.

Stones and minerals of various types and origins were found in great number in the Prague and Ambras collections. Emperor Rudolf II had a special relationship with stones; according to his court physician Anselmus de Boodt, Rudolf was convinced that in them 'you may ever have before your eyes something of the light and appearance of divinity'. Among the testimonies to this passion that have been preserved are the many gemstone vessels and *pietre dure* works from the court workshops in Prague

23 Stone panel with fossilized fish and engraved Latin text, dated 1543. Slab limestone from the Upper Jurassic Period. Vienna, Museum of Natural History, Department of Geology and Palaeontology, inv. no. 1880/c/995.

(pp. 227–236). In the case of Archduke Ferdinand II of Tyrol – who kept more than 1,800 objects in a single library case, including amethyst, azurite and malachite, stephanite, argentite, galena, turquoise, chrysolite as well as gold and silver ore – parts of his mineral holdings can be admired today in the collections of Vienna's Museum of Natural History. Among them is a large specimen of Colombian emerald [22], formed from several emerald samples from two different Colombian mines, which were cemented together with pitch in the 16th century to create a larger composition.

According to early modern museum theory, products of the earth included not only minerals in the modern sense of the word but also antiquities, fossils and prehistoric finds. Fossils were regarded as petrified testimonies to and victims of the Biblical Flood, as is expressed in the inscription on a framed stone plaque with a fossilized fish [23]. It was located originally in the Ambras collection, as was the ammonite fossil [24], which was recorded in the inventory of 1596 as being in the sixth display case and described as *Ain schlangen, so zu ainem stain worden* – 'a snake that turned into a stone'. A snake's head was carved into it to underscore this image visually.

By the 17th century a growing number of natural scientists were devising clear, scientific classification criteria and systems. Scholars, physicians and chemists, for their part, created *Naturalienkabinette,* or cabinets of natural curiosities, which became spaces for scientific experiments and the acquisition of new knowledge. Polymaths were increasingly replaced by specialized scientists. Researchers

24 Ammonite fossil carved with a snake's head. From the Lias Period (Lower Jurassic) in Württemberg (southern Germany). Vienna, Museum of Natural History, Department of Geology and Palaeontology, inv. no. 1880/c/998.

25 *Emperor Ferdinand III*. Jan van den Hoecke, Vienna,
c. 1643. Oil on canvas. Vienna, Kunsthistorisches
Museum, Picture Gallery, inv. no. GG 3283.

such as Carolus Linnaeus designed systems that gave even
the smallest species a classification and a name. Strange
and exotic natural objects lost much of their mysterious attraction as well as much of their aura as magical remedies.
On the way to the modern world of science, the element
of wonder was lost and with it most of the unworked,
unadorned natural objects that had filled the Habsburgs'
Kunstkammer in the 16th and 17th centuries.

The imperial collections from the 17th to the 19th century

When he died in 1612, Emperor Rudolf II left behind no
instructions in his will regarding his possessions and art
treasures. Following intensive negotiations, his brothers,
Matthias, Albrecht and Maximilian, decided that same
year to repay the court's outstanding debts, but then to
use the Prague holdings as the basis for the founding of a
joint *Kunstkammer* of the House of Habsburg that would
remain with the current eldest male member of the family. In the years 1621 and 1635, with his establishment
of the right of primogeniture (*Majoratsstiftung*), Emperor

Ferdinand II further defined ownership laws with regard
to this family treasure. He decreed that all imperial insignia, jewels and art treasures were the inalienable property
of the Habsburg dynasty, no longer bound to 'the land and
the people' but rather to the first-born male as head of the
family. With this measure, he created the legal basis for
uniting these Habsburg treasures in Vienna, the imperial
capital, which would be of utmost importance for the later
collections of the Kunsthistorisches Museum.

Only a few months after Rudolf II's death, in 1612, his
successor as emperor, his brother Matthias (1557–1619),
had the imperial insignia and a number of precious objects
brought to Vienna. Further shipments followed, as shown
by entries in the estate inventory of Emperor Matthias,
who died in 1619, pertaining to items that were clearly
from the collection of Rudolf II. Because of this reloca-
tion, which was continued during the reign of Matthias's
successor, Emperor Ferdinand II (1578–1637), at least
parts of Rudolf's collection were preserved for the House
of Habsburg. The holdings that remained in Prague, on
the other hand, were largely plundered or destroyed in the
wake of the Thirty Years' War. The contents of the Prague
Kunstkammer were decimated first by the Bohemian
estates, then by Duke Maximilian I of Bavaria and the
Saxon prince-elector, and finally – and most devastatingly
– by the Swedish troops. In 1648 the Swedes ransacked
the fortress and the collections, with the result that a large
number of paintings, sculptures, coins and medals, books,
clocks and musical instruments as well as natural objects and exotic rarities from Rudolf II's collection passed
into the possession of Queen Christina of Sweden, from
whose estate they were then scattered among numerous
European collections.

The holdings that had been brought to Vienna in the
previous decades were stored in the old Hofburg palace
complex, probably in the wing behind the Real Tennis
Court (Ballhaus) known as the Kunsthaus (art house),
which had been built in the late 16th century and restored
in several stages beginning in 1610. A description in Latin
from 1637, the year Emperor Ferdinand III (1608–57)
[25] came to the throne, is the first written reference to
the multi-room 'Galeria' located on the second level of
this wing, '*quem Thesaurum vocant*' ('that which they call
the Treasury'): 'Here is stored a multitude of all manner
of precious things made of gold, with gems and mounts
as well as works of the highest craftsmanship, paintings,
also outstanding examples of natural and human power
and very many other rare and remarkable objects'. The
author especially emphasized the imperial crown [17]
and the Agate Bowl. Documents pertaining to renovation
plans in 1640–41 show that the second-level gallery was

situated above a row of closed, vaulted rooms and had twelve windows that opened onto the old Burggarten, today the Summer Riding School. Emperor Ferdinand III had the building restored and the Treasury furnished with new cases. He also had the holdings expanded, with an eye to the types of art objects particularly popular in the 17th century. Numerous ivory objects in the form of lathe-turned vessels and carved statuettes were added, taking the place of the small bronzes that had been held in such high esteem in the 16th century. Many precious stone vessels were also acquired, the loveliest of which were created in the Prague workshop of Dionysio Miseroni (pp. 256–259), the son of the famous Ottavio Miseroni, who had been active in the era of Rudolf II. While inventories of the treasury holdings of this period are mentioned in contemporary documents, none has been preserved.

A reasonably accurate impression of the types of objects found in the collection and their arrangement can, however, be gleaned from reports by visitors to the imperial Treasury in the second half of the 17th century. Among the earliest accounts is that of Johann Sebastian Müller, a civil servant to the Duke of Saxe-Weimar who in 1660 was given a tour of the rooms by the treasurer. His report suggests that the holdings were displayed separately – as they still are today – in a Secular and an Ecclesiastical Treasury in various rooms on the second level of the gallery wing. In the large hall of the Secular Treasury stood thirteen black wooden cases decorated with eagles holding the monograms of Emperor Ferdinand III. Paintings hung on the walls; by the windows stood tables and cabinets as well as sculptures.

The contents of the cases were ordered according to the customary principle of shared material. The first and second cases held objects of rhinoceros horn, ivory, amber and coral, including the splendid goblet by Nikolaus Pfaff (p. 203) from Rudolf II's Prague collection and the tall ivory centrepiece by Marcus Heiden [26]. The third and fourth cases were filled with clocks, while the fifth, seventh and eighth cases each contained magnificent vessels of gold and silver that were valuable both in material as well as artistic terms, such as the precious christening set of the archdukes of Austria. The sixth, ninth and tenth cases displayed vessels and cameos made of precious stones. Among these objects was a necklace with portraits of many members of the House of Habsburg as emperors of the realm and archdukes of Austria, symbolizing the authority of the dynasty's political claims [27].

26 Tall ivory table centrepiece. Marcus Heiden, Coburg, Eisenach or Weimar, signed and dated 1634. Vienna, Kunsthistorisches Museum, Kunstkammer, inv. no. KK 4775.

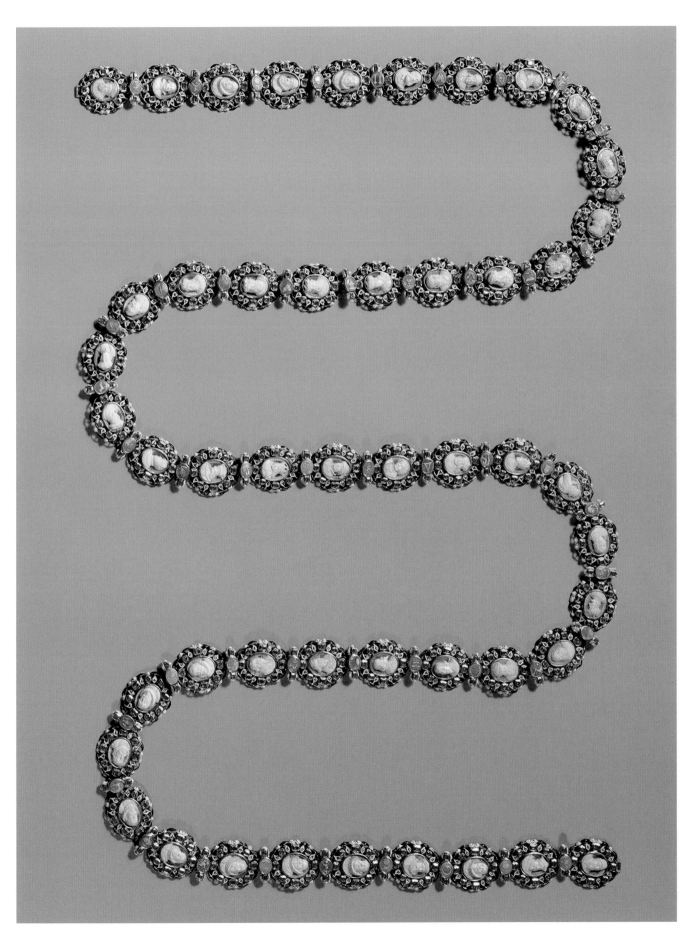

27 Necklace of forty-nine shell cameos with Habsburg portraits. Southern German,
c. 1650/60. Gold, enamel, shell cameos. Vienna, Kunsthistorisches Museum,
Kunstkammer, inv. no. ANSA XII 53.

28 *Archduke Leopold William in His Gallery in Brussels.* David
Teniers the Younger, Brussels, *c.* 1651. Oil on canvas. Vienna,
Kunsthistorisches Museum, Picture Gallery, inv. no. GG 739.

The eleventh and twelfth cases held vessels of rock crystal, including Dionysio Miseroni's famous Pyramid Vase
(p. 259), whose valuable material and technical virtuosity
made it a characteristic showpiece of the early Baroque.
Finally, the thirteenth case showed off the crown jewels of
the House of Austria, with the imperial crown of Rudolf II
as the thematic centrepiece [17].

A similar description, even more precise in some details,
is provided by an anonymous visitor in an account printed
in 1677. Both contemporary witnesses mention additional
objects in this hall and in two adjoining rooms: bronze
statuettes, Turkish weapons, copper engravings, medals,
pictures made of wood and wax, furniture, more clocks
as well as natural specimens such as 'adder's tongues' (fossilized shark's teeth), bezoar stones, and rhinoceros and
'unicorn' horns. The Ecclesiastical Treasury contained primarily precious reliquaries, devotional pictures and vest-
ments. However, it also included examples of the belief

in miracles, in the form of two humanoid-shaped mandrake roots depicting Christ on the cross. The famous
'Eppendorf Mandrake', which is associated with an ancient and convoluted legend, was obtained by Emperor
Rudolf II for his Prague collection in 1602.

On his visit in 1660, Johann Sebastian Müller was able
to view not only the '*Kayserliche Schatz-Cammer*' (imperial treasury) but also the '*Kunst Kammer und Schilderey*'
(art chamber and picture gallery), which had only recently been installed by the most significant Habsburg collector in the period after Emperor Rudolf II, Archduke
Leopold William (1614–62). As the second eldest son
of Emperor Ferdinand II, the young archduke originally
trained to become a priest. In 1646 he became governor of
the Habsburg Netherlands, where in the ensuing years he
amassed an extensive collection of paintings, drawings and
sculptures [28] in Brussels. In 1656 he returned to Vienna
and began work on the installation of his collection on the

Porticuum prospectus.

illust. tres porticus feré æqualis longitud: palmor: restricet 185 latitud: 17. His correspondent treé officinæ majores longitud: eiusdem, latitud ±6, insuper duæ mediocres longitud: et latitud ±6, et duæ minores, tabulæ, in vniuersum sunt 1700,statuæ 260. N. v. Hoy del.' F. vande Steen S. C. M. sculp

29 'View of the Picture Gallery of Archduke Leopold William in the Vienna Stallburg'. From: David Teniers the Younger, *Theatrum pictorium*, Brussels, 1660, fol. 215. Copperplate engraving.

second level of the Stallburg, a building in the Hofburg complex. The project was completed in 1659. The inventory compiled as part of this undertaking mentions 1,397 paintings, 343 drawings, and 542 antique and modern objects of marble, bronze, wax and wood, with only isolated entries for rare or exotic pieces.

Leopold William was the first Habsburg to focus his collecting activities primarily on paintings. The designations *Kunstkammer* ('art chamber') and *Schatzkammer* ('treasure chamber'), which in the context of the Habsburg collections had been used more or less interchangeably since the 16th century to refer to the same holdings, were applied by Leopold William in a much more nuanced manner. He used the term *Kunstkammer* for the collection of paintings and sculptures, while *Schatzkammer* referred to the holdings of precious objects and rarities. These two collections were also kept physically separate. The holdings of Leopold William's *Schatzkammer* inventoried in

1660 were placed in a vaulted room in what was then called the Neue Burg, known today as the Amalienburg. In the archduke's spaces at the Stallburg, however, where his collection of paintings and sculptures was presented [29], only a single room, the library, displayed 'rarities'.

In 1664 Leopold William's art treasures – to which the present-day collections of Vienna's Kunsthistorisches Museum, particularly the Picture Gallery, owe much of their splendour – passed to his nephew Emperor Leopold I (1640–1705), who the next year also inherited the estate of the last male representative of the Tyrolean collateral line, Archduke Sigismund Francis. Among the loveliest objects of the Vienna Kunstkammer's present-day holdings are the sculptures and carvings of the Italian Renaissance and Flemish early Baroque from the collection of Leopold William. These include such key works as the various small bronzes by the Mantuan sculptor Antico (p. 102) and the bust of a woman by Francesco Laurana (p. 92).

41

30 *King Joseph I Vanquishing Fury*. Matthias Steinl, Vienna, dated 1693.
Ivory. Vienna, Kunsthistorisches Museum, Kunstkammer, inv. no. KK 4663.

31 *Emperor Leopold I as Victor over the Turks.* Matthias Steinl, Vienna, *c.* 1690/93.
Ivory. Vienna, Kunsthistorisches Museum, Kunstkammer, inv. no. KK 4662.

32 *Leopold I in the Circle of his Family.* Charles Boit, Vienna,
dated 1703. Copper, enamel. Vienna, Kunsthistorisches
Museum, Kunstkammer, inv. no. KK 3242.

However, this collection was also the source of the 10th-century ivory relief depicting St Gregory (p. 53), which, after being purchased by Heiligenkreuz Abbey in the 19th century, was reacquired by the Kunsthistorisches Museum in 1928. Also of great significance among the holdings of the Vienna Kunstkammer are the many tapestries that the archduke commissioned or purchased for his residences.

Under Ferdinand III and especially under his son and successor Emperor Leopold I, the Treasury was given a significantly greater role as a means of glorifying imperial power, as a tool of propaganda and as an illustration of the political and religious ideologies espoused by the House of Habsburg. While both the diversity of the objects and their grouping according to material were largely preserved, as recorded in the contemporary accounts discussed above, a growing number of works with a pointed emphasis on idealistic and political messages were finding their way into the Treasury, such as the above-mentioned necklace with the Habsburg portraits [27] and the famous 'indoor monuments' [30 and 31]. With this allegorical double memorial to Emperor Leopold I and his son King Joseph I, the themes of continuity and renewal in the Holy Roman Empire under the rule of the House of Habsburg on the one hand and the triumph over the foreign enemies of the dynasty on the other were placed literally at the centre of the Treasury, directly addressing all the visitors who – for a fee – were granted admission to view the imperial collections.

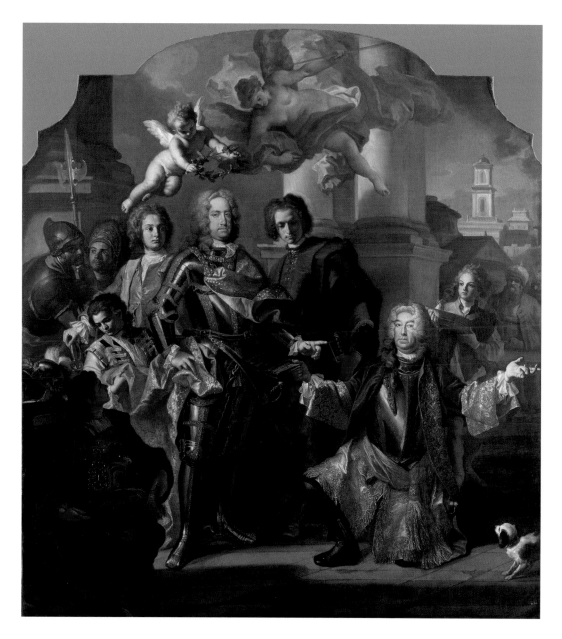

33 *Count Gundacker Althan Presents Emperor Charles VI with the Inventory of the Imperial Picture Gallery in the Stallburg.* Francesco Solimena and others, Naples and Vienna, dated 1728. Vienna, Kunsthistorisches Museum, Picture Gallery, inv. no. GG 1601.

In the same way, many other works were interpreted on a higher semantic level as symbolizing the tradition and continuity of the family as well as the legal foundation for its claim to universal power. These include the many relics in the Ecclesiastical Treasury as testimonies to the renowned piety of the dynasty *(pietas Austriaca)* and the mementoes of the Protestants and Ottoman Turks in the Secular Treasury as symbols of victory over the vanquished foe. Under Leopold I, the Treasury also significantly expanded its holdings in the field of decorative gemcutting and precious metals [32], and particularly its ivory collection (pp. 271–78). The emperor was particularly fond of this material and was himself proficient in the technique of ivory lathing.

In the decades before and after 1700, scholarly curators increasingly took over the administration and supervision of the imperial collections, evaluating and organizing their holdings in a critical, systematic manner. In 1712 Emperor Charles VI (1685–1740) appointed the Swedish academic Carl Gustav Heraeus (1671–1725 or 1730) as Inspector of Medals and Antiquities, charging him with the task of merging the holdings from the Court Library, the gallery at the Stallburg and Ambras Castle to create a unified imperial coin cabinet. Charles VI had Leopold William's collection at the Stallburg, whose layout had remained largely unchanged during the era of Emperor Leopold I, rearranged over a larger space and commissioned a three-volume illustrated inventory [33], which

34 'Black Cabinet in the Gallery in the Stallburg'. From: *Neu eingerichtes Inventarium der Kayl. Bilder Gallerie in der Stallburg welches nach den Numeris und Maßstab ordiniret und von Ferdinand à Storffer gemahlen worden*, vol. 2, 1730, fol. 2–11. Gouache on parchment. Vienna, Kunsthistorisches Museum, Picture Gallery.

again shows the cases with objects organized according to material. These items were installed in two rooms, where cabinets displayed coins, medals, a number of sculptures and examples of the goldsmith's art, and 'antiquities and rarities from the realm of nature' [34].

Only a few years after the death of Charles VI, his daughter and successor as ruler of the Austrian hereditary lands as well as Bohemia and Hungary, Empress Maria Theresa (1717–80), initiated an extensive reorganization of the Treasury. This was necessary because due to the building of the new Imperial Chancellery Wing, the Secular and the Ecclesiastical Treasury were forced to move to a different area of the Hofburg, where parts of these collections can still be found today. In 1747, magnificent walnut display cases were constructed for the redisplay; the objects in the thirteen cases, however, continued to be organized according to material, following the model of the collection's 17th-century predecessors, and the thirteenth and

final case of the redesigned Treasury still contained 'rarities, among them many works of gold and silver as well as minerals'.

The ensuing decades brought comprehensive and fundamental innovations in terms of the make-up of the imperial collections, which resulted in forward-looking and lasting changes. Maria Theresa's husband, Francis I Stephen, Duke of Lorraine (1708–65), who in 1745 brought the title of Holy Roman Emperor to the newly founded House of Habsburg-Lorraine, had a special passion for the natural sciences. He used his own money to have a Cabinet of Natural Curiosities (*Naturalienkabinett*) and a Physics Cabinet (*Physikalisches Kabinett*) installed and outfitted. To house the emperor's new collections, a building, known as the Augustinian Wing, was specially constructed near the Court Library [35]. Several rooms in the Augustinian Wing were given over to the Cabinet of Coins and Medals, which was one of the first imperial collections

35 *Emperor Francis I Stephen in His Natural History Collections.* Johann Zoffany, *c.* 1776/77.
Oil on canvas. Vienna, Kunsthistorisches Museum, Picture Gallery, inv. no. GG 6389.

36 *The Ambras Collection in the Lower Belvedere: Family Tree Room.* Carl Goebel, Vienna, dated 1888. Watercolour. Vienna, Belvedere Gallery.

to have a permanent curatorial staff, and which in 1798 was renamed the Cabinet of Coins and Antiquities. Maria Theresa contributed greatly to the expansion of the holdings of the natural history collection, as did her son Emperor Joseph II (1741–90). Scientific expeditions and research trips were financed, objects were purchased, and extant holdings from other collection were appropriated. Many examples of precious gems and minerals, gold and silver ore, fruits and stuffed animals made their way during this period from the Treasury to the Cabinet of Natural Curiosities, while mechanical objects and scientific instruments were moved to the Physics Cabinet.

In 1776 the widowed empress ordered the transfer of the gallery at the Stallburg to the Upper Belvedere and the establishment of an independent picture gallery. The holdings for the new gallery were examined and inventoried at the various palaces and residences from which they were to be taken. The majority of the paintings in the

Treasury were removed as well. Conversely, during these decades of restructuring, the treasures from the collection of Archduke Leopold William, which up to that time had been kept in the Stallburg gallery, were transferred to the Treasury. Unlike the Cabinet of Natural Curiosities, the Cabinet of Coins and Antiquities and the Picture Gallery, which had all commenced with the methodical, scholarly organization and re-evaluation of its holdings as early as the 18th century, the Treasury remained purely an administrative office, with no curators engaged in academic work, until well after the mid-19th century. The staff were primarily responsible for procuring valuables and medals as gifts and testimonials. In the course of the preparations for the founding of the new Kaiserlich-Königliche Kunsthistorisches Hofmuseum (Imperial and Royal Court Museum of Art History), the resolution was made – and is still largely valid today – that the only objects to remain in the Treasury in the Hofburg Palace would be those whose historical and symbolic nature adequately reflected the power and status of the imperial dynasty.

Among the Vienna imperial collections in the 19th century, the Ambras holdings had the role, according to the former archivist of the Kunsthistorisches Museum Alphons Lhotsky (1903–68), of 'preserving medieval and modern art and cultural history'. The collection was transferred to Vienna in 1806 and placed under the administration of the Cabinet of Coins and Antiquities. The curator Alois Primisser supervised the installation of the collection in the rooms of the Lower Belvedere Palace, which was opened to the public in 1814. Primisser's description of the Ambras collection, published in 1819, records that the holdings were divided into four sections: armour and weapons; paintings; manuscripts, books and graphic works; and the *Kunst- und Wunderkammer* – the 'cabinets of art and wonders'. In his description, the curator expressly refers to the traditional designation of this group, which contained what he described as 'rarities of nature and art'.

Objects from this latter group were classified and displayed largely according to material, as they had been at Ambras Castle. Alongside the groups of antique sculpture, glasswork, clocks and mathematical instruments, and musical instruments, there was at this time also a separate subgroup of natural objects, including stuffed animals, horns and teeth, cedar cones, seed pods, and stag's antlers around which a tree trunk had grown. However, like the other imperial collections, these holdings, which were still very much in keeping with the spirit and history of the Ambras Chamber of Art and Curiosities, were to undergo significant changes in the following decades as well. As a result of the efforts to 'relieve' the Treasury of all object groups not considered to be historical mementoes in the strictest sense, the Ambras collection became a kind of catch-all for these works. A series of watercolours created after 1870 by the painter Carl Goebel [36] vividly illustrates the changes and expansions this meant for the holdings displayed in the Lower Belvedere. The paintings document that by this time several bronze sculptures from the *Kunstkammer* of Rudolf II and Leopold William had already found their way into the display cases of the Ambras collection, and new acquisitions had been added to the display, including the set of Habsburg busts by Paul Strudel (p. 268), acquired in 1832, and the regalia of the Order of the Golden Fleece, which had been evacuated from Brussels in 1794 and brought to Vienna in 1797.

Carl Goebel's paintings, executed only a few years before the opening of the former Ambras collection in the newly constructed K. K. Kunsthistorisches Hofmuseum under the name of the 'Collection of Art-Industrial Objects', serve as a graphic illustration of the state of the holdings at that time: a juxtaposition of objects from widely divergent historical contexts. There was still a great awareness that the art treasures of the most important parts of the collection dated back to Habsburg collectors of the past, and this was clearly expressed in visual terms through the large ceiling painting in the Golden Room of the new museum (pp. 10–11). The objects at this time, however, were still largely arranged according to material and technique. It was not until the redisplay in 1935 that the holdings were for the first time placed in a chronological sequence and accompanied by notes on their relationships to individual members of the House of Habsburg and to the historical era in which they were created.

The current reorganization of the Vienna Kunstkammer represents the most comprehensive attempt since 1891 to make the extant artworks more accessible by presenting them in the context of their relationship to the historical *Kunstkammer* and the most important collectors. Nevertheless, the historical developments described above, as well as the collection's present-day location in a 19th-century museum building, are parameters that make a plan to reconstruct a historical *Kunstkammer* neither feasible nor sensible. At the same time, however, it is certainly possible to explore and emphasize these historical links within the context of a modern museum presentation.

The selection of masterpieces presented in this book generally follows the chronological order of the new arrangement of the Vienna Kunstkammer and uses the historical figures who collected and commissioned the works as thematic focal points. An exhaustive history of the Habsburg collections can neither be written nor conveyed in an exhibit based solely on the extant holdings of the Vienna Kunstkammer. These works do, however, provide visitors with unique insights into the many historical collections of the House of Habsburg and the treasures that have been incorporated into these holdings, masterpieces that no other museum in the world can match in terms of form and quality.

Two Ivory Reliefs

St Gregory with the Scribes (opposite)
Master of the Vienna Gregory Tablet
Lorraine (?), late 10th century
Ivory, H. 20.5 cm (8 in.), W. 12.5 cm (5 in.)
Inv. no. KK 8399

The Ascension of Christ (front and rear views)
Metz, 10th century
Ivory, H. 20.6 cm (5 in.), W. 14.4 cm (5⅝ in.)
Inv. no. KK 7284

Following the age of classical antiquity, when ivory was a material much valued for its colour and lustre, the Christian world also made use of ivory to create and decorate items used for religious purposes. Among the objects that have survived in the greatest number are ivory reliefs featuring sacred motifs, which were used to adorn the bindings of liturgical books. The two upright, rectangular panels in the Vienna collection, which are among the most important extant works of their kind from the early and high Middle Ages, once served this function. The plaque that depicts Pope Gregory the Great (r. 590–604), bent over a desk composing liturgical prayers, probably once served to adorn a copy of the 'Gregorian Sacramentary', a book of liturgy attributed to Gregory the Great. This relief is fascinating for its realistic detail that even allows us to decipher the first words of the prayer in Gregory's book,

as well as for the virtuosity of the carving technique with its deep undercuttings. *The Ascension of Christ* is impressive above all for its composition: Christ is shown from the back, ascending through a tunnel of clouds, while the group of the Apostles and Mary, the mother of God, shown in various states of agitated motion below, express their astonishment at the miraculous event. In both works, the images are framed by an elegant acanthus frieze that, like a number of other details here, reflects the influence of Byzantine models.

The high value of ivory and the esteem that it consquently enjoyed are demonstrated by the fact that the rear side of *The Ascension of Christ* was recarved in the 17th century with a scene that depicts the Holy Family's flight into Egypt.

FKi

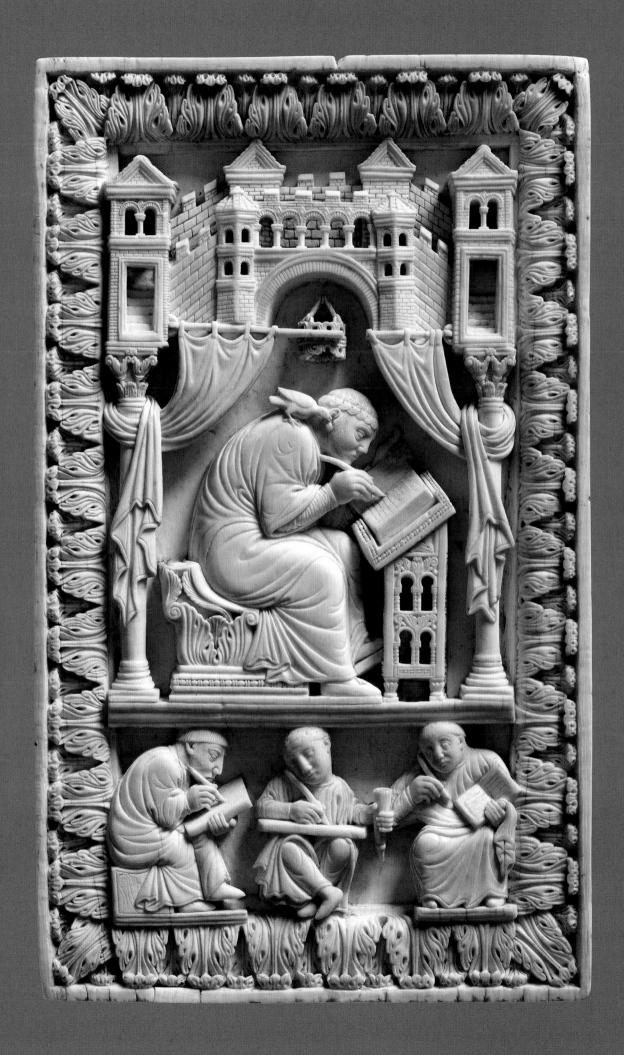

Aquamanile in the Form of a Griffin

Helmarshausen, *c.* 1120/30
Gilt bronze, silver, niello, garnet,
H. 17.3 cm (6⅞ in.)
Inv. no. KK 83

An aquamanile is a type of ewer that was used in the high Middle Ages for the washing of hands during mass. Later it was also used during secular banquets. Frequently these vessels were in the form of animals, hybrid creatures or chimeras. The bronze griffin aquamanile in Vienna is one of the earliest and most celebrated of those that are still extant. It is rightfully considered a masterpiece of animal depiction in the high Middle Ages. The powerful tension of its posture and the lively expression of the head impressively present the wild and powerful nature of this fabulous beast. Practical elements of the design have been skilfully incorporated into the animal's shape: the open beak is the spout while the tail that arches elegantly up the creature's back serves as a handle, and also has an opening for filling the vessel with water. It is closed by a movable palmetto lid at the top.

The importance of this object is indicated by the unusually elaborate decoration of the cast bronze. Most of the surface is covered with an ornamental pattern in bluish-black niello, and the wings and eyes are inlaid with silver. Together with the gilding, this creates a particularly colourful appearance. The combination of the various materials and the refinement of the execution give this bronze piece the look of a precious product of the goldsmith's art, a characteristic feature of a group of objects whose creation can be attributed to Helmarshausen Abbey in northern Hesse.

FKi

The Wilten Chalice

**Communion Chalice with Paten and Straw,
known as the Wilten Chalice**
Lower Saxony (?), *c.* 1160/70
Silver, partly gilt, niello; chalice: H. 16.7 cm (6½ in.);
paten: Diam. 23.5 cm (9¼ in.)
Inv. no. KK 8924

This communion set from Wilten Abbey, Innsbruck, consists of a chalice, a paten and two silver straws, which in the high Middle Ages were used by the congregation to drink the consecrated wine at Holy Communion. The direct and symbolic relationship between chalice and paten is underscored by the complex sequence of images decorating their outer surfaces. The close succession of scenes begins on the base of the chalice with events from the Old Testament, continues on the cup with episodes from the New Testament, and reaches its narrative culmination on the paten, which in the course of the mass was placed over the chalice. The paten's underside (overleaf, right) shows Christ on the cross as a vivid expression of the Christian doctrine that the blood shed by Jesus on the cross becomes present in the Eucharist. On the paten's top side (overleaf, left), the series of sacred images from the Resurrection to Christ's Ascension is completed, with commentary on the narrative in the form of a number of engraved inscriptions.

This richness of content finds a counterpart in the splendid visual appearance of the chalice set: nearly all of its surfaces are filled with figurative engravings that are partly left silver and partly gilded and set against a nielloed background. Because of the inscription 'BERTOLDVS' on the chalice's base, the ensemble is generally believed to have been a gift from Count Bertold III of Andechs-Merania (d. 1188) to Wilten Abbey, from where it was purchased in 1938 by the Kunsthistorisches Museum.

FKi

Two Rock-Crystal Vessels

Two-Handled Vase
Palermo, 1st half of
13th century
Rock crystal; setting: gilt
silver (mid-18th century),
H. 40.5 cm (16 in.)
Inv. no. KK 2316

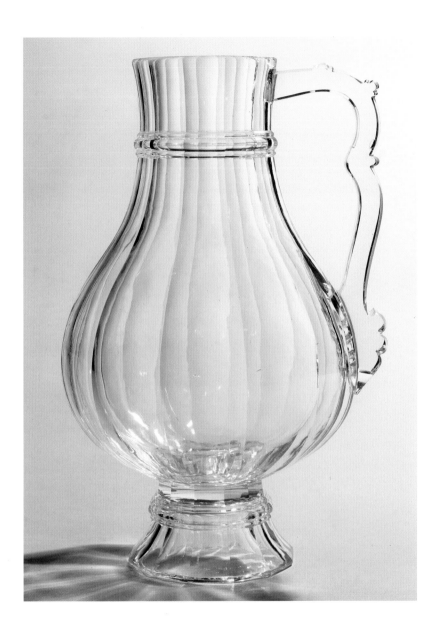

Jug with Handle
Paris, 1st half of
14th century
Rock crystal,
H. 26.3 cm (10⅛ in.)
Inv. no. KK 2272

These two rock-crystal vessels form the centrepiece of the extraordinarily rich holdings of medieval hardstone objects in Vienna's Kunstkammer. The monolithic – meaning carved from a single block – vase with two handles weighs 12.8 kg (28 lbs) and is thought to be the largest extant medieval vessel of its kind in the world, while the smaller jug with a single handle is regarded as one of the most important testimonies to the high level of artistic and technical skill attained by the art of hardstone carving in medieval Europe.

During the Middle Ages, Constantinople, Palermo, Venice, Paris and Prague were all centres for the manufacture of costly vessels of this kind, which found their way from these cities to the sacred and secular courts of the west. The monumental double-handled vase is presumably an example of the highly developed art of gem-cutting that flourished in Sicily under the Hohenstaufen Emperor Frederick II (1194–1250). The superbly made one-handled jug, on the other hand, made of particularly pure rock crystal, is likely a product of the equally exacting Parisian court artists of the first half of the 14th century.

The large vase is mentioned for the first time in 1598 in the inventory of King Philip II of Spain's estate, where it is valued at a price several times higher than that of paintings by such major painters as Titian. In 1666 the vase came to Vienna as part of the dowry of Infanta Margarita Teresa, the first wife of Emperor Leopold I.

FKi

Two Cameos with Mythological Motifs

Poseidon as Master of the Isthmian Games (?)
Cameo: Southern Italy, *c.* mid-13th century
Sardonyx; setting: gold (18th century),
cameo: H. 7 cm, W. 8.8 cm
Inv. no. ANSA IXa 62

Poseidon and Athena
Cameo: Southern Italy,
2nd quarter of the 13th
century
Onyx; setting: enamelled
gold, precious stones
(Spain, early 17th
century), cameo:
H. 3.5 cm (1½ in.),
W. 2.6 cm (1 in.)
Inv. no. ANSA XII 143

As early as classical antiquity, the art of cutting small-scale images into precious stones of great hardness, such as onyx, sardonyx and chalcedony, was held in high esteem. In the Middle Ages, ancient cameos and intaglios were frequently reused as ornaments for ecclesiastical objects. They also occasionally served to inspire newly created works, as in the case of these two outstanding cameos.

Poseidon, the Greek god of the sea, appears in both scenes: in the one scene he battles Athena for sovereignty over Attica; in the other, which is more difficult to interpret, he stands at the centre of the composition, presumably as the founder of the Isthmian Games. In the case of the scene showing the contest between Poseidon and

Athena, not only has the antique cameo that served as the model for the work survived but so has another replica from the 13th century, whose inscription makes it clear that the man and woman beside the tree with the serpent at their feet were intended to be Adam and Eve.

With regard to the time and place of these masterpieces' creation, scholars have argued persuasively that the works are related to the court of the Hohenstaufen Emperor Frederick II (1194–1250) and his circle in southern Italy. There are, however, no unequivocal historical sources pertaining to the manufacture of cut stones of this kind in that region.

FKi

The Krumau Madonna

Madonna and Child, known
as the Krumau Madonna
Prague (?), *c.* 1390/1400
Calcareous sandstone, partly painted
and gilded, H. 110 cm (43¼ in.)
Inv. no. KK 10156

In the art of the late 14th century, a style of depicting the Madonna and Child became established in which the mother of God was bestowed with childlike grace and great charm, aptly described by scholars as the *schöne Madonna* or 'beautiful Madonna'. The so-called 'Krumau Madonna' in the Vienna collection, discovered in the early 20th century in a house in the South Bohemian city of Český Krumlov, is among the most famous extant examples of this type. It splendidly combines the idealized portrayal of the Queen of Heaven with the image of a loving mother and realistic observation from nature in its portrayal of the naked infant. Mary's crown, parts of her veil, and the left arm and right hand of the young Jesus, in which he presumably held an apple, have been lost. The polychromy of the garments, originally white, blue and gold, has also been nearly completely lost. The gilding of the hair, however, and the sublime and subtle coloration of the skin have fortunately been largely preserved.

Mary's body almost completely disappears beneath the fullness of her garments, whose cascades of folds were a characteristic feature of the International Gothic style of the period around 1400. The Krumau Madonna, which itself served as the model for several other Madonna statues, is generally considered to be associated with the courtly art of Prague under the emperors of the House of Luxembourg.

FKi

The *Wiener Musterbuch*

Musterbuch (Sample Book) with Leather Case
Prague, *c.* 1410/20, with later additions: Vienna, *c.* 1430/40
Silverpoint heightened in colour, ink, maple, paper; leather;
drawings: each H. 9.5 cm (3¾ in.), W. 9 cm (3½ in.)
Inv. nos. KK 5003, KK 5004

This sketchbook, known as the *Wiener Musterbuch*, is a compilation of fifty-six individual drawings that a miniaturist presumably assembled to use as models for his studio work or for presentations for potential clients. The drawings, masterly executed with silverpoint, ink and a few accents of colour on green tinted paper, were glued in groups of four in recessed sections of concertina-like wooden panels. The sketches are arranged loosely into groups of animal depictions and human heads; this indicates connections with sacred Christian themes as well as with subjects related to the secular world of the court. The creator of these drawings can with certainty be placed in the field of book illumination and in the artistic circle of the book-lover King Wenceslas IV (1361–1419) in Prague.

Still in the second quarter of the 15th century – probably in Vienna – the portraits of a man and of a woman with a bonnet were added to the somewhat older series of drawings in the collection, attesting to the particularly high regard in which the *Musterbuch* was held as early as the late Middle Ages. This esteem is confirmed by the fact that a leather case, with carved decoration, was custom-made for the book to protect the delicate paper. Eyelets punched into the sides were originally intended for the attachment of a cord, which could be used to draw the case closed and transport it.

FKi

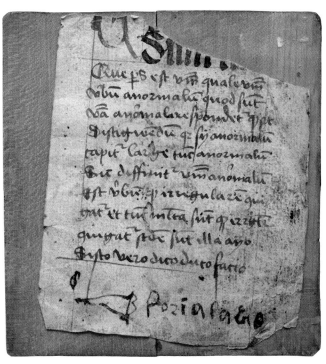

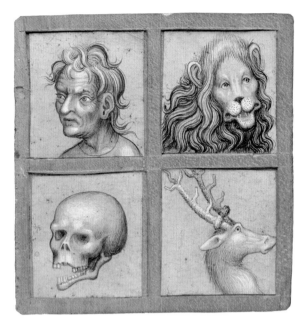

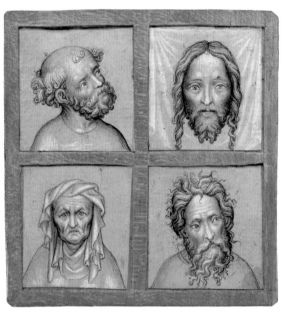

Four Cards from the
Ambras Court Hunting Pack

Workshop of Konrad Witz
Basel, *c.* 1440/45
Pen drawings, watercolour, opaque paint, shell gold,
paper, H. 15.6 cm (6⅛ in.), W. 9.5 cm (3¾ in.)
Inv. nos. KK 5019, KK 5022, KK 5041, KK 5049

The deck of cards known as the Ambras Court Hunting
Pack or *Hofjagdspiel* is – along with the *Hofämterspiel*
or Ambras Court Officials Pack (KK 5077–KK 5124), also
found in Vienna's Kunstkammer – among the earliest extant card games from the region north of the Alps. Of
the original fifty-six cards of the Court Hunting Pack,
comprising four suits, fifty-four have been preserved. The
cards from Ace to Ten are followed by Knave, Knight,
Queen and King. This structure matches the Venetian
Tarot; however, the twenty-two trump cards are omitted.
The four suits are derived from falconry motifs: the falcon
as a hunting bird, the silver heron as prey, the hunting
dogs, and the bait to lure the falcon back to its master.

The painters of these cards, who in all likelihood were
active in the workshop of the noted Basel-based painter

Konrad Witz, created depictions of contemporary hunting life that in terms of both their figural composition and their landscape design show a richness of variety and high degree of realism that are unparalleled in their time and in this medium.

The paintings remain unfinished, however. In several spots, the preparatory sketch, executed with pen and ink, is visible. The reasons for this are unknown. Nevertheless, the fact that the cards' motifs were related to hunting, an important courtly pastime and symbol of status, meant that even in their incomplete form they were apparently so highly prized that the set was later acquired for the art collection of Archduke Ferdinand II of Tyrol (1529–95) at Ambras Castle, where they still remain.

FKi

'Adder's Tongues' and 'Griffin Claws'

Drinking Horn, known as the 'Griffin Claw'
Low German, 2nd half of 15th century
Buffalo horn; setting: gilt silver and gilt bronze
Inv. no. KK 80

Shark's Tooth Table Ornament
Nuremberg (?), *c.* mid-15th century
Gilt silver, fossilized shark's teeth, citrine, H. 27 cm (10⅝ in.)
Inv. no. KK 89

In the Middle Ages and the early modern period, unusually shaped objects and exotic materials spawned countless mythical tales about their origins and powers. Thus the sharply bowed form of buffalo, bison and aurochs horns led to fanciful speculation that they were actually the claws of the griffin, the mythical creature with a lion's body and an eagle's head and wings that had been a familiar figure since antiquity. These drinking horns were thought to be endowed with the power to make visible and neutralize any poison in the beverage they contained. Thus, the name 'griffin claw' came to designate the type of drinking vessel used for this purpose. In the case of the specimen in the Kunstkammer, this connection is alluded to by a small winged griffin that supports the 'claw'.

The ability to detect poison was also ascribed to fossilized shark's teeth, which were believed to be the teeth of dragons or the tongues of snakes. Known as *Natternzungen* ('adder's tongues') in German or as tongue stones in English, they were used as amulets or affixed to eating or drinking vessels. In the form of an ornament called a *Natternzungen-Kredenz* or 'adder's tongue credenza', they were placed in the dining room on a side table, to test the food and drink of high-ranking people for poison. Today, only three of these unusual objects are known to exist. The example in Vienna's Kunstkammer takes the form of a pedestal bearing a small tree whose branches are set with fifteen shark's teeth. At the top is a large citrine.

FKi

The *Prunkbecher* of Emperor Frederick III

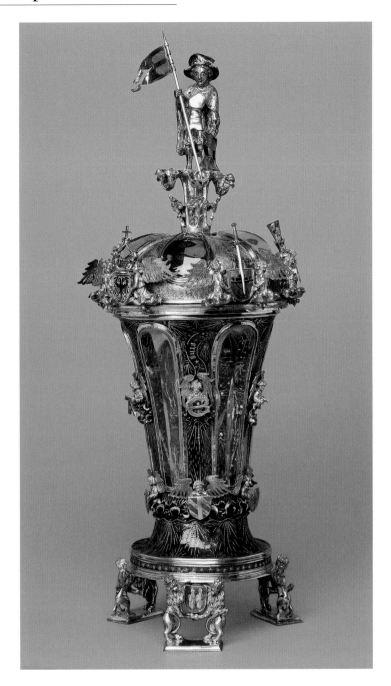

Burgundian Netherlands,
3rd quarter of 15th century
Gilt silver, translucent enamel,
metal foil, rock crystal,
H. 41.5 cm (16¼ in.)
Inv. no. KK 65

This magnificent lidded beaker counts among the highlights of the late medieval goldsmith's art found in the Vienna Kunstkammer. It not only possesses a particularly rich and ornate decoration of coloured translucent enamel with fused, stamped gilt foil; it also makes a direct reference to Emperor Frederick III (1415–93). Three pairs of lions holding coats of arms bear the base of the lidded beaker, whose outside wall, between the rock crystal windows, is painted with violet and green enamel, while the inside surface is coated with blue enamel. Angel busts affixed near the bottom of the beaker and on the lid hold coats of arms representing the territory of the Habsburg empire and glorifying Frederick as ruler of the Holy

Roman Empire. The angel busts that encircle the middle of the beaker bear the letters 'AEIOV', the famous cryptic formula used by Frederick III. Above the busts, the same series of vowels appears again in fused metal foil; in this case, its message is written out: '*aquila eius iuste omnia vincet*', meaning 'His eagle is destined to conquer all'.

Scholars have long surmised that this beaker was presented to Frederick III as a gift at his famous meeting with Duke Charles the Bold (1433–77) in Trier in 1473. While no historical evidence has as yet emerged to support this conjecture, the enamel decoration technique does suggest a provenance in the region of the Burgundian Netherlands.

FKi

75

Vanitas or *Allegory of Vanity*

Jörg Syrlin the Elder (Ulm, *c.* 1425–Ulm, 1491),
or Michel Erhart (*c.* 1440/45–Ulm, after 1522)
Ulm, *c.* 1470/80
Limewood with original paint, H. 46 cm (18⅛ in.)
Inv. no. KK 1

The *Vanitas* group in Vienna's Kunstkammer is among the most famous small-scale carvings from Northern Europe dating from the period before and around 1500. Sharing a round base, three naked figures stand back to back: a young woman, a young man and an old woman. The figures were carved as a group from a single piece of wood, with the women's long hair crafted in a virtuoso manner to cover the join at their backs. The differentiation between the stages of life as a symbol of transience is accentuated by the harsh realism in the depiction of the body of the old woman and further heightened through the masterly polychromy. The pale, rosy hue of the young couple's flawless skin stands in stark contrast to the yellowish brown tone of the old woman's vein-streaked form, on which painted flies serve to intensify the image of a decrepit body.

It is not known what the intended purpose of this group was at the time of its creation in Ulm. In the 19th century it was mounted on a revolving base in a windowed case; for this reason scholars have speculated that it may originally have served as part of a mechanical clock with revolving figures. Historians also consider it possible that the group was created as a small sculpture with no specific purpose other than to ornament a *Kunstkammer*.

FKi

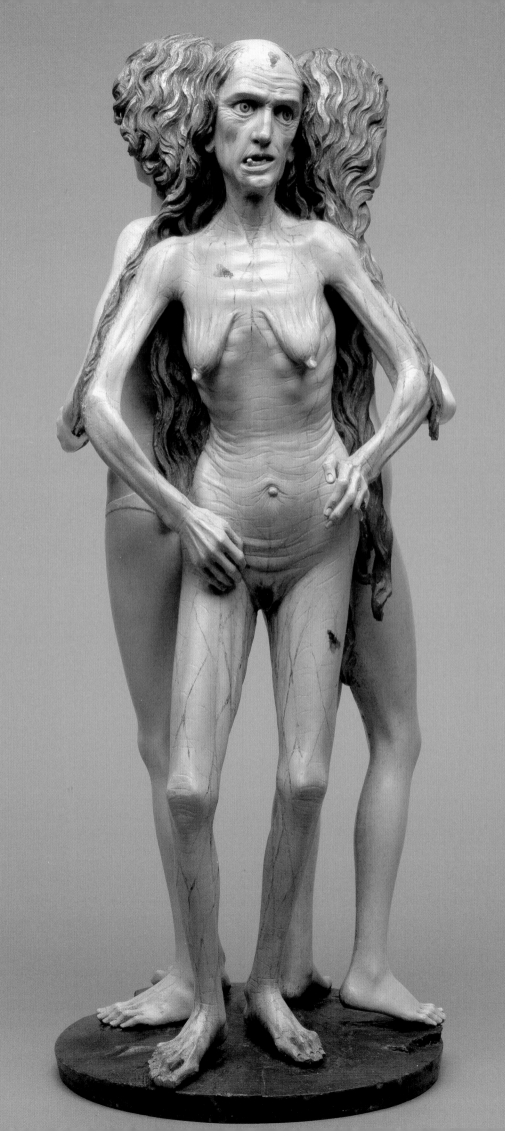

Virgin and Child

This statue of the Virgin and the Christ Child, hollowed out at the back and designed strictly to be viewed from the front, was doubtless originally part of a larger work. It presumably constituted the centrepiece of an altar retable that was later lost.

Art historians have long attributed this Madonna to Tilman Riemenschneider, the most important sculptor north of the Alps during the transition from the late Gothic period to the Renaissance. Master Tilman, who had his workshop in Würzburg, created numerous sacred sculptures of wood and stone, such as portal sculptures, tombs, altarpieces and devotional pictures. Riemenschneider was one of the first woodcarvers to forego the polychrome finish that had been obligatory until then, thus preparing the way for the use of bare wood as an artistic device.

The Vienna group was fully painted in the traditional manner by a polychromist, and the extensive gilding emphatically underscores the dignity and status of the Madonna as the venerable Queen of Heaven and Mother of God. This type of depiction of the Virgin, with the Christ Child held crossways in front of her chest, recurs in several other works by Riemenschneider.

FKi

Tilman Riemenschneider
(Osterode/Harz, c. 1460–Würzburg, 1531)
Würzburg, c. 1500
Limewood with original paint,
H. 145 cm (57⅛ in.)
Inv. no. KK 8899

The Dürer Goblet and the Maximilian Goblet

Among the most significant works of the German gold-smith's art in the late Gothic and Renaissance periods are *Buckelpokale*, or 'lobed cups', whose distinguishing characteristic is the rounded bosses protruding from the vessel's walls. These lobes lend stability to the cup while at the same time enhancing its appearance, as they reflect the light more intensely and in a more differentiated manner than would a flat surface.

The impeccably designed and executed form of the Dürer Goblet, with its distinctive motif of three intertwined bosses, exactly matches a cup sketched by Albrecht Dürer (1471–1528). For this reason, scholars have long assumed that the cup in Vienna's Kunstkammer was also designed by Dürer, who is known to have completed an apprenticeship as a goldsmith; it therefore bears the name of the great German Renaissance artist.

The second cup was made only ten years later: its designation as the Maximilian Goblet derives from the coat of arms, bearing the imperial double eagle, found on the inside of the lid. As early as the late 16th century, Habsburg inventories assigned this coat of arms specifically to Emperor Maximilian I (1459–1519). In the case of this cup, the design has been transformed entirely in keeping with the spirit of the Renaissance: the geometric lobes have been replaced by realistically depicted pears on the base, cup and lid. The lid is crowned by a masterfully conceived tendril bearing lifelike thistle blossoms.

FKi

Albrecht Dürer Sketchbook

Cover: brown calfskin (over cardboard) with blind-tooled lines and gold stamping, H. 47.5 cm (18¾ in.), W. 37 cm (14⅝ in.)
Contents: 230 drawings and prints; an additional four folios from Dürer's *Apocalypse* are enclosed as loose sheets
Inv. no. KK 5127

Nymph of the Spring (opposite)
c. 1514
Pen on brushstroke outline, lightly painted with watercolours

Dream Vision (left)
1525
Watercolour

This sketchbook was part of the art collection of Archduke Ferdinand II of Tyrol (1529–95) at Ambras Castle. The book contained a set of woodcuts and prints from metal plates by Dürer, who played an important role in elevating these media to the ranks of artistic respectability. Also included are thirteen sketches: eight of these are by Dürer himself, four are attributed to Hans Ritter, known as Döring, and one is by an anonymous artist. Döring, who was active between 1514 and 1557, studied under Dürer and was possibly responsible for compiling the works. This collection may have served him, among other things, as a ready stock of model motifs, a personal art collection in a practical format.

Four drawings by Dürer with mythological themes represent a separate group in this artist's oeuvre. The outlines of the depictions are executed here with a brush using red and blue paint and subsequently traced over with a pen. Among this group is the *Nymph of the Spring*.

The famous *Dream Vision,* another original work by Dürer, documents in both visual and written form a nightmare in which Dürer witnesses the earth being flooded by deluges of water falling from the sky. The sketch, executed in watercolour, shows an astounding expanse of space in which the small houses and trees are rendered nearly indistinct.

KSvL

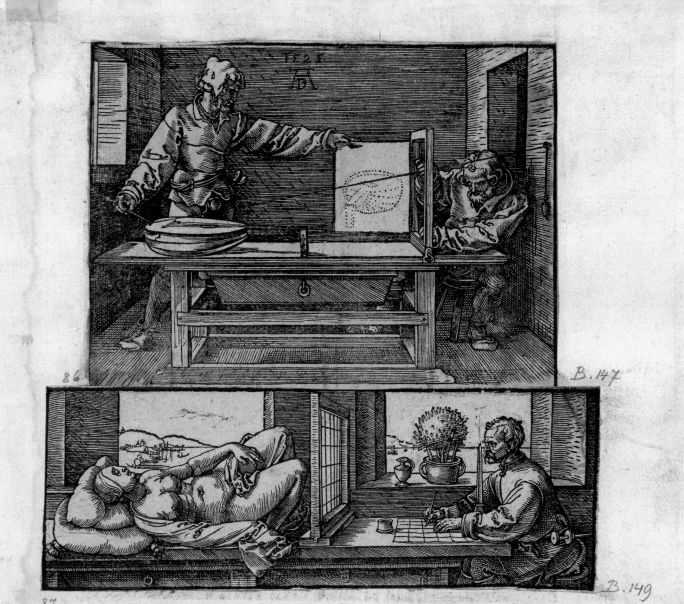

86   B.147

87   B.149

88   L.415.

Virgin and Child by Donatello

Donatello (Florence, 1386–
Florence, 1466), tondo
Gilt bronze, Diam. 27 cm
(10⅝ in.)
Desiderio da Settignano
(Settignano, *c.* 1429/30–
Florence, 1464), frame
Florence, *c.* 1445
Marble, originally partly
gilded, H. 88 cm (34⅝ in.),
W. 51 cm (20⅛ in.)
Inv. no. KK 7462

This house altar, intended for private devotion, consists of a masterfully crafted marble frame, probably an early work by Desiderio da Settignano, and set into it, a gilt bronze tondo by Donatello depicting the Mother of God as the 'Madonna of Humility'. The retable, quite remarkable in terms of its form, was undoubtedly created for Cosimo de' Medici the Elder, Donatello's friend and most important private patron. The highly gifted Desiderio may have trained with Donatello, and the two collaborated frequently until the younger artist's early death.

With his ingenious design for the aedicula-like frame, Desiderio seems to express his admiration for the work of the older sculptor. His youthful eagerness to experiment manifests itself in the bold openwork candelabras flanking the frame, the unorthodox combination of the architectural elements, and the liberal variation of the ornaments. With his virtuoso rendering of the two angels holding the banderole, Desiderio pays homage to the technique of *rilievo schiacciato*, or 'flattened relief', developed by Donatello. The altarpiece is crowned by a fruit bowl that at first glance appears somewhat crude; however, it was probably intended to be coloured with a polychrome glaze. This technique was becoming fashionable at the time, as the glazed terracotta works of Andrea della Robbia demonstrate.

CKG

Laughing Boy

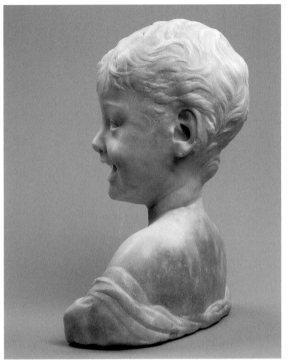

Desiderio da Settignano (Settignano, *c.* 1429/32–
Florence, 1464)
Florence, *c.* 1460/64
Marble, H. 33 cm (13 in.), W. 21.5 cm (8½ in.)
Inv. no. KK 9104

In the second edition of his book on the lives of Italian artists, published in 1568, Giorgio Vasari extolled the style of
Desiderio for its delicate grace and reported that the artist's
statue of the *Christ Child*, which crowns his Tabernacle of
the Sacrament in San Lorenzo, Florence, was so popular
that every Christmas it was placed on the high altar for
veneration. Desiderio's gift for evoking tenderness thus
predestined him for works to be used for private devotion.
A genre apparently invented by him is that of small-scale
busts of young boys as idealized depictions of Christ and
St John the Baptist. According to contemporary writings
on education, encouraging children to identify with these
divine role models served to promote virtuous behaviour.

Desiderio is credited with the execution of a group of
touching busts of boys that, although idealized, are so
realistic that they have often been assumed to be portraits.
Particularly in the case of this boy in the Kunstkammer,
whose cheerful, carefree laughter lends the bust a delight-
ful liveliness, it is difficult to see anything but the portrayal
of a beloved child – Desiderio himself was the father of
four children. Even the execution of the boy's wavy, silky
hair is of such striking individuality that this bust could
well be seen as one of the earliest portraits of a child in
the history of art. Works such as these, as well as his sensi-
tive busts of women, made Desiderio a pioneer of portrait
sculpture. Through his subtle treatment of stone, coupled
with exceptional powers of observation, he succeeded in
breathing warm life into the hard marble.

CKG

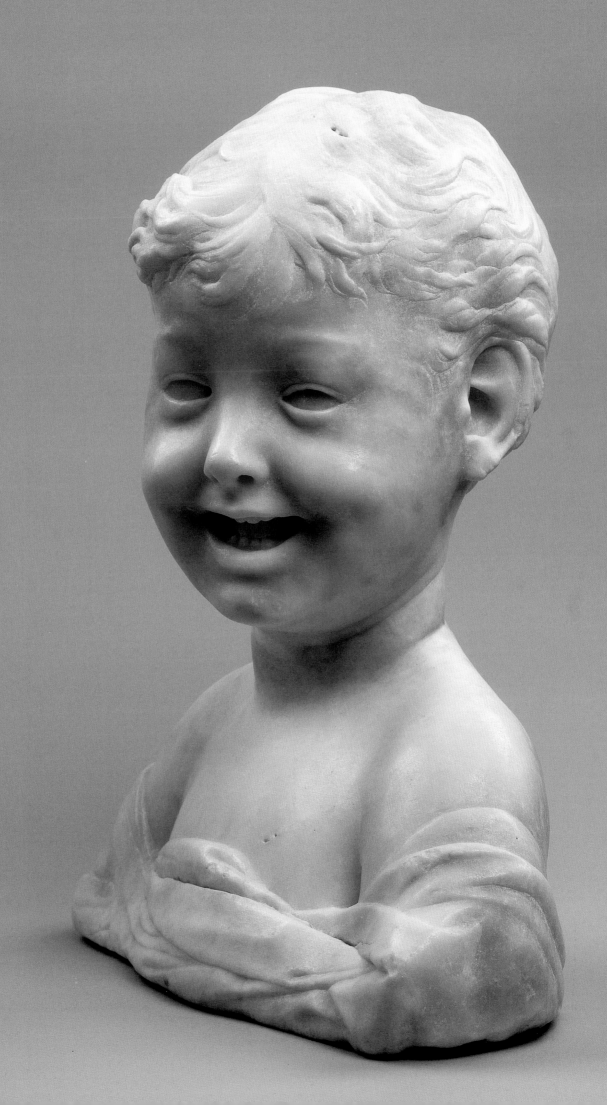

Madonna and Child by Antonio Rossellino

Antonio was the youngest member of a family of stone-cutters named Gambarelli. 'Rossellino' is actually a nick-name ('little redhead'), originally used only for Antonio. Today, however, he and his elder brother Bernardo – also a noted sculptor – are both known by this name.

This relief in the Kunstkammer is among Antonio's love-liest creations as well as representing one of the outstanding examples of early Renaissance Florentine sculpture. It depicts the seated Madonna, holding the boy Jesus on her lap, with two adoring angels in the background. Mother and child gaze seriously and pensively at the bird, symbolizing the Passion, that Christ holds in his left hand. These types of depictions were intended for private devotion; for this reason, tender intimacy and a nearly tangible physical presence were important criteria. The relief therefore ends below the Virgin's knees, with no distinct edge, in order to bring the figures as close as possible to the viewer and thus close the divide between the beholder and the image. The artist also achieves a remarkably convincing three-dimensional effect that results from the skilful alternation between sections in high relief and those with a flatter surface. The subtle delicacy of his treatment of the marble – which seems to purge the stone of its hardness, as can be seen in the gently flowing folds of the drapery as well as in the soft, chubby cheeks of the child – is characteristic of Antonio's finest work. In the 15th century, copies of this Madonna were being made with cheap materials such as painted plaster or stucco, whereas the execution in marble suggests a commission for a special client.

CKG

Antonio Rossellino (Settignano, 1427–Florence, 1479)
Florence, c. 1465/70
Marble, H. 69.5 cm (27⅜ in.), W. 52 cm (20½ in.)
Inv. no. KK 5455

Bust of a Woman

Francesco Laurana (Vrana, 1430–
Avignon, 1502)
Last quarter of 15th century
Polychromed marble, wax
applications, H. 44 cm (17⅜ in.),
W. 42.5 cm (16¾ in.)
Inv. no. KK 3405

Francesco Laurana was born in Dalmatia, at that time part of the Republic of Venice. Laurana was an itinerant artist who worked in Naples, Sicily and France, where he was an early disseminator of the Renaissance style. Among his most important works are half a dozen female busts whose strict stylization exerts a mysterious attraction. As two of these busts can be recognized through their inscriptions as portraits of Battista Sforza and Beatrice of Aragon, scholars have been tempted to identify the remaining busts as members of this family as well. Although the element of idealization in the execution of female portraits in this period makes a conclusive identification virtually impossible, there have been various suggestions that this bust depicts Eleonora or Isabella of Aragon, or perhaps Ippolita Maria Sforza – speculations that have yet to be confirmed.

Due to the close resemblance of the Vienna bust to a portrait, preserved in a manuscript, of Laura, the unattainable beloved of the Italian poet Petrarch, she too has been suggested as the subject. It is quite plausible that Laurana was interested in this theme, if only because of the play on words related to his own name. In any event, thanks to the original, largely preserved polychromy of this bust, it is evident that its golden hair and dark eyes match the qualities that Petrarch extolled in Laura. These features can be conveyed only with paint and cannot be chiselled; for this reason the sculptor may have wished to demonstrate with his painted marble bust that his work could unite the two rival genres in the *paragone*, the ongoing debate regarding the relative merits of painting and sculpture.

CKG

Poet Singing to his Beloved

Poet Singing to his Beloved (Allegory of Music?),
formerly known as *Bacchus and Ariadne*
Tullio Lombardo (Venice, 1455–Venice, 1532)
Venice, *c.* 1505/10
Marble, traces of paint, H. 56 cm (22 in.),
W. 71 cm (28 in.), Diam. 20 cm (7⅞ in.)
Inv. no. KK 7471

This relief is one of the most beautiful works of the Venetian Renaissance and a key work by Tullio Lombardo, one of Venice's leading sculptors in the period around 1500. Through the invention of a new genre – idealized portraits in the form of reliefs – Tullio sought to broaden his field of activity. While his work had traditionally been limited to altars and tomb sculptures, he also wished to produce works that would appeal to private collectors, such as antique objects and paintings. The format of this relief resembles an easel painting. In the style of ancient tomb stelae, it shows two busts – recognizable by the cut-off upper arms – placed on a narrow baseplate. Tullio, however, plays a trick of illusion on the viewer: although he is actually depicting a sculpture within a sculpture, he models the busts with such sensuality that they seem to be feeling, living beings: gazing dreamily into the distance, the two lovers lean their lovely heads close together while the young man, crowned with the ivy wreath of a poet and with his lips slightly parted and Adam's apple in motion, sings a song (pastoral poems were sung) to his beloved, who listens in rapture. Since the love that perceptibly links the two figures represents the inspiration for the poet, his lover is also his muse, which justifies her nakedness. Although the female wears a fashionable hairnet, the classicized style of the relief makes the couple seem oddly disconnected from their time, bringing to mind the poetic suggestiveness of the paintings of Giorgione or Titian.

CKG

The Entombment of Christ

Andrea Mantegna (near Padua,
1431–Mantua, 1506), attributed
Mantua, *c.* 1480
Bronze partly gilt, H. 24.4 cm (9⅝ in.),
W. 44.9 cm (17¾ in.)
Inv. no. KK 6059

There has long been controversy with regard to the creator of this exceptional relief. Although the work is strongly reminiscent of Donatello in its expressiveness, none of his successors would have been capable of this degree of refinement. For this reason, the painter Andrea Mantegna, who according to historical sources also worked as a sculptor, is increasingly considered to be the likely artist. Mantegna, whose pictures exhibit a latent sculptural character, was fascinated by classical carvings and during his time in Padua his art was greatly influenced by Donatello. His work at the artistically inclined Gonzaga court, for which Antico created his partly gilded small bronzes (p. 102), may have supplied the final stimulus for Mantegna not to merely paint clever imitations of sculptures but to actually produce them. Indeed, this entombment scene suggests that it could not have been conceived by a professional sculptor: it is more drawn than modelled, and uses artistic devices that are effective in producing the illusion of space in a painting but not in a relief. Thus the brilliant composition remains bound to the surface and is dominated by lines. The proportions of the figures and the numerous motif parallels corroborate the attribution to Mantegna of the design at least; it is possible that a Mantuan goldsmith assisted him with the execution. The virtuoso relief, whose many touching details are revealed only when viewed at close range, was presumably created not for private devotion but for a sophisticated collector.

CKG

Two Bronzes with Classical Themes

Pan
Adriano Fiorentino (Florence,
c. 1450/60–Florence, 1499)
Florence, c. 1486 (?)
Bronze, H. 41.4 cm (16¼ in.)
Inv. no. KK 5851

Bellerophon Tames Pegasus
Bertoldo di Giovanni (Florence, c. 1440–Poggio a Caiano, 1491)
Adriano Fiorentino (Florence, c. 1450/60–Florence, 1499), casting
Florence, c. 1481/82
Bronze, H. 32.5 cm (12¾ in.)
Inv. no. KK 5596

The group (above) depicts the taming of the winged horse Pegasus, which threw Bellerophon off its back on the way to Mount Olympus, while the statuette (opposite) represents the shepherd god Pan. Thanks to the signatures on the undersides of the two bronzes we know their makers: Bertoldo was a pupil of Donatello and belonged to the circle of artists around Lorenzo de' Medici (1449–92), in whose garden of antique sculptures he taught Michelangelo, while Adriano, who cast this *Bellerophon*, was probably also one of Bertoldo's pupils before he became active as a bronze founder and medal-maker in Naples and Saxony.

These two works are among the earliest and most renowned small bronzes of the Renaissance, a new genre inspired by antiquity that was devoted largely to pagan subjects and brought the revered age of ancient Greece and Rome into the homes of classically educated collectors in a compact form. In this case, the *Dioscuri*, on the Quirinale in Rome, served as the model for Bertoldo's group.

In their heavy, experimental casting and distinctive chasing, these bronzes show the fascinating features characteristic of early works that are still grappling with the problems of balance. In order to support the weight of his body, the long-legged Pan must lean on a tree branch, and the bucking horse in the Pegasus group is propped up by the figure of Bellerophon; however, half of the hero's body is embedded within that of the horse, which is confusing when viewed from the front, although seen from the side, the effect is that of a relief.

CKG

Venus Felix

Pier Jacopo Alari de Bonacolsi, known as Antico (Mantua, *c.* 1460– Gazzuolo, 1528)
Mantua, *c.* 1510
Partly gilt bronze, H. 29.8 cm (11⅝ in.)
Inv. no. KK 5726

In the 15th century, the artistically minded court of the Gonzagas made Mantua a centre for the fine arts; here, key works of the Renaissance were produced that were very much in keeping with the ideals of the rebirth of antiquity. As the coveted classical originals were expensive and usually unattainable, the court sculptor Antico created for his art-collecting patrons small-scale, sometimes rather freely interpreted reproductions of these works, which gave him his nickname. With his technically brilliant bronze statuettes, which for the first time were also reproducible, Antico invented a new genre that quickly became a commercial success. Of the nine Antico works found today in the Kunstkammer, at least five were in the possession of Isabella d'Este, one of the most avid collectors at the Mantuan court.

Antico modelled this superbly executed statuette on a monumental marble sculpture from the Roman imperial period known as *Venus Felix*, after the inscription it bears. In all likelihood it portrays an Antonine princess, which is why her genitals are completely covered by the drapery and her hand. Antico, however, did away with both her modesty and her severe hairstyle: with the finesse of a goldsmith, he gave his *Venus* the loose, upswept hair of a goddess crowned with a wreath of oak leaves. This is presumably a reference to Pope Julius II, a member of the della Rovere family (*rovere* is Italian for oak). In 1509 Julius II, who had an illegitimate daughter named Felice (Italian, 'happy' or 'lucky'; in Latin: *felix*), installed the original *Venus Felix*, which he owned, in the garden of antique sculptures he had established in the Vatican.

CKG

Boy with a Goose

Andrea Briosco, known as Riccio
(Trent?, 1470–Padua, 1532)
Padua, *c.* 1515/20
Bronze, H. 19.6 cm (7¾ in.)
Inv. no. KK 5518

Although Riccio's style was heavily shaped by the ideals of classical antiquity, as was typical in Northern Italy in around 1500, he sometimes tended towards expressive realism. *Boy with a Goose* represents a lone exception in his unconventional oeuvre, in that it is a copy of a famous antique sculpture. The original Greek bronze, *Boy Strangling a Goose*, had long been lost and would have been familiar to the artist's contemporaries only through the description by the Roman scholar Pliny the Elder in his *Natural History* and from several Roman marble copies. The fact that Riccio selected this work, a classical sculpture so exceedingly complex in its composition and so characteristic of its genre, for small-scale reproduction in bronze is indicative of the artist's temperament. It was not only the potential 'in the round' quality of the sculpture – allowing it to be viewed from all sides, something that would not become commonplace until later in the 16th century – that

seemed to attract him, but also the addition of the boy's missing head, which he reconstructed according to the text passage in Pliny's book, complete with a suitably strained facial expression. Through this, and with the omission of the prop beneath the child's buttocks – which was necessary in the marble versions but detracted from the composition – Riccio demonstrated a knowledge of classical literature, which must have impressed the scholarly circles of Padua. With this bronze he was also competing with the copies of antique sculptures that Antico was producing n Mantua (see p. 102), although Riccio sought to surpass these works through his lively surface modelling. With his chasing of the goose's feathers, which would have done credit to any goldsmith, Riccio demonstrated that he was technically on a par with the artist whom Pliny had praised as the creator of the original *Boy*.

CKG

Two Gilded Reliefs by Moderno

Madonna and Child with Saints (left)

The Scourging of Christ (opposite)

Moderno (active *c.* 1500 in Lombardy and Rome) Rome, *c.* 1510 Silver, partly gilt; *Madonna*: H. 13.9 cm (5½ in.), W. 10.2 cm (4 in.); *Scourging*: H. 13.8 cm (5⅜ in.), W. 10.2 cm (4 in.) Inv. nos. KK 1107, KK 1105

These two reliefs are the finest works of a mysterious master who around 1500 signed a series of small plaques with the pseudonym 'Moderno'. Although the identity of the artist, who certainly came from Northern Italy, remains unclear, he can be counted among the most important representatives of the new genre of plaquettes – small, reproducible reliefs of silver and bronze created specifically for collectors. His pseudonym was possibly a conscious response to that of the Mantuan sculptor Pier Jacopo Alari de Bonacolsi, who was known as Antico (see p. 102).

That there is more to the name 'Moderno' than simply a play on words is powerfully demonstrated by these two reliefs: the depictions of familiar Christian themes are 'modernized' in accordance with contemporary taste through the ingenious use of classical references. The posture of the scourged Saviour, for example, is derived directly from the antique sculpture *Laocoön*, excavated in 1506, while the two henchmen paraphrase the famous *Dioscuri* on Rome's Quirinale. Every detail of the architecture, from the so-called grotesques – which cover the rear wall of the *Madonna* relief in the style of the Domus Aurea, the Golden House of Nero, which had also only recently been discovered – to the garments worn by the figures reveals Moderno's precise knowledge of the classical world. This enabled him to transform a Roman imperator into St George and a splendid nude of Bacchus into St Sebastian. These two figures were also cast separately and then affixed to the Madonna relief, an ingenious method of heightening the three-dimensional effect.

CKG

Carvings by Conrat Meit

Adam and *Eve*
Conrat Meit (Worms, *c.* 1475/80–
Antwerp, 1551)
Mechelen, *c.* 1520
Boxwood; *Adam*: H. 25.5 cm (10 in.);
Eve: H. 24 cm (9½ in.)
Inv. nos. KK 9888, KK 9889

Archduchess Margaret, Regent of the Netherlands
Conrat Meit (Worms *c.* 1475/80–Antwerp, 1551)
Mechelen or Brou, dated 1528
Painted clay, Diam. 9.2 cm (3⅝ in.)
Inv. no. KK 3150

Conrat Meit worked as court sculptor to Archduchess Margaret of Austria (1480–1530), daughter of Emperor Maximilian I and Mary of Burgundy. As regent of the Netherlands, the archduchess was a skilful politician and in Mechelen presided over a court with a great appreciation for art. She practised a type of patronage that was conducive to the work not only of sculptors but also of musicians, writers, tapestry weavers and painters. In her, the Habsburg passion for collecting was very clearly manifested for the first time.

The medallion depicts her dressed as a widow, while the inscription around the edge refers to her status as the daughter of Emperor Maximilian I and the aunt of Emperor Charles V. The clay medallion is probably based on a carved wooden model, no longer extant, from which impressions were made in order to disseminate the portrait of the regent.

With his two freestanding statuettes of *Adam* and *Eve*, Meit created apogees of Renaissance sculpture in the Netherlands, showing the newly awakened interest in depicting the human body. The nudes reveal a thorough understanding of corporeality; their muscles are emphasized and anatomically correct. Conspicuous features are the manner in which Adam leans towards Eve, his contrapposto and the crossed legs of the woman – all motifs borrowed from Albrecht Dürer's 1507 panels of *Adam* and *Eve* (currently in the Museo del Prado, Madrid). Even Eve's self-confident gaze and Adam's inquiring gesture together with his slightly open lips derive from these works.

KS

The Reign of Emperor Charles V

Portrait Bust of Emperor Charles V
Leone Leoni (Menaggio, 1509–
Milan, 1590)
Milan, *c.* 1555
Bronze, H. 113 cm (44½ in.)
Inv. no. KK 5504

Seal Signet of Emperor Charles V
Spain, *c.* 1519/30
Gold, enamel, bloodstone, H. 2.84 cm (1 in.),
L. 2.98 cm (1⅛ in.)
Inv. no. KK 2150

Hat Badge with a Portrait of Charles V
Netherlands or Spain, 1520
Gold, enamel, H. 5.72 cm (2⅛ in.)
Inv. no. KK 1610

The empire of Emperor Charles V (1500–58) was one on which the sun never set. In 1506, he became ruler of the Habsburg lands in Netherlands; in 1516, at the age of sixteen, King of Spain; and in 1519 he succeeded his grandfather Emperor Maximilian I as Holy Roman Emperor and Archduke of Austria.

While the golden hat badge shows him – according to the inscription –- at the age of twenty as ruler of the Spanish crown lands, the large-scale bronze bust depicts him at the height of his power. He is portrayed here in the armour he wore in 1547 in the Battle of Mühlberg, one of his most important military victories against the Protestant Schmalkaldic League. At the same time the bust

is very much in the tradition of portraits of Roman emperors and thus creates a link between Charles V and the rulers of antiquity.

Charles V took as his personal symbol the Pillars of Hercules and as his motto *Plus ultra* ('further beyond'). This ambition to keep expanding his rule in Europe, Africa and the Americas is also evident in the design of his signet stamp. The stamp shows a triumphal chariot, pulled by lions, with an eagle as a symbol of the imperial ruler of the world and the initials V.V.V. These can be read as *veni, vidi, vici* ('I came, I saw, I conquered') and interpreted as a claim to complete rule of the world.

FKi

Tapestry with the Coat of Arms of Emperor Charles V

Brussels, c. 1540
Weaving workshop of Willem de Pannemaker
(active from c. 1535–81)
Wool, silk, metal thread, H. 167 cm (65¾ in.),
W. 273 cm (107½ in.)
Inv. no. T XXXIII/3

In front of a luxuriant background adorned with rich floral motifs, a so-called verdure (from the French word *vert:* green), this tapestry shows the imperial double eagle with crowns on both heads. The eagle holds the quartered coat of arms of Emperor Charles V (1500–58), with the divided inescutcheon showing Flanders and Tyrol. The upper left section of the arms is again quartered, depicting Castile and Leon, while the upper right side is divided into Aragon and Sicily, with the pomegranate of Granada in the bottom tip between the two. The lower left quarter is separated into Austria and Old Burgundy and the lower right into New Burgundy and Brabant.

Charles grew up in Brussels, the centre of European tapestry production in the 16th century. This piece, which formerly belonged to him, is one of a series made in around 1540 in Willem de Pannemaker's weaving workshop, one of the most renowned in the city. Charles's acquisitions of extraordinary tapestries attracted a great deal of attention even in his lifetime, as hangings such as the one shown here were among the most costly and coveted symbols of royal prestige. They were portable and could be installed at any time at a desired location, where they served as a sign of the ruler's claim to power even in his absence.

KSvL

Archduke Ferdinand I

Archduke Ferdinand I
Augsburg, *c.* 1522/27
Marble, gilt wooden frame,
Diam. 20.5 cm (8 in.)
Inv. no. KK 4452

Signet Ring with the Archducal Coat of Arms and Sundial
Southern German (Nuremberg?), *c.* 1524/25
Gold, rock crystal, traces of coloured cold enamel, Diam. 2.8 cm (1 in.)
Inv. no. KK 2183

This marble likeness corresponds to the most widespread portrait type of the young Archduke Ferdinand I. He is depicted here in rigid head-and-shoulders profile portraiture, fashionably dressed, wearing the Order of the Golden Fleece, and with his mouth open. This work was modelled after a silver medal (KHM Coin Cabinet, inv. no. MK MD750bß) attributed to the Augsburg sculptor Hans Daucher, a work that was copied frequently using a variety of artistic techniques. The inscription on the portrait's gilded wooden frame makes it possible to date the work with some accuracy. Ferdinand I is referred to here as the deputy to the emperor, which he became only in 1522 through an agreement with his brother, Emperor Charles V. But in the inscription he does not yet bear the title of King of Bohemia and Hungary, which he assumed in 1527 following the death of his brother-in-law Louis II. The portrait thus depicts the archduke at an age between nineteen and twenty-four.

The elegant image of the young ruler in this portrait is further enhanced by his golden signet ring. It bears the archducal arms, surrounded by the chain of the Order of the Golden Fleece. This ring, however, can also be used as a sundial. The inside of the ring shows the faces of the winter and summer clock, and two small holes have been bored in the middle of the band. When the ring is held vertically towards the sun, the light shines though the holes and shows the time on the dials on the back of the bezel.

KS

Tric-Trac Gameboard

Hans Kels the Elder (Füssen, *c.* 1480/85–Kaufbeuren, 1559)
Jörg Breu the Elder (Augsburg, *c.* 1475/80–Augsburg, 1537),
design and workshop
Georg Hörmann (1491–1552), iconographical scheme
Kaufbeuren, 1537
Wood: oak, walnut, rosewood, mahogany, tulipwood, boxwood;
bronze hinges; board: 56 × 56 cm (22 × 22 in.); playing pieces:
Diam. 6.5 cm (2½ in.)
Inv. nos. KK 3419–KK 3449, KK 7257, KK 7258

This gameboard, which belonged to Emperor Ferdinand I, is a very characteristic *Kunstkammer* piece, as its function as a playing board is secondary to its real purpose as a monument to imperial symbolism. Two hinged wooden panels unfold to reveal the playing surface for 'Langer Puff' and 'Tric-Trac', early versions of backgammon. The exterior design, however, propagates the dynastic and territorial claims of the Habsburgs. In the centre of both panels stand the brothers Charles V and Ferdinand I as armour-clad horsemen, surrounded by portraits of ancestors and relatives, the arms of their crown lands and medallions in the corners portraying Roman emperors and rulers of the ancient world – all devoted to the ideal of the continuation of the Roman Empire and its world domination.

The figurative decoration of the playing pieces is based on Ovid and other classical authors, Boccaccio and the Old Testament: the carvings show love scenes and erotic depictions of women, with the portrayal of some couples relating to the theme of *Minnesklaven*, or 'slaves of love' – perhaps a humanistic allusion to the omnipotence of love.

The board is the work of the Kaufbeuren carver Hans Kels the Elder, who followed designs by Jörg Breu the Elder. The creator of the complex iconographical scheme is presumed to be the Kaufbeuren patrician and classical scholar Georg Hörmann, who as a high-level employee of the Fugger family maintained close relations with the House of Habsburg.

KS

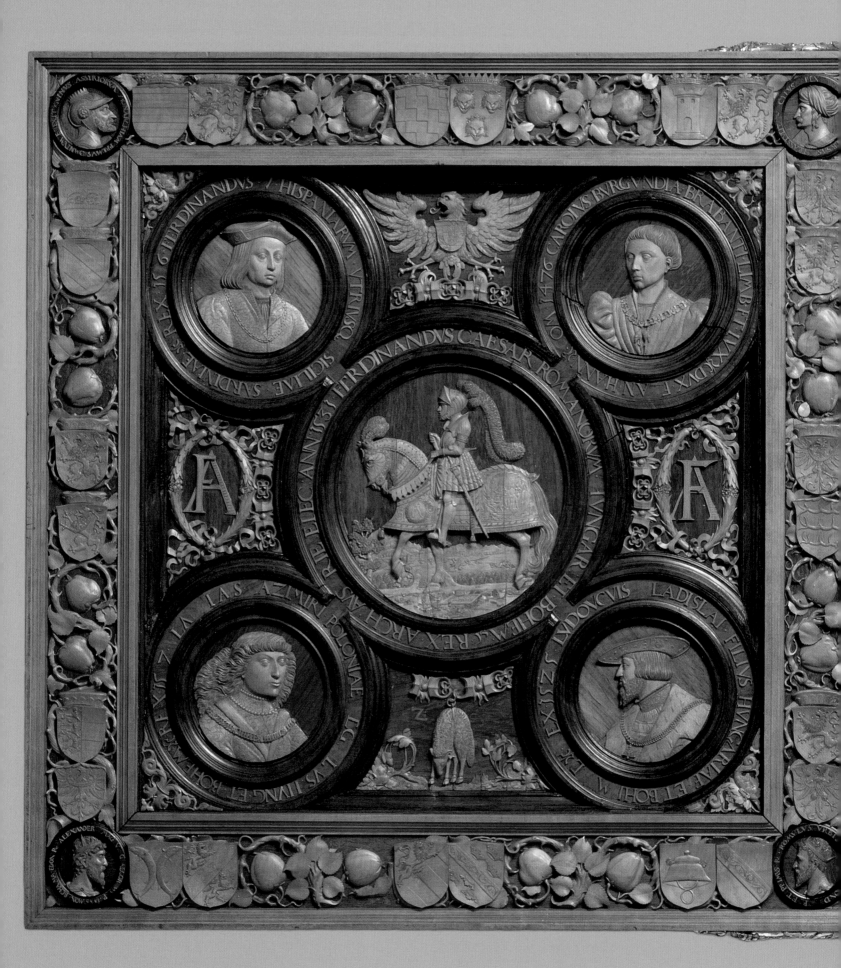

Tapestry: *The Unity of the State*

Francesco Primaticcio (Bologna, 1504–Paris, 1570), design
Claude Badouin, cartoon; Jean and Pierre Le Bries, weavers
Fontainebleau, 1540–50
Tapestry: wool, silk, metal thread, H. 330 cm (130 in.),
W. 620 cm (244 in.)
Inv. no. T cv/6

When the former residence of the kings of France in Fontainebleau was completely renovated between 1528 and 1532, the decoration of the room known as the Gallery of Francis I was entrusted to the Florentine artist Rosso Fiorentino. Later he designed tapestries with mythological themes for Francis I that depict a modified repetition of the decoration of the south wall of this gallery. This instance of existing architecture serving as the model for tapestries is unique in the history of art. Each of the series of six tapestries represents a single wall compartment, and includes not only the central image but also the stucco frame, the edge of the ceiling and the moulding of the wood panelling at the base, creating – particularly when the tapestries are hung alongside each other – an illusionistic impression of a room. This superb series of

hangings was made in Fontainebleau by expert weavers from Paris.

The tapestry shown here portrays the French king as an art-loving, virtuous ruler dressed in the uniform of a Roman emperor and holding a pomegranate, symbolizing life and fertility as well as power and unity. He stands before a backdrop of a splendid palace, while a boy kneeling in front of him offers him another pomegranate.

It is unclear how the Fontainebleau tapestries found their way to Vienna. They were probably presented to Archduke Ferdinand II of Tyrol in 1570 as a token of appreciation for his service to the French king Charles IX: Ferdinand served as Charles's proxy at the latter's wedding that year to Archduchess Elizabeth of Austria.

KSvL

The *Saliera*

Benvenuto Cellini (Florence, 1500–Florence, 1572)
Paris, 1540–43
Gold, partly enamelled, ebony, ivory, H. 26.3 cm
(10⅜ in.), L. 28.5 cm (11¼ in.), W. 21.5 cm (8½ in.)
Inv. no. KK 881

With what he himself referred to as a *Saliera* (salt cellar), Benvenuto Cellini achieved a feat of sculpture that was intended to surpass everything that had come before it, and this masterpiece was his decisive entry into the *paragone*, the ongoing contest for supremacy between the arts. Despite its relatively small size and its conception as a piece of tableware, the *Saliera* is among the most important artworks of the modern age. Moreover, statements by the artist that have been passed down have furnished us with a nearly complete history of its creation. Cardinal Ippolito d'Este, who originally commissioned the piece, initially dismissed Cellini's design as unworkable, but in King Francis I of France, the artist found a patron in possession of the necessary confidence and financial means to have the piece executed in gold. Cellini designed his salt cellar to include a cosmographical programme of images characterized by ambiguities, pairs of opposites and linking elements. The two god-like figures seated opposite each other represent the male and female principle, symbolized by water (Neptune) and earth (Tellus). Neptune is accompanied by a small ship for holding salt, the white gold of the sea, while Tellus has a temple by her side for pepper, the black gold of the earth. Sea and land animals accompany the pair; the four winds, the four times of day and other allegorical depictions complete the complex iconography. Cellini also built ivory balls into the sculpture's base on which the artwork could be rolled back and forth on the table, showing its complexity to its best advantage and allowing it to be viewed from all sides.

PR

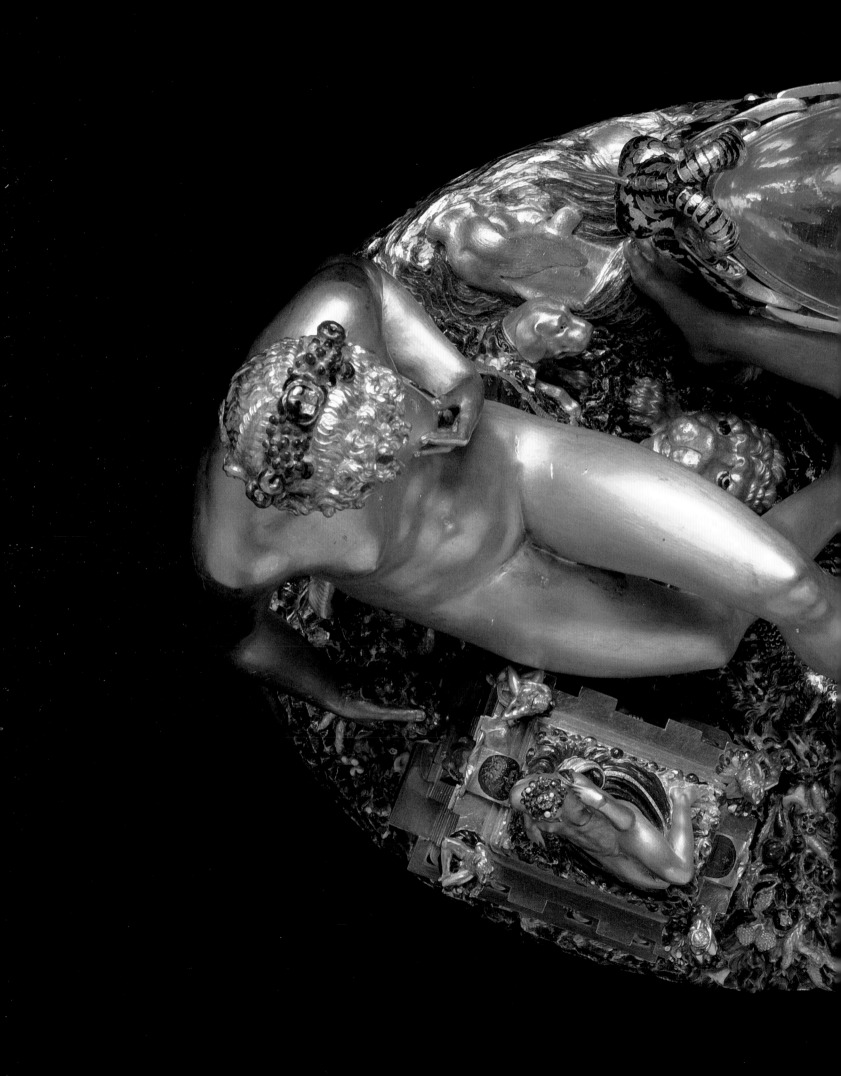

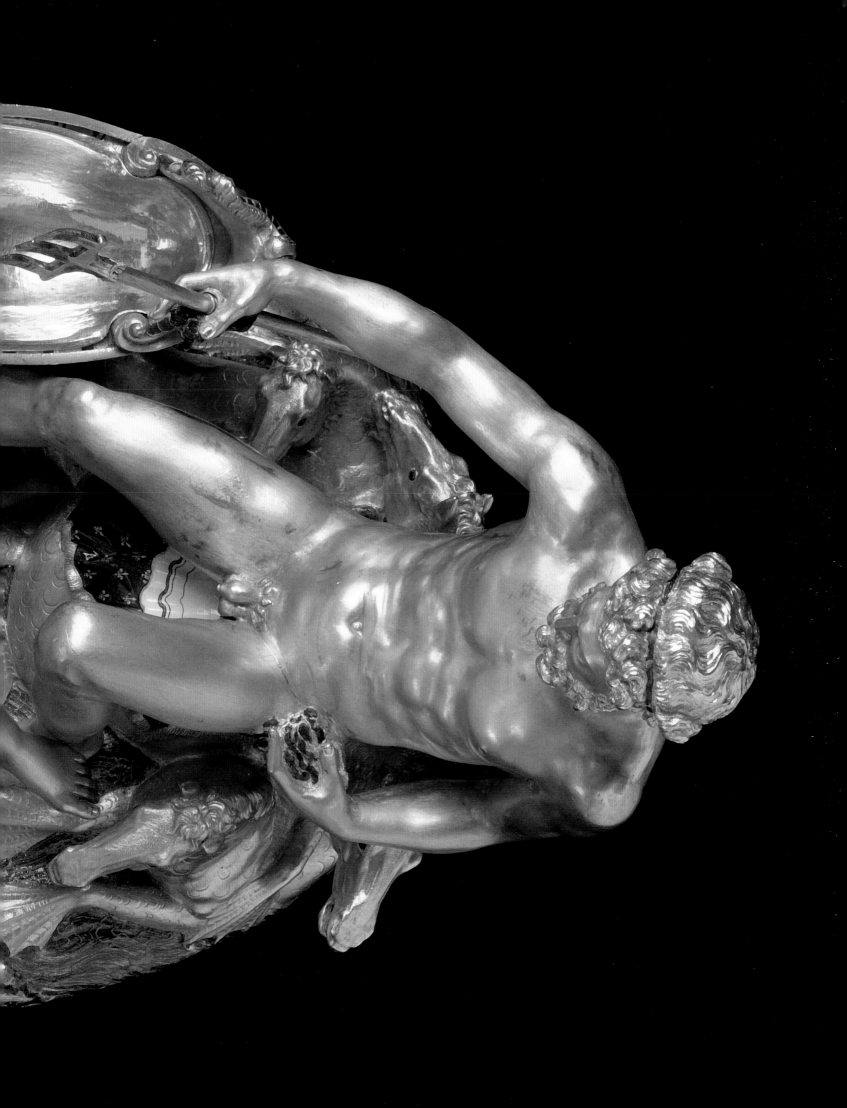

The Burgundian Goblet and the Michael Goblet

Burgundian Goblet ('Burgundischer Hofbecher')
Burgundian Netherlands, between 1453 and 1467
Rock crystal, gold, enamel, champlevé enamel, pearls,
diamonds, rubies, H. 46 cm (18⅛ in.)
Inv. no. KK 27

Michael Goblet
Antwerp, 1532
Gold, partly enamelled, diamonds, emeralds,
rubies, pearls, H. 51.7 cm (20⅜ in.)
Inv. no. KK 1120

These two pinnacles of the gemcutter's and goldsmith's craft in the Middle Ages and Renaissance came into the possession of the Habsburgs in 1570, along with Benvenuto Cellini's *Saliera* (p. 124) and the Onyx Ewer (p. 134), when the French king Charles IX presented them as spectacular gifts to Archduke Ferdinand II of Tyrol. The Burgundian Goblet had previously passed from the estate of Duke Charles the Bold to the French royal treasury, while King Francis I of France purchased the magnificent Michael Goblet from a dealer in Antwerp for the treasury in 1533. These splendid goblets are captivating not only for their material richness and the technical perfection of their execution but also for their balanced and elegant design. The cups are harmoniously enthroned above the slender stems and crowned with elaborate lids. The figure of the archangel Michael, richly studded with diamonds, stands atop the Antwerp goblet and thus gives it its name. Michael is depicted here as the conqueror of Satan, but the name may also be a reference to the French chivalric Order of St Michael. In contrast, the rich gilding of the magnificent rock crystal Burgundian Goblet, with the fire-iron and flint shooting out showers of sparks, bears the personal emblems of the Burgundian duke Philip the Good, which were also used as the emblems of the Order of the Golden Fleece.

PR

Onyx Ewer

Richard Toutain the Younger (master
craftsman from 1558–Paris, 1579)
Paris, 1570
Sardonyx, agate, enamelled gold, diamonds,
rubies, emeralds, pearls, H. 27.9 cm (11 in.),
W. 18.4 cm (7¼ in.)
Inv. no. KK 1096

This extraordinary ewer was one of four gifts – along with Benvenuto Cellini's *Saliera* (p. 124), and the so-called Michael Goblet and Burgundian Goblet (p. 130) – that Archduke Ferdinand II received in 1570 from King Charles IX of France when Ferdinand served as proxy for the French king at the latter's wedding to Archduchess Elizabeth of Austria. The interplay between exquisite goldwork and sophisticated gemcutting makes this a major work of courtly French art of the second half of the 16th century. For this piece, the goldsmith used existing pieces of onyx, combining them with enamelled gold to create a thoroughly homogeneous vessel. Only upon closer inspection is it revealed that the ewer consists of two parts: its upper section with the high handle and spout can be removed from the bottom part and used as a jug with a low foot. The chalice-shaped lower section that remains can, like the upper section, serve as a vessel in its own right.

One reason for this astounding and unique solution was surely the surprise effect created when the ewer was examined more closely. A more important reason, however, was that the goldsmith made the ewer out of pieces of older Byzantine vessels and other fragments, using them skilfully to create something entirely new.

PR

Two Cameos

Leda and the Swan
Paris, c. 1550
Mother-of-pearl opal, gold, enamel, diamonds, rubies
Cameo: 4.7 × 5.5 cm (1⅞ × 2¼ in.); frame: 7.3 ×
7.9 cm (2⅞ × 3⅛ in.)
Inv. no. ANSA XII 123

Moorish Woman
Workshop of Girolamo Miseroni (Milan, 1522–after 1584)
Milan (setting: Prague), 4th quarter of 16th century
Andreas Osenbruck (active in Prague, c. 1610–after 1622), setting
Agate, enamelled gold, diamonds, rubies
Cameo: 3.7 × 5.1 cm (1½ × 2 in.); frame: 6 × 5.9 cm (2⅜ × 2¼ in.)
Inv. no. ANSA XII 120

The renewed interest in classical antiquity that characterized the Renaissance manifested itself, among other things, in the adoption of artistic techniques from that period. With the cameo, Renaissance artists revived one of the most exquisite of ancient art forms, creating magnificent collector's items in this technique. They were increasingly dissatisfied with merely mimicking antiquity; these artists were intent on surpassing it. Characteristic examples of this intent are the two cameos presented here, which were created in Paris and Milan, respectively. With its depiction of *Leda and the Swan*, the Paris piece takes up a theme from Greek mythology; in this interpretation, however, the cameo is combined with delightfully contrasting goldwork, with the colour and lustre of its surface combining to create a harmonious and vibrant work. This is further enhanced by the frame of interlacing tendrils of enamelled gold, studded with diamonds and rubies. The Milan piece, meanwhile, seeks to outdo its ancient predecessors not only in its execution but also in its choice of theme. The natural colour of the rare agate is used here to depict the beautiful dark-skinned woman. In its wonderful interplay of art and nature, the portrait exudes an exotic allure, while the gold frame, which was added in Prague, perfectly complements what is already a splendid stone, creating an exquisite piece of jewelry.

PR

Grisaille Enamel

Footed Bowl, with *The Miracle of St Christopher*
Jean de Court (active 1555–85)
Limoges, 2nd half of 16th century
Copper, enamelled on both sides, Diam. 25.2 cm (10 in.)
Inv. no. KK 3198

Dish
Pierre Reymond (1513–c. 1584)
Limoges, 1558
Copper, enamelled on both sides, Diam. 45.2 cm (17⅞ in.)
Inv. no. KK 3201

The city of Limoges, located in France's northwestern Massif Central region, is renowned for its painted enamel. A particular speciality of the Limoges school was grisaille, in which an image is rendered entirely in shades of grey, a style particularly popular at the court of the French king Francis I. Pierre Reymond, who had his workshop in Limoges, was a prolific artist who made his name primarily with objects decorated in a similar graphic style. The magnificent dish (opposite) was executed in Reymond's workshop; its motif, after a design by Jacques Androuet du Cerceau, shows the triumphal procession of the goddess Diana, framed by a frieze of grotesques.

Among the superb enamel workshops that flourished in Limoges in the 16th century was that of Jean de Court. He is possibly identical with the artist of the same name who was court painter to Mary, Queen of Scots, beginning in 1562 and succeeded François Clouet as painter to the French king Charles IX in 1572. His workshop in Limoges presumably continued to operate during his stay at the French court. The bowl (above) is one of the few extant works that can be linked to de Court; it takes as its theme the story of St Christopher, who on a stormy night carried the Christ Child across a river on his shoulders.

KSvL

Tapestry: *The Seven Deadly Sins: Greed*

Pieter Coecke van Aelst (Aalst, 1502–Brussels, 1550), design
Weaving workshop of Willem de Pannemaker (active from *c.* 1535–81)
Brussels, *c.* 1555
Tapestry: wool, silk, metal thread, H. 450 cm (177 in.),
W. 775 cm (305 in.)
Inv. no. T XXXV/4

The seven-part tapestry series with depictions of the deadly sins is based on designs by the Flemish painter Pieter Coecke van Aelst. In his interpretations, he gives the historical presentation of the sins an innovative and clever new form. A manuscript preserved in Madrid's Biblioteca Nacional de España identifies Coecke van Aelst explicitly as the creator of this series and provides insights into the complex iconography of the tapestries, which incorporate numerous historical, mythological and biblical figures. The hangings bear the mark of the Brussels-based weaver Willem de Pannemaker, who boasted among his clients Emperor Charles V and the emperor's sister Maria of Hungary and also had the honour of bearing the title of '*tapissier* to his Majesty'.

This tapestry is devoted to one of the seven cardinal sins: Greed, Covetousness or Avarice. The personification of Greed, a winged, horned woman, is seated on her triumphal chariot, drawn by a vulture. With both hands she reaches for gold coins in an open casket in front of her. The mounted standard-bearer at the right edge of the composition is a personification of Covetousness with the mole as the symbol of Avarice on her flag. The rider seen from behind is Pygmalion, who according to legend made and fell in love with an ivory statue, which Aphrodite then brought to life (Ovid, *Metamorphoses,* Book 10). The Phrygian king Midas, with his donkey's ears, occupies a prominent place at the centre of the tapestry.

KSvL

Antonio Abondio (Riva del Garda, 1538–Vienna, 1591)
Innsbruck, 3rd quarter of 16th century
Obsidian, wax, pearls, silver, Diam. 11.5 cm (4½ in.)
Inv. no. KK 3074

Emperor Maximilian II (1527–76) is portrayed here in strict profile, the traditional style of coin portraits from antiquity. A laurel wreath crowns his head, a field marshal's baton is grasped in his right hand, and a red sash hangs across his classical-style chest armour. The reverse shows a triumphant Victory with rich spoils of war and a bound, naked figure wearing a turban. The medallion, a monument in miniature, thus celebrates the Emperor of the Holy Roman Empire as vanquisher of the Ottomans. In 1566 Maximilian II did indeed take part in a campaign against the Turks but was not victorious. That same year he took the Northern Italian artist Antonio Abondio into his service as his personal portraitist. Abondio became famous for his naturalistic, polychromed wax reliefs of members of the House of Habsburg and related dynasties.

Maximilian II was known as an exceptionally erudite nobleman, fluent in a number of languages and possessing a great appreciation of art. He inherited the important collection of coins and antiques from his father, Emperor Ferdinand I, and apparently acquired ancient artworks himself. In addition, he was also one of the first Habsburgs to collect paintings – and not merely family portraits – out of an appreciation for the works themselves and their artists, including masterpieces by Titian and Arcimboldo. His *Kunstkammer* also contained an impressive selection of cut gemstones. The bulk of his collection ultimately passed down to his son, Emperor Rudolf II (1552–1612), who kept the works in his own famous *Kunstkammer* at Prague Castle.

KS

Four Gilded Bronze Statuettes

Flora, Ceres, Bacchus and *Vulcan*
(*Allegories of the Four Seasons*)
Johann Gregory van der Schardt
(Nimwegen, *c.* 1530–Uranienborg,
Hven, probably 1591), attributed
Wenzel Jamnitzer (Vienna, *c.* 1508–
Nuremberg, 1585), design (?)
Nuremberg, *c.* 1570
Fire-gilded bronze, H. 71.2 cm
(28⅛ in.), 70.7 cm (27⅞ in.),
71.8 cm (28¼ in.), 71 cm (28 in.)
Inv. nos. KK 1118, KK 1122, KK
1126, KK 1130

These four statuettes are all that remains of a mechanical silver fountain, measuring over 3 metres (10 feet) in height, which the Nuremberg goldsmith Wenzel Jamnitzer began work on in around 1568 as a commission for Emperor Maximilian II. However, the fountain was not completed until 1578, after Maximilian's death, and was instead delivered to his son Rudolf II in Prague. In 1629–30, on the orders of Emperor Ferdinand II, the fountain was brought to Vienna, where it was melted down in the mid-18th century. The four figures of gods representing the seasons survived only because they were made of gilded bronze.

A written description of the fountain dating from about 1640 provides us with a reasonable idea of its original appearance. According to this document it was an indoor fountain in the shape of a monumental imperial hoop crown, supported by caryatids symbolizing the four seasons. This explains why these figures, which held up the entire structure and thus required a degree of stability, are made of bronze. Their slender proportions and elegant poses correspond very closely to the Venetian Mannerist style of the Netherlander Johann Gregory van der Schardt. In view of the outstanding quality of these caryatids, we can imagine what a loss the destruction of the silver fountain represents; it must have been not only a marvel of the silversmith's art but also a tour de force of engineering, as some of the fountain's parts, powered by water, were even movable.

CKG

Writing Cabinet

Nuremberg, c. 1560/70
Ebony, thuja root, mahogany, ash (?), conifer wood,
gilded copper, glass, mother-of-pearl, H. 46 cm (18⅛ in.),
W. 93 cm (36⅝ in.), Diam. 45 cm (17¾ in.)
Inv. no. KK 3402

This writing cabinet, made of a variety of exotic woods, represents a type of small, ornamented furniture probably created in Nuremberg in the mid-16th century. The many drawers and pigeonholes were used to store small and often valuable objects, and the front section was usually closed by means of a panel that dropped down to create a writing table. In the case of this particular cabinet, however, the panel was later replaced by two glass doors (in the 19th century, these doors were replaced by the single large glass door that can be seen today). The glass provides an unobstructed view of the extraordinary decoration of the drawers cabinet the small double doors in the middle. On these doors are gilded and engraved copper plates set with panels of *verre églomisé*, or reverse gilded glass. This

technique, which was particularly common in Nuremberg, involved figures and ornaments being engraved in gold foil that had been applied to glass. Coloured pigment was then applied, with the engraved areas allowing the colours to show through. Finally, the image was backed with a protective layer of metal foil. The result is a textured, shimmering juxtaposition of colours and gold. The images are of muses, virtues, various personifications (based on engravings by Virgil Solis) and the Labours of the Months, as well as assorted bird and border motifs.

The sides and back of the cabinet are decorated with gilded copper plates; the back bears the signature 'CR'.

KS

Gemstone Vessels by Gasparo Miseroni

Dragon Cup
Gasparo Miseroni (Milan, *c.* 1518–Milan, 1573)
Milan, *c.* 1565/70
Lapis lazuli, enamelled gold, rubies, emeralds, pearls, garnets,
H. 17.2 cm (6⅞ in.), L. 18.9 cm (7½ in.), W. 10.9 cm (4⅜ in.)
Inv. no. KK 1851

Prase Cup with Lid
Gasparo Miseroni (Milan, *c.* 1518–Milan, 1573)
Milan, *c.* 1565/70
Prase, enamelled gold, rubies, emeralds, pearls, onyx cameos,
H. 19.3 cm (7⅛ in.), W. 23.9 cm (9½ in.)
Inv. no. KK 2014

Under Gasparo Miseroni, the legendary Miseroni dynasty of Milan became the most important family of stonecutters of the Renaissance. In the second half of the 16th century their technically and artistically unrivalled treatment of hardstone, coupled with a formidable talent for goldsmithing, resulted in the production of magnificent vessels that popes, kings and emperors vied to acquire. These two splendid cups may have been purchased by Emperor Maximilian II, who is documented as being one of Gasparo's clients. The stonecutter designed the Dragon Cup as a synthesis of a drinking vessel and a miniature sculpture. As if preparing to strike, the dragon arches its neck and waits, with head lowered and teeth bared, for its victim. The golden wings set with emeralds and rubies grasp the sides of the vessel, while the creature's fish-shaped legs are cut in low relief directly into the sides of the cup. This creates the impression that the dragon has taken possession of the lapis lazuli cup and intends to defend it against any possible users.

In the case of the wonderful green prase cup, the zoomorphic element is confined to the two handles. The restrained and harmoniously crafted body of the vessel appears to be completely subordinated to the beauty of the prase, a variety of chalcedony that was highly prized from classical antiquity onwards.

PR

Two Rock-Crystal Vessels with Figurative Motifs

Lidded Goblet with Images from the Persephone Myth
Annibale Fontana (Milan, 1540–Milan, 1587)
Milan, before 1569
Rock crystal, enamelled gold, H. 24.6 cm (9¾ in.),
Diam. 12.3 cm (4⅞ in.)
Inv. no. KK 1415

Cup with a Tall Foot
Francesco Tortorino (active in Milan from c. 1550–
Milan, 1573), signed
Milan, c. 1569
Rock crystal, enamelled gold, H. 13.2 cm (5¼ in.),
Diam. 14.3 cm (5⅝ in.)
Inv. no. KK 2248

These two splendid vessels of flawlessly pure rock crystal were ideally suited as a medium for mythological motifs, which their makers painstakingly engraved on the receptacles' sides. Francesco Tortorino and Annibale Fontana were both artists especially known for their figurative intaglio work. Tortorino decorated the shorter vessel with an idyllic depiction of a grape harvest, while the shaft features likenesses of Bacchus, Venus and Ceres. These images illustrate a well-known quotation from the Roman playwright Terence: *Sine Cerere et Baccho friget Venus* – 'Without Ceres (bread) and Bacchus (wine), Venus (love) grows cold.' Ceres, the goddess of agriculture, can also be identified on the second, somewhat taller, rock crystal goblet. With a Mannerist sense of motion, Fontana depicts the story of Persephone, the daughter of Ceres, and the origins of the four seasons according to Ovid (*Metamorphoses*, Book V, 341–570). The two Milanese craftsmen thus created flawlessly executed works of art in which the purity of the raw material, rock crystal, is coupled with the meticulously engraved and compositionally and anatomically attractive figural scenes. They also produced pieces ideally suited for a *Kunstkammer*, vessels whose depictions invite viewers to pick them up or walk around them in order to grasp their complex pictorial narratives and engage in scholarly conversation about them.

PR

VER·

AESTAS

SEX CVM DILECTO
CONIVGE DITE MANET

Throne Baldachin

Hans Vredeman de Vries
(Leeuwarden, 1527–Antwerp,
1604), design
Michiel Coxcie (Mechelen,
1499–Mechelen, 1592), design
Weaver's mark: FNVG
Brussels, dated 1561
Tapestry: wool, silk, metal
thread, H. 419 cm (165 in.),
W. 271 cm (106¾ in.)
Inv. no. T XLV/1

On formal ceremonial occasions, a baldachin was placed over the throne of a ruler, creating a kind of stage backdrop appropriate to the symbolic nature of the event. The canopies made for this purpose, frequently from textiles, are characterized by the use of precious materials, superb workmanship and exquisite design. The magnificent throne baldachin in Vienna's Kunstkammer is among the rare extant specimens of this type. It consists of a rear wall and a canopy that looms up high into the room. At the centre of the rear wall, which is decorated with architectural elements, Pluto, the god of the underworld, and Proserpina (Persephone), his wife, are seated on carved chairs. The four medallions framing this scene illustrate the legend of these two deities, which is closely related to the myth regarding the origins of the four seasons.

The design for this illusionistic composition was by Hans Vredeman de Vries, one of the most popular architectural and ornamental draughtsmen of the second half of the 16th century, while the figures of Pluto and Proserpina are attributed to the painter Michiel Coxcie.

This baldachin was probably owned by Duke Charles II of Lorraine (1543–1608). Documents show that it was in the inventory of the Lotharingian collections from 1575 to 1606. In 1736 the last Lotharingian duke, Francis III (as of 1745 Francis I Stephen of Lorraine, Holy Roman Emperor), brought the baldachin to Vienna on the occasion of his marriage to Archduchess Maria Theresa.

KSvL

Sculptures by Alessandro Vittoria

Zacharias
Alessandro Vittoria
(Trento, 1525–Venice, 1608)
Venice, c. 1585
Bronze, H. 32.2 cm (12¾ in.)
Inv. no. KK 5664

Bust of Angela Loredan
Alessandro Vittoria
(Trento, 1525–Venice, 1608)
Venice, c. 1560/70
Terracotta, H. 83 cm (32⅝ in.)
Inv. no. KK 9905

Alessandro Vittoria and his teacher Jacopo Sansovino were the most important Venetian sculptors of the 16th century. His great forte was the modelling of soft materials such as clay and wax, which is particularly apparent in his brilliant portraits and small bronzes. Greatly influenced by Titian and the works of classical antiquity, Vittoria created a style of portraiture that incorporated elements of classical forms and demonstrated his tremendous grasp of human physiognomy. Vittoria portrayed members of the Venetian upper classes with impressively bold heads on high and very broad upper bodies, which lent the subjects the desired sense of dignity. In this way he also succeeded in stylizing a lady such as Angela Loredan, wife of the Venetian senator Antonio Zorzi, as the embodiment of virtue and noble-mindedness. Her bust originally stood in the family palazzo, where it was installed along with three other portraits in the atrium. This is the reason for the weather-related damage on the bust's right side.

The virtuoso bronze statuette *Zacharias* shows a rangy male figure, twisted and bent and standing on a very small socle. He is wrapped in a heavy cloak whose voluminous folds emphasize the bend of his body while at the same time also delineating the outline of the sculpture and giving the figure a flame-like contour. Although the details of the old man's head are precisely rendered, Vittoria focuses first and foremost on the three-dimensionality of the overall form and thus attains a monumental effect reminiscent of Michelangelo.

CKG

Joanna of Portugal

Elephant with Salt Cellar
India, 15th century; salt cellar: Europe, 14th–15th century; mount: Francisco Lopez, Lisbon, 1550
Rock crystal, gold, jacinth, enamel, H. 7.3 cm (2⅞ in.), L. 9.4 cm (3⅝ in.), W. 4.9 cm (2 in.)
Inv. no. KK 2320

Cameo: *Joanna of Portugal*
Jacopo da Trezzo (Milan, *c.* 1519–Madrid, 1589)
Madrid, *c.* 1566; setting: Spain, 4th quarter of 16th century
Onyx, gold, enamel, H. 4.1 cm (1⅝ in.), W. 3.4 cm (1¼ in.)
Inv. no. ANSA XII 70

This small outstretched elephant, made of rock crystal, was most likely originally used as a receptacle for perfume or incense. Probably created in India in the 15th century, it subsequently found its way to Lisbon, one of the most important European trading centres for precious items from regions in Africa, India, China and Japan, to which the Portuguese had opened up sea routes in about 1500. In 1550 Catherine, the wife of King John III of Portugal, the sister of Emperor Charles V and one of the most important collectors of exotic, precious objects in the House of Habsburg in her time, acquired the elephant from a goldsmith in Lisbon. This artist added the small – and older – salt cellar to the animal's back. In 1553 Queen Catherine presented the unusual piece of tableware to her niece, Joanna, who that year married Catherine's son, John Manuel of Portugal, thus becoming the queen's daughter-in-law as well. Following her husband's death the very next year, Joanna returned to Spain, presumably taking the elephant with her.

The cameo with the portrait of Joanna is based on a portrait by the Spanish painter Alonso Sánchez Coello. The lapidary artist Jacopo da Trezzo, who was active at the Madrid court and very highly regarded by King Philip II, masterfully translated all the details of the original image into the small format of the layered stone.

FK

Ivory Fan and Casket

Fan
Ceylon, mid-16th century
Ivory, horn, H. 43 cm (16⅞ in.)
Inv. no. KK 4751

Casket
Ceylon, c. 1540; mount: Indo-Portuguese, mid-16th
century, and Southern German, c. 1580/90
Ivory, silver, H. 14.9 cm (5⅞ in.), W. 25 cm (9⅞ in.),
L. 16 cm (6¼ in.)
Inv. no. KK 4743

As a result of the increased contact between Portuguese seafarers and non-European cultures, which began around 1500, many products and artefacts from Africa, India, Ceylon and Japan came to Europe, objects that in the 16th and 17th centuries were usually classified by Europeans stereotypically as 'Indian'. The exotic formal and pictorial language of these objects presumably fascinated collectors just as much as the craftsmanship and technique manifest in the working of the material. This certainly applies to the ivory fan, as is evidenced by this entry of 1596 in the inventory of Archduke Ferdinand II of Tyrol's estate: *'ain schener helfenpainer gar khunstlicher windmacher mit aim schön durchgraben langen still'* ('a lovely, quite artistic ebony windmaker with a beautifully carved long

handle'). The sticks, between which the leaves can be folded away, form the handle and are designed in the shape of a peacock's head and neck; when the fan is opened, the bird seems to be fanning its tail. This type of peacock fan has its roots in the Indian tradition; only few examples have been preserved in European collections.

Also from Ceylon is a small ivory casket, which is adorned on all sides with figurative scenes from Singhalese mythology. In 1542–43, a delegation from the kingdom of Kotte presented the Portuguese queen Catherine with an ivory casket of this type. It was possibly even this very container, which, like the ivory fan, was mentioned in 1596 in the inventory list of Ambras Castle.

FK

Exotic Materials

Bezoar
Spanish, 3rd quarter
of 16th century
Gold, emeralds, rubies,
H. 25.5 cm (10 in.)
Inv. no. KK 981

**Covered Goblet of
Rhinoceros Horn**
Spanish or Netherlandish,
c. 1560
Rhinoceros horn, enamelled
gold, H. 20 cm (7⅞ in.),
Diam. 9 cm (3½ in.)
Inv. no. KK 3258

Many of the exotic natural materials brought to Europe from far-flung countries in the Age of Exploration were believed by Europeans to have mystical healing properties or other magical powers. The presentation of this bezoar, which rests on the heads of three lions studded with emeralds, underscores the extraordinarily high regard in which this stone was held in Europe. A bezoar is a hardened, indigestible mass found in the intestines of some ruminant animals, such as wild goats and llamas. It was said to have the power to neutralize poison and to act as an effective cure for melancholy, epilepsy and the plague. Bezoars were often set in gold and worn on a chain as a necklace or mounted inside drinking vessels, so that the stone's powers could work through contact with wine or water.

Rhinoceros horn was also believed to be able to counteract poison, in addition to its legendary powers as an aphrodisiac. Due to the horn's natural shape, it was frequently used for the crafting of drinking vessels. In Europe, horn was frequently lathe-turned. The elaborate decoration of this goblet consists of a trellis-like layer of gold and enamel that protects the horn vessel beneath it and at the same time underscores its costliness. The thin ring that sits loosely at the bottom of the goblet's foot was intended to show off the craftsman's exceptional technical skill: it was lathed out of the horn together with the rest of the shaft.

FK

Decorative Objects in Tortoiseshell

Drinking Horn in the Shape of a Dragon
Cornelius Gross (master craftsman before
1534–75)
Augsburg, *c.* 1560/70
Tortoiseshell, gilt silver, enamel, cold colours,
H. 29.5 cm (11½ in.), L. 35 cm (13¾ in.)
Inv. no. KK 889

**Flask in the Shape
of a Heart**
India, Gujarat (?),
16th century
Tortoiseshell, silver,
H. 33.7 cm (13¼ in.)
Inv. no. KK 4126

Ornamental tortoiseshell, obtained from the curved, upper shell of sea turtles, has from time immemorial been prized for its lovely marbled patterns and translucency. After being soaked in simmering water, shells could be flattened and fused together to form larger plates suitable for making small boxes, bowls, horns, combs and even flasks. Because heart-shaped flasks of this type present the exotic material in such an unusual form, they must have been considered quite a curiosity in Europe at the time.

In the case of the drinking horn, a simple Indian hunting horn was transformed in Augsburg into a bizarre but splendid goblet in the shape of a dragon whose head is turned belligerently toward the viewer. The dragon's gullet originally contained an 'adder's tongue', a fossilized shark's tooth that was believed to counteract poison; it

is even possible that small stems of coral once projected from the dragon's nostrils to represent its fiery breath. The tortoise on which the dragon stands is presumably an allusion to the material; in conjunction with the winged dragon, however, it could also serve as a visual translation of a common folk saying, admonishing the viewer to choose a happy medium between moving too quickly and too slowly.

The Triton seated on the dragon's back holds the coat of arms of Count Ulrich IX of Montfort-Tettnang. It was from his estate that Archduke Ferdinand II of Tyrol acquired this vessel for his collection at Ambras Castle, where the heart-shaped flask – along with a companion piece – is also recorded in inventory lists of 1596.

FK

Showpieces in Shell

Ostrich Egg Goblet
Clement Kicklinger (master craftsman
from 1561–Augsburg, 1617)
Augsburg, c. 1570/75
Ostrich egg shell, coral, partly gilt
and partly painted silver, H. 56.8 cm
(22⅜ in.)
Inv. no. KK 897

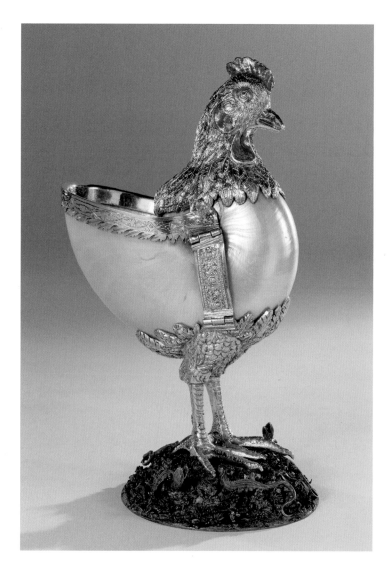

**Drinking Vessel in the
Shape of a Cockerel**
Workshop of Wenzel Jamnitzer
Nuremberg, 3rd quarter of
16th century
Nautilus shell, partly gilt and
painted silver, natural casts,
H. 18.4 cm (7¼ in.)
Inv. no. KK 1060

No Mannerist *Kunstkammer* would have been complete without showpieces made of rare, exotic materials. These objects were further ornamented through exquisite goldwork, increasing their value through a union of stunning products of nature and outstanding human artistry. In the case of these two goblets, the natural materials – an ostrich egg and a nautilus shell – remain recognizable as such while at the same time serving as the body of drinking vessels with extravagant shapes. Coral stems make up the fragile and bizarre-looking foot of the ostrich egg goblet. Above, a Moor leads an oversized ostrich on a chain, while the bird carries its own egg on its back. Although this egg is hollow and closed with a lid, the goblet has been stripped of any functionality. To the viewer, this remarkable showpiece seems much too delicate and fragile to be brought to one's lips without danger of breakage. This applies to the second drinking vessel as well. In this elaborate figure, the exotic natural material is reinterpreted as the body of a cock standing on a base covered in meticulously crafted grasses and shrubs. The base is also populated by lizards, which, like the plants, were cast from life and represent the fusion of nature and art in its purest form.

PR

Archduke Ferdinand II

Archduke Ferdinand II of Tyrol
Francesco Segala (active in Padua and Venice,
1557–97)
Innsbruck, *c.* 1580
Coloured wax, precious stones, rock crystal, pearls,
H. 22.3 cm (8¾ in.), W. 19.9 cm (7⅞ in.), with
frame
Inv. no. KK 3085

Seal Signet of Archduke Ferdinand II
Northern Italy (?), *c.* 1580/90
Emerald, jasper; setting: gold, enamel,
L. 10.4 cm (4 in.), Diam. 5.9 cm (2⅜ in.)
Inv. no. ANSA XII 779

As the second-born son of Emperor Ferdinand I, Archduke Ferdinand of Austria was denied the crown; in 1547, however, his father named him governor of Bohemia, and in 1564, after the death of his father, Ferdinand II became ruler of Tyrol. The coat of arms depicted on his seal signet reflects his territorial claims.

Among the art objects in Archduke Ferdinand II's collection at Ambras Castle was this symbolic portrait in wax. It is one of the oldest extant examples of a type of relief portrait used originally as a model for medals. In the 16th century, these wax portraits evolved into an autonomous genre and became very popular due to the degree of naturalism made possible by the material. The sculptor Francesco Segala, who worked in Padua and Venice, was an early practitioner of wax portraiture, which found its way from Northern Italy to the European courts.

The portrait depicts Ferdinand in a symbolic manner, dressed in splendid armour and holding a baton in his right hand. He is shown in half-length in front of a curtain decorated with pictures of Jonah and the Whale. This motif, together with the motto *vincit potentia fati* ('the power of destiny overcomes'), can also be found on medallions of the archduke. The archducal coronet is prominently displayed beside him.

Ferdinand presumably became acquainted with Segala, who worked at the Gonzaga court in Mantua, through Anne Catherine Gonzaga, the archduke's second wife.

KSvL

Collector's Cabinet

Southern German or Mantua, *c.* 1582
Ebony, maple, walnut, silver, H. 75 cm (29½ in.),
W. 62 cm (24⅜ in.), L. 45 cm (17¾ in.)
Inv. no. KK 883

This collector's cabinet with its elegant contrast of ebony and silver formerly belonged to Archduke Ferdinand II of Tyrol. When the lockable drawer in the base is completely opened, it can be folded out to create a writing surface. The writing implements, including an inkwell and pounce pot, were stored in the top part of the cabinet, which may thus be considered the forerunner of a modern writing desk. Opening the double doors on the front reveals a magnificently designed interior wall with numerous drawers. Here the archduke is known to have kept a wide variety of objects from the natural history and artefact collections of Ambras Castle. Itself a part of this large collection, the cabinet is therefore also a *Kunstkammer* in miniature, reflecting the nature of ensembles of this kind.

For its aristocratic owner, the cabinet was an object of intellectual awareness and contemplation. By viewing and touching the objects, the collector gained insight into the world that he himself had organized in rooms, cabinets and drawers, giving him symbolic power over them. This role was a confirmation of the ruler's earthly power.

The silverwork consists of allegories of the virtues, the seven liberal arts, the four seasons, the four elements, the seven planetary gods, the five senses, the four continents and the twelve labours of Hercules, the hero of antiquity with whom Ferdinand II most closely identified as a Habsburg ruler. Perched above the rest is an allegory of wisdom.

KS

Two Centrepieces in the Form of Herons

Saracchi Workshop
Milan, c. 1590
Rock crystal, partly enamelled gold, emeralds, jacinths,
rubies, pearls, rhinestone, garnets, cameos, heron feathers
(replacement)
KK 2401 (opposite): H. 39.4 cm (15½ in.), L. c. 50 cm
(19½ in.), W. 23.3 cm (9⅛ in.); KK 2238 (above): H. 23.7 cm
(9⅜ in.), L. 29.3 cm (11½ in.), W. 16.4 cm (6⅜ in.)
Inv. nos. KK 2401, KK 2238

These two grotesquely imaginative centrepieces came from the estate of Archduke Ferdinand II. The works are truly princely by virtue of the size and quality of the rock crystal, the flawless artistic workmanship and, not least, the enamelled gold mounts, richly set with precious stones and pearls. In keeping with the characteristics typical of Mannerist collector's items, the vessels are theoretically functional but their forms are exaggerated to the point of absurdity. The bellies of the fantastic animals are hollow for holding liquids, and the tails can be removed to allow the liquid to be poured from them. That task would be made rather difficult, however, by the filigree work and radically exaggerated shape. Thus these impressive rock crystal objects became *mirabilia* ('curiosities'), artworks that existed simply to be admired. Ambiguity and transformation were their most important elements, with the birdlike form also embracing characteristics of dragons and fish. The design resists any attempt to find a simple, spontaneous explanation, demanding that viewers explore its less obvious elements as well, letting their eyes and minds wander in search of new, surprising discoveries.

PR

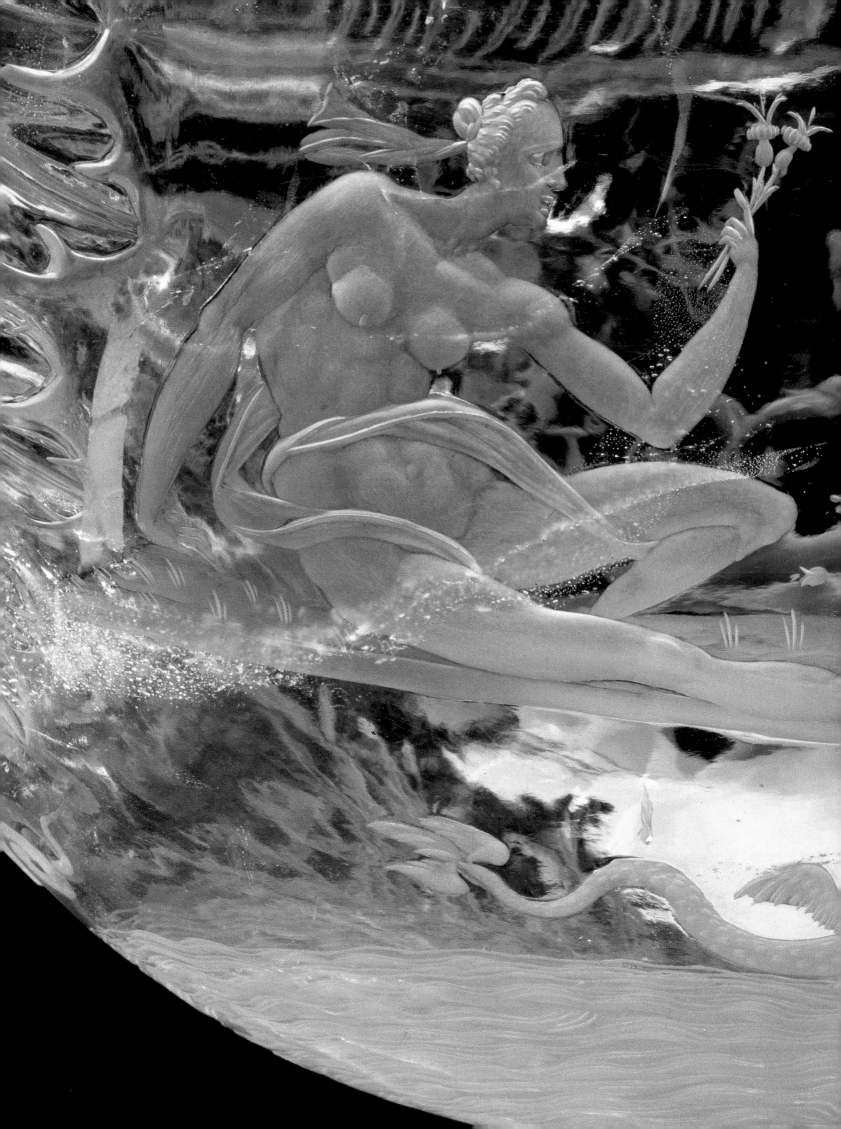

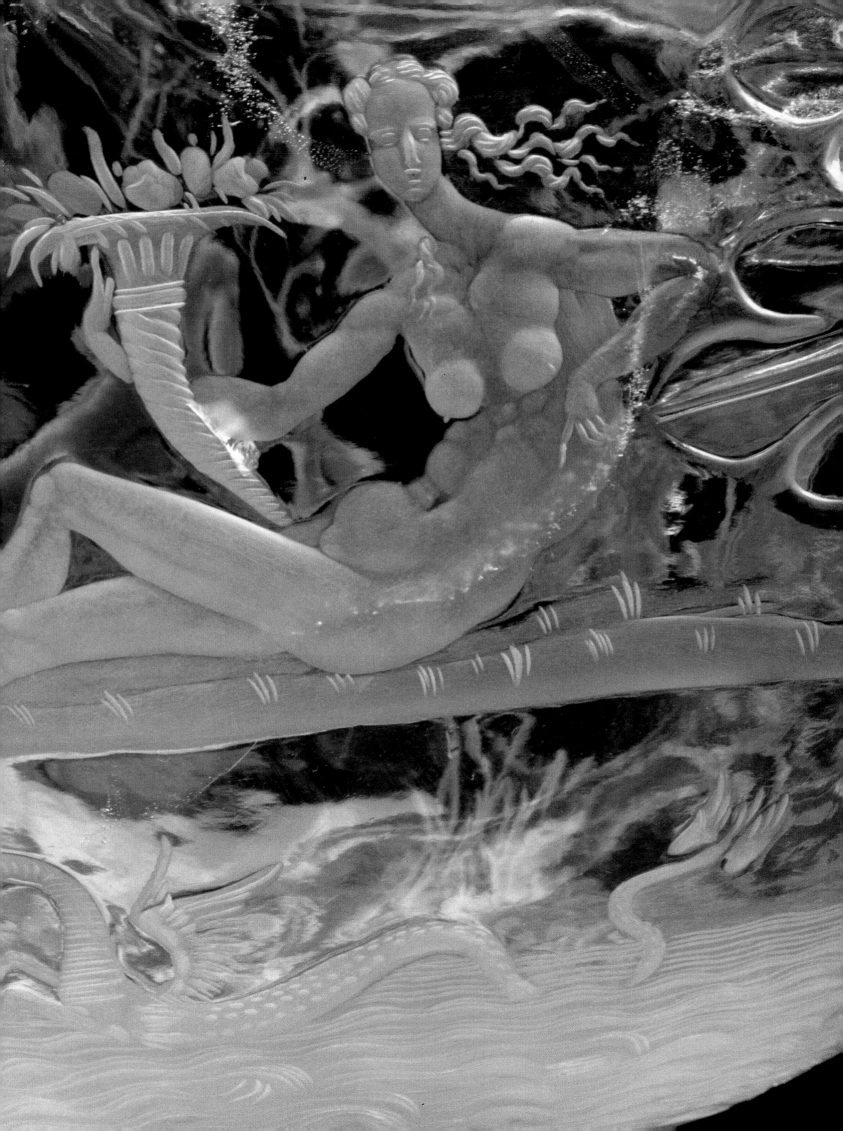

Novelty Vessel: *The Bear as Hunter*

Gregory Bair (Merano, master craftsman
in 1573–Augsburg, 1604)
Valentin Drausch (1546?–1610)
Heinrich Wagner (active 1570–1607)
Augsburg and Munich, *c.* 1580/81
Partly gilt silver, partly enamelled gold, gilded
and silver-plated brass, iron, ambergris, emeralds,
rubies, sapphire, pearls, H. 21.3 cm (8⅜ in.)
Inv. no. KK 1094

The 'Bear as Hunter' was one of the most popular motifs from the popular imagery of the 'topsy-turvy world'. In a reversal of roles, the dangerous prey becomes the hunter: equipped with a rifle, powder flask, spanner and hunter's vest, he is taking aim at his imaginary prey – the viewer. We often find such intellectual games, which question and reverse the familiar and raise to a principle the elements of surprise and deception, in Renaissance and Mannerist collections of cabinet pieces. In this novelty vessel, the joke is taken to the extreme. The bear itself was coated with a paste of ambergris to give it a pleasant scent. Thus the bestial smell of a wild animal was replaced by a highly prized aromatic substance. On its head, the bear is wearing a tiny hat reminiscent of a straw beehive. The head can be detached from the bear's body to reveal a small cup in its neck, thus making the complex figure a drinking vessel. But even more surprises lie in store: in a drawer at the bottom is a miniature enamel board for playing the games of chess, nine men's morris and backgammon. Thus this zoomorphic vessel combines three princely leisure activities: hunting, game-playing and drinking.

PR

Silver Writing Set

Wenzel Jamnitzer (Vienna, 1507
or 1508–Nuremberg, 1585)
Nuremberg, c. 1560/70
Silver, H. 6 cm (2⅜ in.), L. 22.7 cm
(8⅞ in.), W. 10.2 cm (4 in.)
Inv. nos. KK 1155–KK 1164

With the technique of casting metal animals and plants directly from life, Renaissance artists acquired a tool that made it possible for them to recreate nature with the utmost realism. In the 16th century, Nuremberg joined Padua as a major centre for the production of these casts from nature (known as the *style rustique*). Wenzel and Albrecht Jamnitzer were pioneers of the technique, which was new to southern Germany, and perfected the art of casting in silver. In 1547 the Nuremberg mathematician Johann Neudörffer praised the quality of 'the little animals, worms, grasses and snails' that the two brothers were 'casting from silver, decorating silver vessels with them.' Archduke Ferdinand II of Tyrol, to whom this writing set belonged, appears to have had a special fondness for small cast animals. The rectangular casket, the lower part of which was used to store writing instruments, is especially attractive because of the contrast between the clear shape of the box itself and the liveliness of the casts that have been applied to it. The compartments of the lid are decorated with cast insects, shells, a crab, a mouse, a toad and two lizards. The sides of the casket are luxuriantly festooned with casts of a variety of flowers and grasses. In between, other small animals can be seen to romp. Thus nature is flawlessly imitated and at the same time presented in an abstract form.

PR

Two 'Handstone' Ornaments

Handstone in the Form of a Table Fountain with David and Bathsheba
Caspar Ulich (active 1555–Joachimsthal, 1576)
Joachimsthal (Jáchymov), 3rd quarter of 16th century
Various minerals, silver gilt, enamel, H. 60.5 cm (23¾ in.),
Diam. 23 cm (9 in.)
Inv. no. KK 4161

Handstone with the Resurrection of Christ
Caspar Ulich (active 1555–Joachimsthal, 1576)
Joachimsthal (Jáchymov), c. 1560
Acanthite (argentite), silver gilt, H. 31.7 cm (12½ in.)
Inv. no. KK 4148

The term *Handstein* or 'handstone' was originally used to describe samples of ore that were of unusual size or shape. They were held in the hand for viewing and were frequently presented by miners as a gift to the mine owner. Over the course of the 16th century, artists increasingly took striking samples of ore, gave them an artistic treatment and mount, and combined them with other materials, goldwork or organic substances to turn them into cabinet pieces, much in the same way that casts from nature were treated. The first handstones to be presented in this manner probably came from Joachimsthal (now Jáchymov in the Czech Republic) in the Ore Mountains of Bohemia,

and that is the source of most of the handstones in the collections of the Kunsthistorisches Museum. These two examples are variations within the genre. The larger of the two was assembled from several ore samples and depicts miners at work along with the biblical story of David and Bathsheba. The smaller one is made from a single piece of silver ore, but 'small' is hardly the right word since this is the largest known piece to have been preserved as an artwork. The front features a Resurrection scene, based on a woodcut by Dürer. On the back, Charles V is depicted as the victor at the Battle of Pavia.

PR

Three Commedia dell'Arte Figurines

Venice/Murano or the Innsbruck Court Glassworks,
last quarter of 16th century
Iron wire, glass, enamel, KK 2705: H. 21.4 cm (8⅜ in.);
KK 2711: H. 19.6 cm (7¾ in.); KK 2714: H. 20.4 cm (8 in.)
Inv. nos. KK 2705, KK 2711, KK 2714

Archduke Ferdinand II organized his collection of objects at Ambras Castle according to medium, and the eleventh display case of the collection was devoted to glass. Ferdinand's great interest in this material is evidenced by the fact that he established a court glassworks in Innsbruck, which drew on technology from the island of Murano, and by the extensive range of glass objects that he collected. Among them are these three figures based on the commedia dell'arte tradition. This improvisatory theatrical form, which arose in mid-16th century Italy, featured stock characters, masks and situations but was not scripted. Its success therefore depended on the improvisational skill of the actors. One of the best-known characters is Il Capitano, the embodiment of a loudmouth, whose character traits included boasting, malice and greed in combination with cowardice. His attribute is the sword that he wears on his belt but as a rule never uses in a fight.

The manufacture of these figurines required a high degree of skill and precision. Heated glass rods were applied to a structure of iron wire that provided the shape, and a flame was used to fuse the glass to the wire. As early as 1570 Archduke Ferdinand II brought glassblowers to his Innsbruck court from Murano, where the technique had been perfected.

KSvL

Novelty Vessels: *Presumption* and *Tantalus*

Christoph Gandtner
(*c.* 1560/65–Merano, 1605)
Innsbruck, *c.* 1580/90
Clay, multicolour glazed and
cold painted, *Presumption*
(KK 3109): H. 26 cm
(10¼ in.); *Tantalus* (KK 3155):
H. 26.6 cm (10½ in.)
Inv. nos. KK 3109, KK 3155

These two novel and comical vessels are part of a group of colourful, glazed clay objects made by the master potter Christoph Gandtner of Merano. He is best known today for the witty works he supplied to the court in Innsbruck.

Presumption is symbolized by a naked woman holding a horn of plenty and sitting on a hedgehog. The fruit in the top of the horn is a stopper that can be removed for filling the vessel.

The second novelty vessel combines the theme of the punishment of Tantalus with another motif popular in the 16th century, Bacchus eating and drinking while seated on a barrel. Tantalus, a king from Asia Minor, was invited to dine at the table of the gods but aroused their anger by stealing nectar and ambrosia. They punished him with insatiable hunger and unquenchable thirst. Here a table laden with food is placed around the man's neck like a gigantic collar that rests on his shoulders, keeping the food out of reach. This punishment for gluttony also contains an element of irony: the figure's head can be removed so that the object can be used as a drinking vessel.

The barrel bears the coat of arms of Andreas Unterberger, a member of the court of the second wife of Archduke Ferdinand II, Anne Catherine Gonzaga. It was probably her doing that these two vessels entered the archduke's collection at Ambras Castle near Innsbruck.

KSvL

Automaton with Trumpeters

Hans Schlottheim (Naumburg on the Saale
1544/47–Augsburg, 1624/25)
Ebony, blackwood, silver gilt, enamel, gilt
brass, work: iron, H. 33.4 cm (13⅛ in.),
W. 36 cm (14⅛ in.), D. 23.5 cm (9¼ in.)
Inv. no. KK 855

This automaton is surely one of the most important mechanical instruments made during the 16th century. Its fruitful interplay of artistic design and technical and musical ingenuity make this an outstanding example of the Augsburg table automata that became highly popular at European courts. Ten trumpeters stand on a castle-like structure, and above them a military drummer beats time. The real attraction of the object, however, is hidden inside the case, where the complicated mechanism has been fitted into a very confined space. Cogs and springs power a bellows and a wooden disc, which contains the musical information. Metal pins 'read' the disc and transfer the information to shafts that open valves, allowing the air from the bellows to play notes on a reed organ of ten notes. At the same time, the disc drives the beaters, which tap a membrane stretched across the bottom of the device to keep time with the music. The mechanism also makes the musicians move: the trumpeters raise and lower their instruments, while the drummer alternately turns and hits his drum. This automaton entered the Habsburg collections in 1582 when Duke Wilhelm V of Bavaria presented it as a gift to his uncle, Ferdinand II of Tyrol. It was an ideal object for delighting a party of aristocratic diners.

PR

Bust of Emperor Rudolf II

Adriaen de Vries (The Hague,
1545–Prague, 1626)
Prague, 1603
Bronze, H. 112 cm (44⅛ in.)
Inv. no. KK 5506

This portrait of Rudolf II (1552–1612) was created in 1603 by his court sculptor Adriaen de Vries as a companion piece to the bust of Charles V made by Leone Leoni in around 1555 (p. 113). Rudolf had acquired a replica of it a short time before, for his famous art collection at Prague Castle. The emperor admired his famous ancestor and asked de Vries to use the earlier bust as a model, although the artist tried to surpass it in expressive power. Like Charles, the ruler is depicted in magnificent armour. The breastplate, however, is not cut away below the shoulders, as was otherwise common practice, but depicted in its full length all the way to the waist. This impressive torso is mounted on a figurative base, lending the composition a triumphal character. De Vries transformed the shy art collector Rudolf into a monarch with a sense of mission by creating dynamic movement in the shoulders and a determined, distant gaze, which he achieved by flattening the curve of the eyeball. Below this heroic figure are an eagle as an imperial symbol, Jupiter and Mercury, who have astrological significance, and a goat, the symbol for Capricorn, which Rudolf had chosen because it was the zodiac sign of Caesar Augustus. This complex symbolism, which continues on the decoration of the armour, preserves Rudolf for posterity as a victorious general, a prince of peace, and thus the epitome of a perfect ruler.

CKG

Tankard Made from a Narwhal Tusk

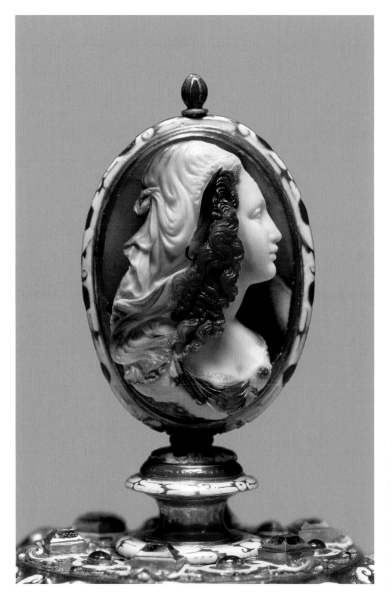

Jan Vermeyen (Brussels, before 1559–Prague, 1606) Prague, c. 1600/5 Miseroni workshop in Milan, double cameo on the lid Narwhal tusk ('unicorn horn'), gold, enamel, diamonds, rubies, double cameo of agate, ivory, H. 22.2 cm (8¾ in.), W. 12.2 cm (4⅞ in.) Inv. no. KK 1113

This unusual vessel, the body of which is made from a piece of narwhal tusk, was among the most valuable items in the collection of Emperor Rudolf II. Its worth derived primarily from the tusk, which was believed at the time to be the horn of the legendary unicorn. It was thought that the mythical beast could be captured only by a virgin, and the horn was said to be capable of raising the dead to life, making it the symbol of divine power. In addition, the horn was believed to have protective and healing powers, including an unsurpassed ability to detect and neutralize poison, as described by Anselmus Boetius de Boodt, the personal physician of Rudolf II. The extraordinary significance that this tusk held for the emperor is reflected in the manner in which the precious natural material was used to create a marvellous artwork. The instructions to the imperial chamber goldsmith Jan Vermeyen were probably to damage the magical horn as little as possible while mounting it in a precious setting. His gold mount is set with a total of 16 rubies and 36 diamonds. The double cameo that crowns the lid is attributed to the Miseroni workshop in Milan.

PR

Bezoar Goblet

Jan Vermeyen (Brussels,
before 1559–Prague, 1606)
Prague, c. 1600
Bezoar, enamelled gold,
H. 14.5 cm (5¾ in.),
W. 9.3 cm (3⅝ in.),
L. 8 cm (3⅛ in.)
Inv. no. KK 3259

This is a very special vessel because the material from which the cup is made is a bezoar stone (found in the intestines of some ruminant animals), which provided the inspiration for this bizarre cabinet piece. The irregularly gnarled natural material that gives the goblet its extravagant shape is mounted on a transverse oval foot and a vase-shaped stem. To keep from damaging the rare and precious bezoar, the goldsmith fastened the body to the mount with three enamelled gold clasps. Tightly hugging the undulating wall of the vessel, they are attached by moveable hinges to the top of the stem and the rim, obviating the need for drill holes. This complicated form of mount indicates the high value that was placed on this natural material, which was worth more than its weight in gold. As a further indication of high esteem, all of the gold was elaborately enamelled. The extensive white ground is enlivened by the shimmering colours of translucent enamel and the elegant splendour of the goldwork. The goldsmith even placed a small enamelled disc in the interior of the lid. In this manner the unaltered natural substance of the bezoar is contrasted with the virtuoso refinement created by human hands, with the two combining to create a harmonious whole.

PR

Ewer Made from a Coco de Mer

Anton Schweinberger (Augsburg, *c.* 1550–Prague, 1603)
Nikolaus Pfaff (Nuremberg, 1556?–Prague, 1612)
Prague, 1602
Coco de mer nut *(Lodoicea maldivica),* silver, partly gilt,
partly decorated with niello, H. 38.5 cm (15¼ in.)
Inv. no. KK 6872

This virtuoso showpiece was surely one of the most important works made for the court of Rudolf II. Two masters in their respective fields – the court goldsmith Anton Schweinberger and the imperial woodcarver and court cabinetmaker Nikolaus Pfaff – took a natural object and with great artistic skill created a vessel that is impressive not only for its unusual shape but also for its strangely exotic character. It invites viewers to embrace its whimsical playfulness, allowing their gaze to explore its complexity, led by its flowing volutes and spirals. Half of a coco de mer, a large palm nut from the Seychelles, provided the inspiration for this consummate artwork. It was used to form the ship-like body of the large jug and at the same time provided the shape and theme of the object. Water, the element in which the exotic nut was found, inspired the design in both content and form. Two sea creatures with human bodies and fishlike tails are seated back to back on the undulating base, where they support the weight of the large nut. Nikolaus Pfaff has echoed these motifs in bas relief, dividing the surface of the nut into four sections, each populated with groups of sea gods, Tritons and Nereids. Schweinberger crowns these scenes with a tall lid that looks like an independent work of sculpture – almost as if he were trying to surpass the decoration of the outer shell in a contextual, formal and artistic sense.

PR

Rhinoceros Horn Goblet with Lid

Nikolaus Pfaff (Nuremberg, 1556?–Prague, 1612), attributed
Prague, 1611
Horn of a white rhinoceros (*Ceratotherium simum*), tusks of an African warthog, silver gilt, partly painted, H. 59.7 cm (23½ in.), W. 27.5 cm (10¾ in.)
Inv. no. KK 3709

The purpose of this bizarre and ornate goblet from the art collection of Emperor Rudolf II was to overcome and subdue potentially harmful forces. The cup and stem of the goblet are carved from rhinoceros horn, which was believed to have qualities that repelled calamity and evil. The warthog tusks on the lid were believed to be the horns of a mythical dragon or wyvern. Here they are used to form the horns of a two-headed composite beast, which has savagely bared teeth on the front while on the back it is held in voluted clasps and thus appears to have been subdued. Along the edge of the lid, which looks as though it were made of soft golden dough, numerous insects, frogs and lizards can be seen roaming around like messengers from the world of darkness, reminding us of the forces of evil. This dichotomy of menace and mollification continues across the entire goblet. The body and stem are encased by sculpted coral branches, interspersed with animals' heads, newts and insects, which seem to have come from the underworld. Above the branches, gentle human faces emerge from the surface as symbols of the healing power of nature and the cosmos.

PR

Ornamental Wash Jug and Basin

Christoph Jamnitzer (Nuremberg, 1563–
Nuremberg, 1618)
Nuremberg, *c.* 1601/02
Partly gilt and enamelled silver; basin: H. 7.5 cm
(3 in.), L. 64.5 cm (25½ in.), W. 52.5 cm
(20¾ in.); jug: H. 43.5 cm (17 in.)
Inv. nos. KK 1104, KK 1128

With this highly refined and symbol-laden wash jug and basin, the Nuremberg master Christoph Jamnitzer transcends the conventional boundaries of the goldsmith's art. Across the surface of the basin, he has created a highly complex iconographic programme, populating the scenes with a large number of figures and turning a vessel whose original function was cleansing into a medium with a message and powerful artistic expression. In order to make a work that was more than a purposeless sculpture, however, the goldsmith made the set potentially functional by lining the jug with an insert with a spout. The complex iconography, designed with great attention to detail and a variety of possible interpretations, is dominated by the six allegorical triumphs described by the poet Petrarch: the triumphs of Love, Chastity, Death, Fame, Time and Eternity. The triumph of Love is shown in a multi-figured scene on the bottom of the basin (overleaf). The culmination of the other triumphs depicted on the jug is found on the lid, in the allegory of Eternity triumphing over Time. This complex programme reflects a grasp of humanist scholarship and would not have been possible without the contributions of a humanist at the court of the client, Emperor Rudolf II. The outstanding artistic execution and the organization that makes the scene legible must be seen, however, as Jamnitzer's own masterly achievement.

PR

Venus Urania or *Allegory of Astronomy*

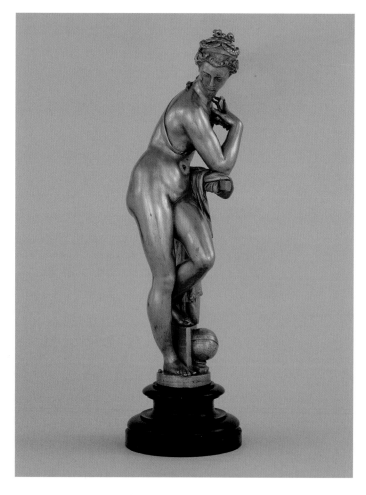

Giambologna (Douai,
1529–Florence, 1608)
Florence, *c.* 1575
Fire-gilded bronze,
H. 38.8 cm (15¼ in.)
Inv. no. KK 5893

Jean Boulogne, known by the Italian name Giambologna, came from the Habsburg-ruled Spanish Netherlands, where he also received his first training. Travelling to Italy as part of his studies, he stopped in Florence and remained there for the rest of his life, becoming court sculptor to the Medici family. His refined compositions were also produced as smaller, more portably sized statuettes that became collector's items and were coveted throughout Europe, and his style thus spread quickly.

The nude female figure in this work is standing on a small, round base that provides just enough room for her right foot, a celestial globe and a prism on which she has gracefully set her left foot. Her upper body is turned sharply to the right and is supported by her left hand, which holds a ruler and drawing compass and, like her right elbow, is resting on a straightedge, which in turn rests precariously on a prism. Her head is turned and inclined gracefully towards her right shoulder. The pose is counterbalanced by movements that result in a screw-like turning of the entire figure; in the art theory of the time this was called *figura serpentinata*. In this statuette Giambologna skilfully embodied the principle of multiple perspectives, which was highly important in 16th-century sculpture: a statue was supposed to have not just one viewing angle but was to be equally interesting from every angle; the composition could be understood only by viewing it from all sides. The *Venus Urania* was therefore an ideal cabinet piece for a collector of the time, who would have gained additional pleasure from the sculptor's brilliant modelling of the figure.

CKG

Mercury in Flight

Giambologna (Douai, 1529–Florence, 1608)
Florence, *c.* 1585
Bronze, H. 62.7 cm
(24⅝ in.)
Inv. no. KK 5898

With his concept of depicting Mercury, the messenger of the gods, taking flight, Giambologna went further than a sculptor had ever dared to go before. The slender youth is balanced almost weightlessly on the toes of his left foot, which hardly seems to touch the ground. His gaze is turned heavenward, and the tension visible in his entire body culminates in his outstretched right index finger: he looks as though he might effortlessly lift off at any moment. No artist before Giambologna succeeded so convincingly in depicting the apparent defiance of gravity, and this daring composition is probably his best-known work. It was often copied, and the master himself repeated it in a wide variety of formats. The design reached its peak, however, as a statuette, which offered the possibility of taking the precarious balancing act on one foot to the extreme.

Along with a version presented in 1586 as a gift from Grand Duke Francesco I de' Medici to the court of Saxony in Dresden, the *Mercury* in Vienna is one of Giambologna's masterpieces. It so closely resembles the one in Dresden that the two must have been made at about the same time. Unfortunately the date it entered the imperial collection is unknown. It first appeared in the inventory drawn up between 1607 and 1611 of Emperor Rudolf II's art collection in Prague. There it was not displayed in a case but rather used to crown an ebony cabinet to great effect. The art-loving emperor so admired Giambologna that he raised him to the peerage in 1588.

CKG

Calligraphic Specimen Book

Georg Bocskay (Rasinja–Vienna, 1575), calligraphy
Joris Hoefnagel (Antwerp, c. 1532?–Vienna, c. 1600), miniature painting
Jan Vermeyen (Brussels, before 1559–1606), workshop, binding
Miniature painting: Frankfurt, 1591–94; calligraphy: Vienna, 1571–73;
binding: Prague, c. 1600/5 (before 1607)
Parchment, watercolours and opaque paint, silver and gold heightening,
binding: leather, bloodstone, enamelled gold, garnets, H. 18.8 cm (7⅜ in.),
W. 14 cm (5½ in.)
Inv. no. KK 975

Between 1571 and 1573, the calligrapher and imperial secretary Georg Bocskay made a calligraphic specimen book at the request of Emperor Maximilian II (1527–76). This magnificent codex consisting of 127 parchment leaves is one of the highlights of calligraphy and illumination in the second half of the 16th century. Its primary sources were books that had been published in the Italian- and German-speaking world since the second quarter of the 16th century. The texts, often extant only in fragmentary form, include prayers, quotations from the Bible, letters, official documents and more.

The illumination in the hand of the Flemish painter and engraver Joris Hoefnagel was created between 1591 and 1594 on a commission from Emperor Rudolf II. In addition to townscapes and naturalistic depictions of flowers, insects and other animals, he decorated the pages with portraits, emblematic images and scenes from the life of Christ. Hoefnagel took his inspiration from passages or sometimes even single words in the book.

The bloodstone binding made in the workshop of Jan Vermeyen was mentioned in the 1607/11 inventory of the art collection of Emperor Rudolf II (1552–1612) in Prague. At that early date, the binding was not yet paired with this book. It was cut down for that purpose sometime after 1611.

KSvL

Mechanical Celestial Globe

Georg Roll (Liegnitz, 1546–Augsburg, 1592)
Johannes Reinhold the Elder (Liegnitz, 1550–
Augsburg, 1596)
Augsburg, 1584
Bronze, gilt brass, partly painted, silver,
enamel, wood stained black; mechanism: iron,
H. 53.8 cm (21⅛ in.)
Inv. no. KK 854

Six versions of this type of mechanical celestial globe made by Roll and Reinhold are known today. With its colourful decoration, however, the one in Vienna is the most richly ornate. Georg Roll's part in the joint enterprise with the clockmaker Johannes Reinhold was primarily in the role of entrepreneur and merchant. In 1584 he sold one globe each to Emperor Rudolf II and his brother Archduke Ernest, with the one for Ernest costing some 300 thalers more than the other. When the emperor got word of this, he decided that Roll had sold him an inferior globe and was so outraged that he had the Augsburg town council throw Roll into prison. We may assume that Rudolf swapped his globe for that of his brother: the one originally in his possession is now in the Victoria and Albert Museum in London. The Vienna globe is the more expensive one that Roll originally sold to Archduke Ernest.

The richly painted sphere of the globe, which depicts the starry sky with forty-nine constellations, can be rotated on its axis with the poles at either end. The horizontal frame divides the sphere exactly in half, with each half displaying the visible stars of the respective hemisphere. Two steel rings represent the courses of the Sun and the Moon. On several levels inside the sphere, clockwork powers the movement of the sky as well as the display of the minutes, hours and days.

PR

Automaton in the Form of a Ship

Hans Schlottheim (Naumburg on the Saale, 1544/47–
Augsburg, 1624/25)
Augsburg, 1585
Silver gilt, brass, cold enamel, oil painting; mechanism:
iron, H. 67 cm (26⅜ in.), W. 66 cm (26 in.)
Inv. no. KK 874

The tradition of making table centrepieces in the form of a ship dates back to the Middle Ages. Ships were symbols of power, expansion and the thirst for discovery. A vessel that could not only inspire enthusiasm with its appearance but also had a crew that performed a cleverly devised dance to music coming from the hull could hardly be surpassed as a form of banquet entertainment. With a mechanical marvel like this, the owner – in this case Emperor Rudolf II – could impress his guests, using the choreography and iconography, which made personal reference to him, to demonstrate his power. The emperor himself, in the form of a small statuette, stands on the deck of this unusual ship, accompanied by trombonists, timpanists and drummers. The flags on the masts bear the imperial double eagle; the

open cabin in which the emperor sits is decorated with the imperial crown. When the automaton is activated, several different mechanisms inside the hull of the ship begin to run, either simultaneously or in sequence, creating the complex programme of music and movement via a series of cogs, gears and shafts. The first piece of music signals the arrival of the emperor as the helmsman of the ship: the trombonists take it in turns to raise their instruments, and a timpanist provides the beat. The ship begins moving across the table, and small organ pipes play a second melody as the vessel puts to sea. The highlight is a salvo fired from two cannon.

PR

Clock: *Diana on a Centaur*

Hans Jakob I Bachmann (Memmingen, 1574–
Augsburg, 1651)
Augsburg, *c.* 1602/06
Silver partly gilt, partly enamelled, pearls, garnets,
wood; mechanism: iron, H. 39.5 cm (15½ in.),
max. L. 32.5 cm (12¾ in.), W. 18.3 cm (7¼ in.)
Inv. no. KK 1166

This automaton clock is one of the earliest and at the same time most remarkable works by the Augsburg goldsmith Hans Jakob I Bachmann. An example of a type of object known as a *Trinkspiel* (drinking game), it is closely related to similar automata that portray Diana seated on a stag, of which around thirty have been preserved. The iconography of the centaur is more unusual, and only two such automata are known today: this example and another in the Grünes Gewölbe in Dresden. What both of them have in common is that a centaur armed with a bow and arrow serves the huntress as a mount and that they are accompanied by dogs. By analogy with the automata showing Diana and a stag, the huntress here can also be identified as the goddess of the hunt. In addition to the excellent goldwork and the magnificent partly gilt, enamelled accessories set with pearls and garnets, the piece is also a mechanical wonder. Hidden inside the wooden base and the body of the centaur is a complex mechanism that allows the automaton to move across the table at a specified time. The heads of the rider and one of the dogs turn while the other dog opens its mouth and the centaur rolls his eyes and shoots an arrow. The latter is what makes this elaborate automaton into a drinking game: the guest towards whom the arrow flies is required to make a toast and empty his glass.

PR

Rolling-Ball Clocks

First Rolling-Ball Clock (opposite)
Christoph Margraf (Augsburg, active in Prague 1595–1612),
signed
Prague, dated 1596
Wood covered with velvet, gilt brass, glass, unrefined silver,
opaque paint on parchment; mechanism: iron, H. 40.3 cm
(15⅞ in.), W. 28 cm (11 in.), L. 23 cm (9 in.)
Inv. no. KK 845

Third Rolling-Ball Clock (left)
Christoph Margraf (Augsburg,
active in Prague 1595–1612)
Hendrick van Steenwyck the
Elder (Steenwijk, Overijssel,
c. 1550–Frankfurt am Main,
c. 1603), interior painting, signed
Prague, c. 1600
Wood, partly stained, silver, gilt
brass, glass, H. 59 cm (23¼ in.),
W. 36 cm (14⅛ in.), L. 39 cm
(15⅜ in.)
Inv. no. KK 859

The imperial clockmaker Christoph Margraf is considered the inventor of the rolling-ball clock, which was fundamentally different from other clock mechanisms previously in use: a ball runs down a slope between two steel wires, always completing the same distance in the exact same time. On arriving at the bottom, it triggers the release of a second ball and then is raised back to its initial position to be released again when the second ball has arrived. The movement of the balls is recorded by a counter, which transfers the information to a clock face, where the hand is moved forward mechanically. In Margraf's clocks, the movement of the balls is visible, part of a fascinating game of deception that made the technology seem of secondary importance to the viewer. Margraf's rolling-ball clocks have a mirror mounted in the lid. When it is raised, the mirror reflects the view inside the clock in front of one of two interchangeable scenes. In the mirror image, it seems to the viewer as if the balls are floating from bottom to top across the scenes. Thus the rolling-ball clock became a mysterious, almost magical moving showpiece.

PR

Planetary Clock

Jost Bürgi (Lichtensteig, 1552–Kassel, 1632), clockwork, attributed
Jan Vermeyen (Brussels, before 1559–Prague, 1606), case
Prague, c. 1605
Gilt brass, silver, partly painted, rock crystal, glass; mechanism: iron, brass, H. 39.3 cm (15½ in.)
Inv. no. KK 846

This outstanding object is the first astronomical clock to include a mechanical depiction of the heliocentric model of the solar system. This groundbreaking innovation is the visible result of cooperation between the imperial chamber clockmaker Jost Bürgi, who today is still considered one of the most important clockmakers of all time, and the astronomer Johannes Kepler at the court of Rudolf II in Prague. The mechanical masterpiece is hidden inside a magnificent case, and only the dial, hands and a rotating ball in the tower that tops the clock suggest its presence. The most important mechanical innovation featured in this clock is a winder; it raises a weight, which, as it descends, powers the clock. That permitted the clock to run for several weeks at a time with a drive that supplied constant power. More important to the maker than keeping accurate time, however, was displaying the motion of the planets. They are prominently displayed on a face on the front, with five hands indicating the revolving of Mercury, Venus, Mars, Saturn and Jupiter around the fixed Sun. The 'old' geocentric system with the Earth at its centre, which was considered inferior to the newer heliocentric model, is depicted on a smaller face below. In addition, there was an indicator for predicting solar and lunar eclipses. A complete revolution took almost nineteen years.

PR

Pietre Dure Landscapes

View of Prague Castle (Hradčany)
Giovanni Castrucci (active in Prague, 1598–1615),
attributed
Prague, after 1606
Commesso of various types of agate and jasper on slate,
H. 11.5 cm (4½ in.), W. 23.8 cm (9⅜ in.)
Inv. no. KK 3060

Landscape with the Sacrifice of Isaac
Giovanni Castrucci (active in Prague 1598–1615),
attributed
Prague, *c.* 1600
Commesso of various types of agate and jasper on slate,
H. 43.3 cm (17 in.), W. 57.7 cm (22¾ in.)
Inv. no. KK 3411

These two pictures were created using the technique of *commesso di pietre dure* (lit.: 'assembled from hard-stones'), also called Florentine mosaic. In this extremely complicated and time-consuming form of lapidary art, coloured stones were ground and polished to make pieces that were then mounted seamlessly on a slate background, the varied colours of the stones thus producing an artistic image. In the 16th century, this technique experienced a great boom in popularity, mostly in Florence and Rome. Emperor Rudolf II was so fascinated by the technique that in 1585 he instructed his ambassador in Rome to hire a *pietre dure* master for whom he intended to open a special court workshop in Prague. The initial attempts failed, but Rudolf succeeded in opening a court workshop in the 1590s when the Florentine master Cosimo Castrucci moved to Prague. The workshop of Cosimo and his son Giovanni remained active in Prague until the 1620s. Rudolf II seems to have been mainly interested in landscapes, and these two works are characteristic examples.

PR

Jasper Jug

Ottavio Miseroni (Milan, 1567–Prague, 1624), jug
Paulus van Vianen (Utrecht, c. 1570–Prague, 1613),
mount
Prague, c. 1590/1600, mount dated 1608
Chalcedony, gold, H. 35.5 cm (14 in.), W. 22 cm
(8⅝ in.)
Inv. no. KK 1866

This monumental jug of brownish yellow chalcedony is one of the early works that the imperial lapidary artist Ottavio Miseroni completed in Prague. He carved the jug – foot, handle and body – in one piece from a single large block. With a creative will typical of the second half of the 16th century, the artist chose a hybrid creature with a dragon's head for the shape of the handle. The ornamental design of the handle merges into a female torso attached to the dragon's head. The bat-like wings of this hybrid creature are wrapped around the neck of the jug, thus connecting it with the handle. No goldwork was really required for this monolithic masterpiece because all the functional parts are fashioned from the same piece of stone with no need for connecting elements. Nevertheless, the artist Paulus van Vianen created a golden base and lid for the vessel. The reason for this was probably that the precious jug suffered an accident while in the emperor's collection. The dragon's head at the top of the handle has proved to be a later addition, and its join with the handle is concealed by a gold cuff. In making the cuff, Paulus van Vianen also gave the vessel a base and a lid, perpetuating his name by marking the piece with his monogram.

PR

Prase Dish with Lid

Jan Vermeyen (Brussels, before 1559–Prague, 1608)
Probably the workshop of Ottavio Miseroni, gem cutting
Prague, c. 1600/05
Prase, bloodstone, partly enamelled gold, garnets, citrine,
amethyst, jacinth, H. 23.5 cm (9¼ in.), D. 17.6 cm (7 in.)
Inv. no. KK 1918

Like the elegant bowl by Gasparo Miseroni (p. 150) this vessel is likewise made of prase (green chalcedony) and features a striking colour contrast between the dark green of the stone and the gleaming gold of the mount. In contrast to Gasparo's bowl, in which the point of departure was the cut piece of stone that a goldsmith completed to create a masterpiece, the lapidary work here was made to fit the goldsmith's design, which provided both the shape and the decoration for the elegant vessel. That is the origin of the unusual style, which is unique with regard to lapidary work. The elegant vessel is comprised of a number of individually worked pieces of prase, which are connected to one another either with pins or by the elaborate mount.

The surface is covered with a network of gold clasps and bands, which for the most part have been generously enamelled and in some cases have been further adorned, either with rows of garnets or individual stones of the same material. The lid provides a precious and colourful top to the vessel with a large citrine as a finial. Compared with the lid, the other parts of the bowl are decorated in a fairly restrained manner. Here the green of the rare stone is dominant, interrupted only by the gold of the clasps. This system continues inside the vessel, where rows of garnets set in gold lend structure to the design.

PR

The Art of Gemstone Engraving

Woman with a Fan
Ottavio Miseroni (Milan, 1567–Prague, 1624)
Prague, c. 1610
Jasper, cornelian, agate on a black chalcedony ground,
gold, enamel, pearls, H. 8.5 cm (3¼ in.), W. 5.3 cm
(2⅛ in.)
Inv. no. ANSA XII 140

Venus and Cupid
Giovanni Ambrogio Miseroni (Milan, c. 1551/52–
Milan, 1616), attributed
Milan or Prague, between 1600 and 1610
Chalcedony, H. 8.3 cm (3¼ in.), L. 11.4 cm (4½ in.),
W. 10.1 cm (3⅞ in.)
Inv. no. KK 1730

Probably no other work in the entire field of gemstone engraving can approach the technical, artistic, and aesthetic perfection of this *Venus and Cupid*. The sculptural problems of depicting human anatomy and motion in space have been resolved in a masterly fashion. The delicate treatment of the details is amazing to viewers, and the power of the tender loving expression of the group could hardly be surpassed. The work is also unsurpassed in the interplay of nature and art as well as in the exploration and exploitation of the natural colours of the material, a block of chalcedony. Giovanni Ambrogio Miseroni incorporated the reddish brown, grey, yellow and milky white parts of the hardstone so masterfully into his composition

that it almost seems that the stone has changed colour to fit the design of the sculpture instead of the other way around.

While Giovanni Ambrogio carved his group from a single stone, Ottavio Miseroni created his depiction of a lady with a fan using a new and different technique, one which he is considered to have invented. He combined the technique of *commesso di pietre dure* with that of cameo cutting, assembling pieces of polished agate and jasper in a manner that created a cameo-like depiction in low relief in a variety of different colours.

PR

235

Cameos by Alessandro Masnago

Cameo: *Lucretia*
Alessandro Masnago (active in Milan from *c.* 1560–Milan, 1620), gem cutting
Milan, last quarter of the 16th century
Jan Vermeyen (Brussels, before 1559–Prague, 1608), mount
Prague, *c.* 1602
Agate, enamelled gold, cameo: 3.7 × 2.5 cm (1½ × 1 in.); frame: 5.9 × 5 cm (2⅜ × 2 in.)
Inv. no. ANSA XII 97

Cameo: *The Rape of Proserpina*
Alessandro Masnago (active in Milan, *c.* 1560–Milan, 1620), gem cutting
Milan, *c.* 1590
Andreas Osenbruck (active in Prague, *c.* 1610–after 1622), mount
Prague, *c.* 1610
Agate, enamelled gold, rubies, diamonds, cameo: 3.1 × 4.1 cm (1⅛ × 1⅝ in.);
frame: 5.4 × 6.3 cm (2⅛ × 2½ in.)
Inv. no. ANSA XII 30

These two cameos were created in Milan towards the end of the 16th century by Alessandro Masnago. No other cameo cutter was more skilled than he in using the varicoloured layers of agate to pictorial effect. The greyish-blue layer provided the background while the pink layer above it was used in both cases to depict the subject. In the case of Lucretia, this layer provides the flesh tones of the beautiful Roman woman while Masnago used the white upper layer of stone for her flowing dress. Especially refined is his use of the existing red specks in the stone for the place where the dagger pierces her flesh. This mastery in incorporating the colours of the material into the design was probably the reason that Emperor Rudolf II so highly esteemed Masnago, who worked almost exclusively for the art-loving ruler. After the cameos arrived in Prague, Rudolf had *Lucretia* set by his court goldsmith Jan Vermeyen and *Proserpina* by Andreas Osenbruck, later court goldsmith to Rudolf's successor, Matthias. Their enamelled gold settings are just as magnificent as the cameos themselves.

PR

Masterpieces of the Florentine Court

Small Domestic Altarpiece with *Christ and the Woman of Samaria*
Cristofano Gaffuri (d. Florence, 1626), *pietre dure*
Bernardino Gaffuri (d. Florence, 1606), walls of aedicula
Ambrogio Caroni (d. Florence, 1611), frame
Jacques Byliveldt (Delft, 1550–Florence, 1603), goldsmith's work
Florence, 1590–1600
Jasper, agate, lapis lazuli, emerald, amethyst, rock crystal, partly enamelled gold, silver gilt, 39 × 23.4 × 7.4 cm (15⅛ × 9⅛ × 2⅞ in.)
Inv. no. KK 1542

Lapis Lazuli Vessel
Gian Stefano Caroni
(d. Florence, 1611),
gem cutting
Jacques Bylivelt (Delft, 1550–
Florence, 1603), mount
Florence, 1575/76–81
Lapis lazuli, enamelled
gold, H. 36.7 cm (14½ in.),
W. 17.8 cm (7 in.)
Inv. no. KK 1655

These two works are among the most outstanding accomplishments of the Florentine court workshop under Grand Duke Ferdinando I de' Medici. The classic, restrained shape of the large lapis lazuli vessel is captivating. It seems to have been chosen to show the beautiful blue surface to its best advantage. Caroni cut the vase in one piece from a large block of high-quality lapis lazuli and then gave the work for completion to the goldsmith Jacques Byliveldt.

The latter was also involved in the creation of the domestic altarpiece. It combines the work of three professions in which the craftsmen of the Florentine court workshop were for a long time leaders in their field: gem cutting, goldsmithing and, especially, the art of *pietre dure*, or hardstone mosaic. The latter technique was used to create the central field of the picture, the background for Christ's encounter at the well with the woman from Samaria. Both works came into the possession of the House of Habsburg as gifts from the grand dukes of Tuscany. The lapis lazuli vessel was a gift to Emperor Ferdinand II in 1628 while the small altarpiece was presented to Emperor Charles VI more than a hundred years later.

PR

The Master of the Furies

Phoenix and *Fury*
Master of the Furies
Salzburg (?), *c.* 1610/20
Ivory, *Phoenix*: H. 23.8 cm (9⅜ in.)
Fury: H. 37.4 cm (14¾ in.);
Inv. nos. KK 3721, KK 3727

The Master of the Furies was an outstanding artist who, even today, has not been identified. Probably this ivory carver was active in the circle of the prince-archbishop of Salzburg. With the highest degree of virtuosity, he carved unusually expressive and dynamically moving figures that have an eerie, unsettling effect. This places his works among the most interesting and unusual small sculptures created around 1600. Thus far, some twenty-five works are believed to be by this unknown master.

His name is taken from this *Fury* from the collections of the Kunsthistorisches Museum, and it displays all the characteristics of his highly individual style. The figure's skinny body seems almost disfigured. The long, emaciated arms and legs and the scarf behind the figure's neck seem to flutter, expanding into space in various directions.

Screaming in a strained manner, the androgynous being seems to be expressing anger or the pain of fear, but the context is impossible to interpret.

The bird listed in the old inventories as a phoenix can be described in a similar manner. With its wings outstretched and its beak open wide, it seems ready to peck aggressively at anyone who approaches. The figure was assembled from countless individual parts that are mounted on a wooden core. The treatment of the ivory is unusual: the material's charm usually derives from the gleam of its polished surfaces, but here the effect is undermined by the shaggy appearance of the feathers. The contrast they make with the smooth beak and claws illustrates the wide range of possible treatments of this material.

KS

Portrait in Wax: *Emperor Ferdinand III*

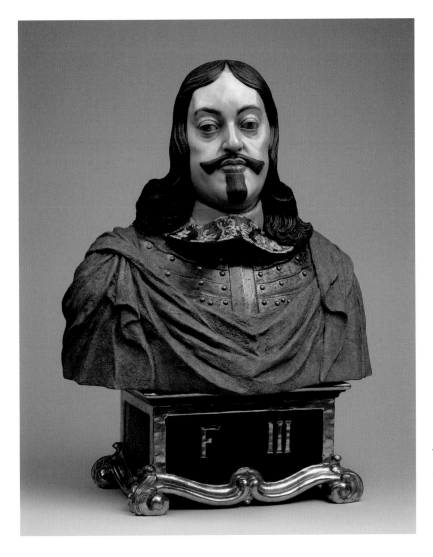

Justinus Psolmayr (active
in the 2nd quarter of 17th
century), attributed
Vienna, *c.* 1643 (?)
Wax, painted, wooden base,
H. 66 cm (26 in.) with base
Inv. no. KK 10.161

Three-dimensional wax portraits of rulers were highly popular during the Baroque period, and were in keeping with the interest in theatrical illusion typical of the time. Some of them are even decorated with human hair, making them seem almost real. In this manner the medium of the portrait was taken to the extreme in an effort to reflect reality. The function of these wax busts was to preserve the symbolic presence of the ruler beyond the boundaries posed created by the transitoriness of human life. Some of them were displayed next to the body of the ruler lying in state. It is said that a life-sized, body-length wax figure of Emperor Ferdinand III once existed that could be dressed in his clothes. An internal clockwork mechanism made its glass eyes roll and made the seated figure stand up and sit down again. It is also reported that the Hungarian chancellor was once so fooled by the automaton emperor that he fell to his knees before it.

While this bust of Ferdinand III lacks such a high degree of realism, it nonetheless reflects the fascination of the illusion of life being recreated in coloured wax. It is attributed to a wax sculptor named Justinus Psolmayr about whom nothing is known apart from the fact that in 1643 he received the grand sum of 300 thalers for a portrait of the emperor.

Emperor Ferdinand III (1608–57) was considered to be kind and just. He was a patron of the arts and sciences, composed music and wrote poetry. Among his political accomplishments was bringing the Thirty Years' War to a close.

KS

Sculptures by Leonhard Kern

The works of the sculptor Leonhard Kern, known almost exclusively for his small-scale sculptures, combine meticulous detail with inner monumentality. His cabinet pieces perfectly suited the tastes of aristocratic collectors at the time. This statuette of the Old Testament's King David playing the harp – an early work by Kern – clearly reflects Michelangelo's corporeal ideal, but the fact that the king is playing music lends the imposing figure a lyrical note.

In stark contrast is the *Scene from the Thirty Years' War*, which explores the aesthetics of terror and is unusual because of its direct reference to a specific period. The officer stabbing a naked young woman from behind can be identified by the three roses on his shoulder strap as a member of the van Rosen family of Livonian aristocrats.

During the Thirty Years' War, Reinhold von Rosen was fighting on the side of the Swedes when they captured the free imperial city of Schwäbisch Hall, where Leonhard Kern lived. Thus the woman being stabbed must be interpreted as an allegorical figure rather than a historical one. The group was first described in 1659 in the inventory of Archduke Leopold William's collection. The art-loving Habsburg archduke was an imperial general in the Thirty Years' War and saw himself as the protector of the free imperial cities. Thus this scene could be viewed as an allegory of the threat posed to Schwäbisch Hall by the Swedish enemy and may have been commissioned by the archduke himself.

KS

Objects in Amber

Six-Sided Bowl with Handles
Jakob Heise (active in Königsberg, 1654–67)
Königsberg, *c.* 1660
Amber, H. 12.8 cm (5 in.), L. 30.5 cm (12 in.), W. 21.4 cm (8⅜ in.)
Inv. no. KK 3535

Since time immemorial, amber has inspired the human imagination, but for a long time the origin of the material remained unknown. Many mystic legends grew up around this 'gold of the sea', as amber was once called. When the Enlightenment finally provided a scientific explanation for this fossilized tree resin, interest in the material abruptly declined. Up to that time, however, amber's mysterious aura made it a highly coveted natural material that was artistically treated to create cabinet pieces for the princely collections of Europe. When turned in the light, beautifully made vessels of translucent amber blaze with a glory that makes a collector's heart beat faster, especially when several shades of amber are combined or used alongside other materials. On this lidded tankard, for example, the colourfully enamelled gold mount with its rich floral decoration is truly eye-catching.

The largest deposits of amber occur along the shores of the Baltic Sea on the Samland Peninsula. The Teutonic Knights established a monopoly on the amber trade, and the rights to the precious material later passed to the House of Hohenzollern, which ruled Prussia. During the Baroque period, Königsberg (now Kaliningrad, Russia) was a major centre for amber processing. The artists of the area, such as Jakob Heise, worked for Prussian dukes and kings, and many of the works were brought to the imperial court in Vienna as diplomatic gifts.

KS

Ivory Tankard: *Drunken Silenus*

Georg Petel (Weilheim, 1601/02–Augsburg, 1634),
ivory carving, attributed
Andreas Wickert (Augsburg, 1600–Augsburg, 1661),
goldwork
Augsburg, 1629
Ivory, silver gilt, H. 38.4 cm (15⅛ in.)
Inv. no. KK 4519

During the Baroque period, Bacchanalian scenes were a popular motif for decorating drinking vessels. These exuberant compositions depicted boisterous merriment, alcoholic excess and lust. The dominant motif on this ivory tankard is the figure of Silenus. So drunk he can hardly stand, he needs a pair of satyrs to support his massive body. Astonishingly, the carver has taken a hard material, elephant tusk, and created the impression of soft flesh, as may be seen in the way the hand of a satyr is gripping the flabby skin of Silenus's side. The idea for the composition may be traced back to Peter Paul Rubens, who was a great master in the depiction of voluptuous corporeality. Rubens not only depicted an obese and drunken Silenus in his paintings but also supplied designs for ivory carvings, including some for this exact same scene.

Georg Petel, a craftsman from Weilheim in Upper Bavaria, was considered in the 18th century to be the 'German Michelangelo'. As a young sculptor he worked for some time in Rubens's studio in Antwerp. Rubens, who collected contemporary sculpture, regarded Petel highly and bought some of his works. The mount for this tankard was made by the Augsburg goldsmith Andreas Wickert. Archival documents record a payment made by Count Ottheinrich Fugger to the two artists in 1629 for an ivory drinking vessel. For stylistic reasons, however, some doubts have been expressed about whether Petel executed this vessel himself.

KS

Four Lathe-Turned Ivory Vessels with Lids

Lathe-turned work is a genre of its own in ivory art. The turner holds a sharply honed tool against the piece to be turned, which is mounted on a lathe where it rotates on its own axis. The material to be turned could be rotated in a variety of pre-set ways. Designs executed in this manner were quite different from those of an ivory carver because the use of a mechanical lathe allowed the material to be given a very regular shape. In the 17th century, ivory turning developed into a highly specialized production technique. With the exacting goal of using mechanical precision to overcome the obstacles presented by nature, lathe-turners executed increasingly difficult designs. Their attitude was, the more difficult the task the better: they were trying to arouse the interest of aristocratic collectors in pieces that, whether symmetrical or asymmetrical, were as complex as possible and sometimes took bizarre and daring architectural forms. Lathe-turning became a hobby for some members of the aristocracy as well, and rulers at many European courts enjoyed working at the lathe.

KS

Ivory Vessels (from left to right)

Marcus Heiden (active 1618–64)
Coburg (?), 2nd quarter of 17th century
Ivory, H. 60 cm (23⅝ in.)
Inv. no. KK 4676

Southern German, 1st third of 17th century
Ivory, H. 54 cm (21¼ in.)
Inv. no. KK 4777

Johann Eisenberg (1600–40)
Coburg, dated 1637
Ivory, H. 34.2 cm (13½ in.)
Inv. no. KK 4772

Johann Eisenberg (1600–40)
Coburg, dated 1630
Ivory, H. 58.8 cm (23⅛ in.)
Inv. no. KK 4671

The Wrangel Cabinet

Collector's Cabinet, known as the Wrangel Cabinet
Ulrich Baumgartner (*c.* 1580–Augsburg, 1652)
Georg Haupt (Stockholm, 1741–Stockholm, 1784)
Augsburg, 1631–34, body
Stockholm, 1776, base
Ebony, precious stones, copper, enamel painting, bronze,
ivory, mother-of-pearl, shells, coral, H. 183 cm (72 in.)
Inv. no. KK 3403

This cabinet was the last one to be designed and sold by the Augsburg art dealer Philipp Hainhofer (1578–1647). As a businessman, Hainhofer specialized in ordering ornamental cabinets from Augsburg furnituremakers, filling the drawers and compartments with cabinet pieces, and selling the entire ensemble as a sort of collection in miniature. Aristocratic clients throughout Europe paid him well for his services.

The original contents of this cabinet have not been preserved, but according to an inventory they must have comprised objects of all kinds related to stone and metal: fossilized plants and animals, artefacts and natural phenomena in various metals and precious stones, and a variety of objects in horn, ivory or coral. The same materials were used to decorate the outside of the ebony cabinet, which thus had the character of a collection of minerals and other materials.

The cabinet was first purchased in 1647 by August, Duke of Braunschweig-Lüneburg who, as the Thirty Years' War was drawing to a close, needed a prestigious gift for the Swedish military and naval commander, Count Carl Gustav Wrangel. The duke's intention was to induce the count to take a lenient attitude towards his duchy as the Swedish troops withdrew. Thus the imposing cabinet was taken to Sweden, where the classical-style base was made in the 18th century. In the early 19th century, the cabinet was purchased and brought to Vienna.

KS

Tapestry: *Riding Lessons: The Creation of the Horse*

Jacob Jordaens (Antwerp, 1593–Antwerp, 1678), design
Everaert III Leyniers (1597–1680), weaver/manufactory
Brussels, *c.* 1650
Tapestry: wool, silk, metal thread, H. 410 cm (161½ in.),
W. 521 cm (205 in.)
Inv. no. KK T XL/1

The famous French riding instructor Antoine de Pluvinel (1555–1620) founded an equestrian school in Paris, where he taught the future King Louis XIII *haute école* riding. In 1623 his instructions were published with illustrations by Crispin de Passe the Younger, and those designs later served as a model for the figures of the individual riders in an eight-part series of tapestries. Emperor Leopold I probably acquired them in 1666 on the occasion of his marriage to Princess Margarita Teresa of Spain.

The first in the series deals with the mythological theme of the creation of the horse, a legend based on the writings of the authors of antiquity. At the centre of this tapestry, which was derived from a design by the Flemish artist Jacob Jordaens, stands the god of the sea, Poseidon. At the depicted moment – as described by Philostratus – the god is gliding across the water in a shell; with his trident he strikes – according to Ovid's *Metamorphoses* – against a rock, causing a fiery steed to rise from the earth. The almost naked wife of Poseidon, Amphitrite, may be seen at the right of the picture. She is sitting in a chariot beneath a baldachin flanked by two dolphins.

Since antiquity Poseidon has been viewed as the god of horses, and according to Pausanias and Diodorus Siculus he was considered the father of equestrianism. The scene is thus a perfect introduction for a series of tapestries depicting *haute école* riding.

KSvL

Gemstone Masterpieces by Dionysio Miseroni

Flower Vase
Dionysio Miseroni (Prague, *c.* 1607–Prague, 1661), vase
Paul Pertz (d. 1661), flowers; Prague, 1647/48
Citrine (yellow quartz), agate, jasper, chalcedony,
rock crystal, partially enamelled gold, enamelled
silver, H. 46.5 cm (18¼ in.), H. without flowers 26 cm
(10¼ in.), W. 20.2 cm (8 in.), D. 11 cm (4⅜ in.)
Inv. no. KK 1330

Emerald Unguentarium
Dionysio Miseroni
(Prague, *c.* 1607–
Prague, 1661)
Prague, 1641
Emerald (2680 carats),
enamelled gold,
H. 10.9 cm (4⅜ in.),
L. 8.5 cm (3¼ in.),
W. 7.2 cm (2⅞ in.)
Inv. no. KK 2048

Along with the rock-crystal Pyramid Vase (p. 259), these two works are among the most remarkable accomplishments of Dionysio Miseroni. The Flower Vase is one of his most elegant vessels made of semiprecious stone. Carved from a large block of clear citrine (a form of quartz), the vase is attractive not only for the intensity of its colour but also for its clear structure, accomplished surface decoration and the harmonious way that it is combined with its enamelled gold mounts. Light reflects off the gently undulating surface but also passes through the vessel, resulting in an always fascinating and constantly shifting play of light and shade, depending on the lighting and the viewing angle. The splendid citrine vase is topped with a magnificent bouquet of flowers, for which Paul Pertz, the imperial cutter of diamonds and other precious stones, also used quartz.

The Emerald Unguentarium is another striking masterpiece. Its captivating appearance is owed to the material used, a huge Colombian emerald. Emperor Ferdinand III commissioned Miseroni to create a vessel from it, and when the highly risky work was completed in 1641, he was rewarded with the truly princely sum of 12,000 florins. The grand duke of Tuscany is said to have offered three tonnes of gold for this wonder, which has long been among the most admired objects in the Treasury.

PR

The Pyramid Vase

Dionysio Miseroni (Prague, *c.* 1607–
Prague, 1661), gem cutting
Hanns Reinhardt Taravell (from 1648
court goldsmith in Prague), mount
Prague, 1651–53
Rock crystal, silver gilt, enamel, total
height (lower vase and four stacking
segments) 145.4 cm (57¼ in.),
maximum W. 29.3 cm (11½ in.)
Inv. nos. KK 2251–KK 2254

In the Pyramid Vase, Dionysio Miseroni created a work of lapidary art that soon after its creation had become famous throughout Europe and provided its creator with a lasting legacy. The German painter and art historian Joachim von Sandrart described this rock crystal in his *Teutsche Academie* (1675) as follows: 'Particularly famous is the fabulous vessel as tall as a man / which…remains superior to all other comparable works of art.' This deserving praise is based on the technical virtuosity used to create the monumental vessel. Cut from a single huge block of rock crystal, it consists of five individual elements that can be stacked on top of one another to create a tower. The artist used a tubular drill to cut each smaller piece from the interior of the next larger one. The monumental piece of pure and almost streakless rock crystal used for making this masterpiece was found in Switzerland in 1651 and presented to Emperor Ferdinand III as a gift. We know from a memorial addressed to the emperor that Miseroni began work on the Pyramid Vase the same year and had fashioned two of the pieces by the end of 1651. It took several more years to complete; the object is dated 1653.

PR

Shell Cameos

Pendant Medallion with a Portrait of Emperor Ferdinand III
Southern Germany, *c.* 1650
Shell; setting: gold, enamel, rubies, shells, H. 7.9 cm (3⅛ in.),
W. 5.2 cm (2⅛ in.)
Inv. no. ANSA XII 79

Pendant Medallion with a Portrait of Archduke Leopold William
Southern Germany, *c.* 1650
Shell; setting: gold, enamel, rubies, shell cameos, H. 11.7 cm
(4⅝ in.), W. 4.6 cm (1⅞ in.)
Inv. no. ANSA XII 77

Shell cameos, which feature reliefs carved into mussel or cowrie shells, are part of the tradition of lapidary art. Initially they served as substitutes for the cameos made from precious stones, such as onyx or agate, which had been made in Italy since the 15th century, in the style of the cameos of antiquity. In the 17th century, portrait shell cameos became fashionable, and workshops in Nuremberg in particular specialized in their manufacture. For the most part they served as jewelry, as was the case with these two medallions.

In the first example, the cover of the medallion case bears a portrait bust of Emperor Ferdinand III (1608–57). His image is crowned with an eagle and surrounded by portraits of twelve of his Habsburg predecessors as kings and emperors of the Holy Roman Empire. The outer frame is composed of twelve rubies alternating with twelve smaller shell cameos bearing the emblems of the rulers who surround Ferdinand III at the centre. While the focus here is on legitimizing imperial rule by including predecessors within the dynasty of the current ruler, the other medallion depicts the emperor's brother Archduke Leopold William (1614–62) as an ecclesiastical and secular prince and member of the House of Habsburg. Here the imperial double eagle decorates the lid of the case, which has a portrait bust of the archduke with his armour on the inside.

FK

The Collection of Archduke Leopold William

Archduke Leopold William
Jérôme Duquesnoy the
Younger (Brussels, 1602–
Ghent, 1654)
Brussels, dated 1650
Marble, H. 68 cm (26¼ in.)
Inv. no. KK 8932

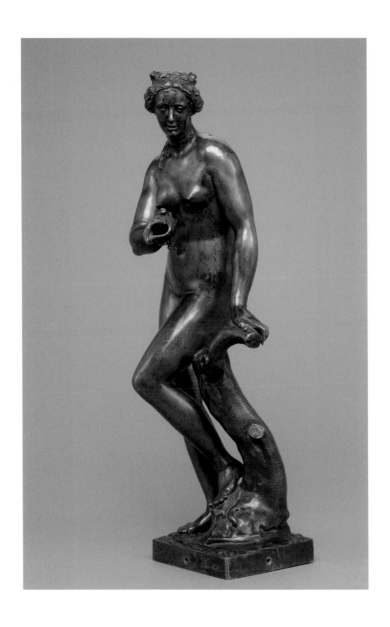

Venus or *Amphitrite*
Francesco Fanelli (Florence,
last quarter of 16th century?
–Paris, 1661), attributed
Italian, *c.* 1645 (executed
in England?)
Bronze, H. 49.2 cm (19⅜ in.)
Inv. no. KK 5850

As the second son of Emperor Ferdinand II, Archduke Leopold William (1614–62) initially trained to become a priest. He was grand master of the Teutonic Order, and he was invested with a number of prince-bishoprics. That, however, did not prevent his serving as a general in the Thirty Years' War. From 1647 to 1656 he was regent of the Spanish Netherlands. There he began an extensive collection of artworks, which ultimately contained some 1,400 paintings. About half of those are now in the Kunsthistorisches Museum, where they provide the foundation of the Picture Gallery. The archduke, however, also collected drawings, tapestries and more than 500 sculptures, statuettes and other cabinet pieces. These included the medieval ivory relief of *St Gregory with Scribes* (p. 53) and this *Venus* (or *Amphitrite*), a bronze figure of the goddess with a shell in her hand. It is depicted in David Teniers the Younger's famous painting of the archduke's picture gallery in Brussels (KHM, Picture Gallery, inv. no. 739). Until only a few years ago it was attributed to Jérôme Duquesnoy, the archduke's court sculptor in Brussels, who also created the marble bust of Leopold William. Then a replica of the *Venus (Amphitrite)* in a private collection was found to bear the signature of Francesco Fanelli, an Italian sculptor who spent most of his career in England. The Vienna sculpture is now likewise attributed to him.

KS

The Martyrdom of St Sebastian

Master of the Martyrdom of St Sebastian
Vienna, dated 1655
Ivory, H. 54.3 cm (21⅛ in.), W. 80.4 cm (31⅝ in.)
Inv. no. KK 3654

Assembled from ten narrow, rectangular ivory panels, this work depicts the martyrdom of the Roman officer Sebastian. Because he was a Christian, he was ordered to be killed by being shot with arrows, but Sebastian survived, and a Christian widow named Irene nursed him back to health. He then criticized Emperor Diocletian, who condemned him to be beaten to death. His body was thrown into a cesspit but later reburied in a catacomb.

The foreground is dominated by the figures, some three-dimensional, of the main scene. The archers take aim at Sebastian, who is bound to a tree with two fellow Christians lying lifeless at his feet. Two putti are coming down from heaven to bring him a victor's laurels and a martyr's palm branch. As in a puzzle picture, the detailed landscape of the background is depicted in flat relief with hunting scenes and other episodes from the saint's life. It is unusual to find such a narrative depiction of the martyrdom of St Sebastian, and it is also impressive for the expressiveness with which the figures are portrayed. This applies in particular to the expression of suffering on the face of the saint – the Laocoön of antiquity appears to have been a model – and the coarse brutality of the soldiers' faces. Along with the precise carving technique, this is a stylistic hallmark of the unknown artist. The Master of the Martyrdom of St Sebastian got his name from this work and a second one on the same theme. He probably came from southern Germany, perhaps from the area of Lake Constance, and moved to Vienna, where he worked for the imperial court.

KS

Emperor Leopold I

Paul Strudel (Cles?, 1648–Vienna, 1708)
Vienna, 1695
Laas marble, H. 86 cm (33⅞ in.),
W. 64 cm (25¼ in.)
Inv. no. KK 5458

With his imperial bearing and severe gaze, the emperor is turning away from the viewer. He wears a magnificent suit of armour with a brocade cape over it, the chain of the Order of the Golden Fleece, a fashionable Baroque full-bottomed wig and a laurel wreath in the style of an ancient Roman caesar. The manner in which the sculptor, Paul Strudel, has used the brittle material of marble and yet differentiated between the various materials and surfaces is impressive. The portrait is from a series of busts of the imperial family, which Strudel made for Johann Wilhelm, Elector Palatine, the brother-in-law of Leopold I. They were intended to be displayed at the elector's residence in Düsseldorf, but the emperor liked the portraits and allowed only the one of the elector himself to be sent to his residence. Leopold I purchased the others, and a year later appointed Strudel to be the imperial court sculptor.

No attempt was made to flatter Emperor Leopold I (1640–1705) in this bust, which indicates that he was of rather unattractive appearance. He was considered to be shy and indecisive but also intelligent and very musical with a talent for languages. He particularly enjoyed Italian opera and even composed himself. During the almost fifty years of his rule, he conducted numerous wars against France, the Ottoman Empire and internal opponents in Hungary. Under his reign, Austria rose to become a great power and absolutism reached a pinnacle.

KS

King Joseph I Vanquishing Fury

Matthias Steinl (Mattsee/Salzburg?,
1643/44–Vienna, 1727)
Vienna, dated 1693
Ivory, H. 47.5 cm (18¾ in.)
Inv. no. KK 4663

The youthful rider in armour is powerful and dynamic as he leaps with an unmoved facial expression over a vanquished enemy. The initials 'JI' on his breastplate identify him as Joseph I. The figure beneath him is Fury, representing the horrors of war, who may be identified by the attributes of a serpent, a torch, the fetter on his raised arm, and the quiver with arrows. Here the young king is thus a prince of peace and a saviour. This piece has a counterpart (see p. 43), which depicts the father of Joseph I, Emperor Leopold I. He, too, is on horseback and seems similarly unmoved as he leaps over an Ottoman archer. The two works belong together and are united by a common concept. Together they form an allegorical monument, meant less to glorify the emperor and his son as individuals than to symbolize the rule of the House of Habsburg as well

as the continuity and renewal of the Holy Roman Empire under the two men, who at the time were the empire's current and future rulers. The occasion for the creation of this double monument was probably the election and coronation in Augsburg in 1690 of the eleven-year-old Joseph as King of the Romans, thus ensuring that the imperial crown and power would remain in the family. Afterwards, father and son returned triumphantly to Vienna, and the imperial ivory engraver Matthias Steinl set to work, creating these two statuettes (larger format versions were never planned) with admirable virtuosity. Despite the meticulous design of every detail, they possess impressive monumentality and are highlights of Western ivory art.

KS

Lidded Tankard with Hunting and Fishing Scenes

Balthasar Griessmann (Wasserburg, c. 1620–
Vienna or Salzburg, 1706)
Vienna or Salzburg, 3rd quarter of 17th century
Ivory, H. 29.8 cm (11⅝ in.), Diam. 11.5 to 8.5 cm
(4½ to 3¼ in.)
Inv. no. KK 4472

A masterpiece of Baroque ivory art, this delicately carved tankard was created for purely decorative purposes. The elaborate decoration of the handle makes it far too delicate to be picked up, revealing that it was never intended for practical use. The vessel also has no metal framework to provide stability. Luxury items of this kind were presented as gifts at European courts, where they were displayed on buffets and credenzas to impress the guests. The figurative decoration is also in keeping with the courtly environment in which the tankard, formerly in the imperial collections, was created. The theme of the detailed relief, the hunt, was a quintessential aristocratic pastime. The pictorial landscapes are densely populated. Along with a few scenes of fishing on the base of the vessel, duck hunting, a wild boar hunt and deer hunting are featured on the sides while the lid depicts hawking and even an ostrich. The finial depicts water-spewing putti riding on dolphins. Hunters and dogs can be seen climbing up the handle, along with a pair of young lovers. On the spout is a grotesque mask, composed in part of snail shells. The decoration alternates between low and high relief with some fully three-dimensional elements.

The ivory carver and turner Balthasar Griessmann was active in Salzburg and Vienna. In addition to relief panels, it is believed that he mostly made ivory tankards and other ornamental vessels. The Vienna Kunstkammer contains a representative sample of his works.

KS

Relief Carvings by Ignaz Elhafen

The Judgment of Paris
Ignaz Elhafen
(Innsbruck, 1658–
Innsbruck, before 1715)
Vienna, after 1700
Ivory, H. 10.4 cm (4 in.),
W. 16.7 cm (6⅝ in.)
Inv. no. KK 4178

Battle of the Amazons
Ignaz Elhafen (Innsbruck,
1658–Innsbruck, before
1715)
Innsbruck (?), c. 1680/85
Cedar wood, H. 12.8 cm
(5 in.), W. 19.7 cm (7¾ in.)
Inv. no. KK 3932

The Innsbruck carver Ignaz Elhafen specialized in small-format reliefs. Early in his career, they were made of hardwood; later he preferred to use ivory. His presence in Vienna is not documented before 1697. There he worked primarily for the princes of Liechtenstein and for other aristocratic families, and no direct link to a patron at the imperial court has yet been found. The ruling family probably acquired his reliefs from dealers or received them as gifts from other aristocrats. In 1704 Elhafen became a court artist to the Electors Palatine in Düsseldorf. His style is eclectic, and he used printed designs as his models.

Battle of the Amazons depicts one of the twelve labours of Hercules: the legendary hero can be seen on the right, wearing the skin of the Nemean lion and wielding a club.

The dense battle scene, which fills almost the entire surface of the artwork and opens at the top into an undefined distance behind a sea of countless lances, is based on a work by the Roman copperplate engraver Antonio Tempesta. Elhafen's detailed depiction of the figures is striking.

The Judgment of Paris is one the artist's most progressive works and was probably created during his final years in Vienna. Paris is shown awarding the apple to Aphrodite as the most beautiful of the three goddesses. Hera seems to be disappointed while Athena is turning her back on the scene of her perceived humiliation. Here Elhafen has combined various Dutch engravings. The psychological differentiation of his figures is remarkable.

KS

Apollo and Daphne

Jakob Auer
(Haimingersberg,
c. 1645–Grins, 1706)
Vienna, before 1688
Ivory, H. 43.9 cm
(17⅜ in.)
Inv. no. KK 4537

According to Ovid's *Metamorphoses*, the nymph Daphne prayed to her father, a river god, to rescue her from pursuit by the god Apollo, who was in love with her. Her father transformed her into a laurel tree (*daphne* in Greek means laurel) as Apollo was attempting to embrace her.

The theme, which combined pursuit and transformation in a single motif, was very popular in Baroque art. Gianlorenzo Bernini's famous marble group at Galleria Borghese in Rome set the standard. Here the carver Jakob Auer has created a virtuoso piece of art with countless tiny details to capture the moment of metamorphosis. Daphne's toes are taking root; her slender fingers and strands of her hair are becoming leafy twigs. The detailed folds of cloth that seem to caress the two lovely figures

echo the substance of tender leaves. The man and woman, hunter and prey, complement one another as equivalents in the complete harmony of their internal and external movement. The figures were carved from a single elephant tusk, and the original shape can still be perceived. The elaborate openwork of the twigs and leaves illustrates perfectly the dissolution of the natural form of the material.

Jakob Auer came originally from Tyrol but during the reign of Leopold I, he moved to Vienna, which at the time was undisputedly the most important centre of ivory craftsmanship. The emperor and many other affluent art collectors greatly admired the precious material for the silky sheen of its surface.

KS

Breakfast Service and Washing Set of Empress Maria Theresa

Anton Matthias Domanek (Domanöck)
(Vienna, 1713–Vienna, 1779)
Vienna, c. 1750
Gold, ebony, porcelain, glass
Inv. nos. KK 1197–KK 1266

First mentioned in the imperial inventories on 16 January 1781 as 'a gold service belonging to Her Late Imperial and Royal Apostolic Majesty' (Maria Theresa, who had died less than two months earlier), this set of more than seventy pieces was used by the ruler during the morning reception called *Lever* (literally 'getting up'). The composition of the washing set suggests, however, that at least some of the items must have been intended for use by her husband, Emperor Francis I Stephen. Among those items are six razors, mirrors, candlesticks with wick trimmers, bottles, a case with toiletries, a complete shaving set with a jug and basin as well as 'five boxes, two large and three small'.

The service that Maria Theresa herself probably used for the *Lever* is made up of various pots for tea, coffee and chocolate as well as the appropriate cups and bowls of Japanese and Meissen porcelain, sugar bowls, spoons and so on. In practice, such precious and elaborately designed sets were likely created for decorative rather than functional purposes. For that reason, the individual objects here show almost no signs of wear. For everyday use the monarchs had smaller services, which were frequently made of silver.

PR

Centrepiece of Duke Charles Alexander of Lorraine

Pierre-Joseph Fonson (Mons, 1713–Brussels, 1799)
Jacques-François Van der Donck (Brussels, 1724–
Brussels, 1801)
Brussels, Sèvres and Vienna, 1755, 1770 and 1794
Gold, porcelain
Inv. nos. KK 1268–KK 1284

In 1755 the court silversmith in Brussels, Pierre-Joseph Fonson, created a golden dining service for Duke Charles Alexander of Lorraine, the brother of Emperor Francis I Stephen and governor-general of the Austrian Netherlands. Of the many individual pieces, only the centrepiece, four candlesticks and two sauceboats have been preserved. The extensive set of golden and gilt dishes was lost over the years. The containers for oil and vinegar, mustard, spices and sugar that remained on the table throughout a banquet were placed on this magnificent centrepiece, originally the focal point of the service and marked with the duke's coat of arms. The central motif that rises above the tray-like base is a basket supported by four candlesticks

and filled with a bouquet of extremely delicate porcelain flowers. The sixty gossamer-fine blossoms are made of soft-paste china, and their naturalistic colours and shapes mark them as a characteristic product of the royal porcelain factory at Sèvres in France. Originally the bouquet was part of the centrepiece of a gold service that Emperor Francis I commissioned on the occasion of the marriage of his son Joseph with Isabella of Parma in 1760. That service was melted down in 1797, but the porcelain bouquet was preserved, later becoming part of this centrepiece for the duke of Lorraine.

PR

Three Sculptures in Lead

Prometheus Bound
Johann Baptist Hagenauer (Strass,
Bavaria, 1732–Vienna, 1811)
Vienna, dated 1759
Lead, tin, H. 41.4 cm (16¼ in.)
Inv. no. KK 5825

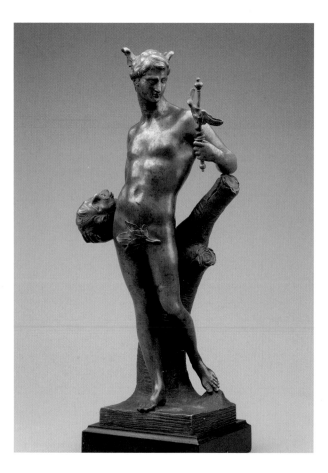 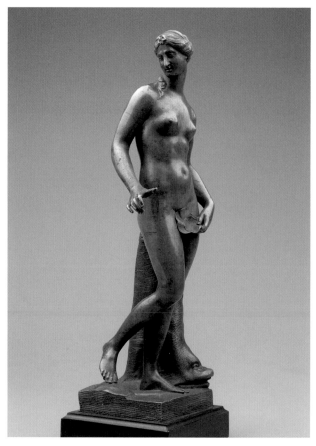

Mercury and *Venus*
Georg Raphael Donner, workshop or successor
Vienna, *c.* 1740/55
Lead, tin, *Mercury*: H. 40 cm (15¾ in.);
Venus: H. 39 cm (15⅛ in.)
Inv. nos. KK 7181, KK 7182

In conscious contrast to the late Baroque sculptural art of Central Europe, Georg Raphael Donner patterned his works more closely on the sculpture of antiquity. Classical influences can be identified in these statuettes of Mercury and Venus. From the extent to which they are mirror images of one another with their bodies in contrapposto poses, it is clear that they were conceived as counterparts to one another. In keeping with common workshop practice, they were produced in several slightly different versions. This pair of statues was either created in the workshop of Georg Raphael Donner or perhaps after his death in the circle of his brother Matthäus.

Donner's preference for lead casting was adopted by his successors and soon became a characteristic of mainstream Viennese sculpture in the 18th century. Thus Johann Baptist Hagenauer, who trained at the Vienna Academy under Matthäus Donner, also used this material. His *Prometheus Bound* is entirely in keeping with contemporary Academic ideals. Pain and emotion are depicted in the form of a naked heroic figure. It could also be understood as a symbol of suffering artists, particularly sculptors, since it was Prometheus, one of the immortal Titans, who fashioned the human race from clay. Against the will of the chief god, Zeus, he then gave them the gift of fire. In revenge, Zeus had Prometheus chained to a rock and sent an eagle to eat his liver, which continually grew back.

KS

Gerard van Swieten

With large, questioning eyes and a tense forehead, the elderly man gazes critically at the viewer. His lips are slightly open, as if he were about to speak. Gerard van Swieten (1700–72), a famous medical doctor from Leiden in Holland, was the idiosyncratic personal physician of Empress Maria Theresa and an assertive reformer of healthcare in the Habsburg empire. This powerful portrait was created by the sculptor Franz Xaver Messerschmidt, who was born in Bavaria but spent most of his working life in Vienna. He is especially known for his fascinating caricatural character studies, which are completely divorced from the classic ideal of beauty, confronting the viewer with grotesque, repulsive faces. Van Swieten's portrait is also unflattering, depicting authentically the physiognomy of a man with a fleshy face and double chin. The bust is also conspicuous for being unclothed. Van Swieten's hairstyle seems natural and departs from the fashion of wearing a wig, which was customary at the time. Here the highly erudite physician and Enlightenment philosopher is in a sense reduced to his naked human existence. The bust probably came from van Swieten's tomb in Vienna's Church of the Augustinians. From there it was moved to the Court Library, where van Swieten had been the director for almost thirty years. The portrait bust has been in the Kunstkammer of the Kunsthistorisches Museum only since 1936. Within the oeuvre of Franz Xaver Messerschmidt, it marks a turning point from the late Baroque to Classicism.

KS

Franz Xaver Messerschmidt
(Wiesensteig, 1736–Bratislava, 1783)
Vienna, c. 1770/72
Marble, H. 47 cm (18½ in.), W. 30 cm
(11¾ in.), D. 22 cm (8⅝ in.)
Inv. no. KK 8921

GERARDVS
L. B.
VAN SWIETEN

Archduchess Marie Antoinette, Dauphine of France

Here the fifteen-year-old daughter of Maria Theresa is an elegant Rococo figure, charming but cool, as she gazes unapproachably past the viewer. The portrait was created soon after her marriage to the French Dauphin, who succeeded to the throne as Louis XVI. Twenty-two years later, 'la pauvre Marie Antoinette' met her end at the guillotine of the French Revolution. Because of her tragic fate she is perhaps the most famous queen France ever had.

This portrait from the young lady's happier days was created on a commission from her husband's grandfather and predecessor, King Louis XV, and was intended as a gift for her mother in Vienna. The artist was the renowned and prolific French court sculptor Jean-Baptiste Lemoyne, who had already created portraits of numerous members of the French royal house and high aristocracy. The bust was sculpted from life: we know that Marie Antoinette sat for Lemoyne while the court was spending the summer at Compiègne. The king and the art critics of the Salon in Paris praised the bust as the elderly artist's most important work. Maria Theresa put it on display in her audience chamber at Vienna's Hofburg Palace. There the portrait continued to be greatly admired, so much so that a copy, a casting and a smaller version in porcelain were made in the 18th century. The latter is now on display in the Millions Room of Schönbrunn Palace.

KS

Jean-Baptiste Lemoyne (Paris, 1704–Paris, 1778)
Paris, dated 1771
Marble, H. 76.5 cm (30 in.), W. 50 cm (19⅝ in.), L. 36 cm (14⅛ in.)
Inv. no. KK 5478

Tapestry: *Les nouvelles Indes: The King Carried by Two Moors*

Alexandre-François Desportes (1661–1743), design
Jacques Neilson (1714–88), manufacture
Paris, Manufacture des Gobelins, 1774–78
Tapestry: wool, silk, H. 418 cm (164½ in.),
W. 498 cm (196 in.)
Inv. no. KK T XV/7

In 1636 John Maurice (or Johan Maurits), count of Nassau-Siegen (1604–97) was named governor-general of the Dutch colony in Brazil and secured control of vast regions of the country for the Dutch West India Company. The sketches and paintings he commissioned from Frans Post (1612–80) and Albert Eckhout (1610–65) are testimony to his interest in natural history and ethnographic subjects. Post was a landscape painter who concentrated mainly on milieu studies; Eckhout painted the inhabitants of Brazil along with its exotic flora and fauna. John Maurice sold a series of the two artists' paintings with 'Indian' motifs to the elector Frederick Wilhelm of Brandenburg (1620–88), who commissioned tapestries to be made from them in Delft in 1667. In 1678 John Maurice presented several other paintings to Louis XIV of France, suggesting that they also be reproduced as tapestries. In 1687 they served as models for cartoons from which the Manufacture des Gobelins in Paris made tapestries. The successful series of *tentures des Indes* ('Indian wall hangings') was reissued several times. In 1692 Alexandre-François Desportes, a specialist in portraying animals, restored the worn cartoons, and in 1735 he created new ones. The tapestries made from the new cartoons, which include the impressive eight-part Vienna series, are known under the name *Les nouvelles Indes* ('The New Indies'). In 1777 the set now in Vienna was presented by King Louis XVI and his queen consort, Marie Antoinette, as a gift to Emperor Joseph II.

KSvL

CLEMENS XIV·P·M
AVGVSTÆ MATRI
IVCVNDISSIMVM DONVM

Celebrations of Habsburg Glory

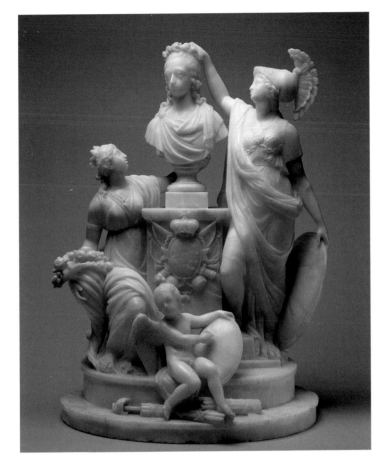

Emperor Joseph II and Peter Leopold, Grand Duke of Tuscany
Bernardino Regoli (active 1759 and 1772 in Rome), mosaic
Lorenzo de' Caporali (c. 1712–Rome, 1777), frame
Rome, 1772
Rhinestone, lapis lazuli, stucco marble, gilt bronze, H. 305 cm (120⅛ in.), W. 180 cm (70⅞ in.)
Inv. no. KK 877

Allegorical Portrait of Ferdinand III, Grand Duke of Tuscany
Florence, c. 1791
Alabaster, H. 56 cm (22 in.), W. 33 cm (13 in.), L. 20 cm (7⅞ in.)
Inv. no. KK 10185

This technically brilliant mosaic is a copy of a painting by Pompeo Batoni (KHM Picture Gallery, inv. no. 1628) depicting the two eldest sons of Maria Theresa: Emperor Joseph II (1741–90) and Grand Duke Peter Leopold of Tuscany (1747–92), the future Emperor Leopold II. The two brothers were in Rome for the conclave that elected Pope Clement XIV in 1769. The new pontiff had the papal mosaic workshop make this copy as a gift for the mother of the two subjects. The magnificent frame is crowned by a double eagle topped by a crown and holding the imperial sceptre and orb, thus underscoring the symbolic nature of the picture. On the right Joseph II is standing with Castel Sant'Angelo and St Peter's Cathedral in the background, extending his hand to his brother, who established the principle of Habsburg secundogeniture (succession of the second-born son) in Tuscany. Thus the brothers are expressing their dynastic and political solidarity. Among the objects lying on the table is the two-volume work *L'Esprit des lois (The Spirit of the Laws)* by Montesquieu as an indication of the intellectual world of the Enlightenment, which was favoured by both Habsburgs.

After Joseph's death in 1790, Peter Leopold succeeded him as Leopold II, and the latter's second-born son thus became Grand Duke Ferdinand III (1769–1824). This finely worked allegory in alabaster, a typical Tuscan material, is dedicated to his accession to the throne. A bust of the young ruler is crowned with a laurel wreath by Minerva while a personification of the city of Florence holds a horn of plenty and pays tribute to him.

CKG

Emperor Francis II

In 1802 the Vienna court commissioned Canova to create this bust, which was put on display in 1805 in the Biblioteca Marciana in Venice. Francis II (1768–1835) was the last Holy Roman Emperor (1792–1806) and from 1804 to 1835 was also emperor of Austria as Francis I. In this portrait he is depicted as the protector of the cultural legacy of Venice, which he had acquired in 1797. In 1805, when the Treaty of Pressburg awarded the recently acquired territory to Napoleon's Kingdom of Italy, the bust was brought to Vienna, where it found a new home in the Imperial Collection of Minerals.

Although Canova had been commissioned to create a bust of the monarch in contemporary uniform, the famous sculptor was able to convince his patron – as he had previously done with Napoleon Bonaparte – to accept his own artistic vision and allow him to create a heroic portrait inspired by the art of antiquity. Thus Emperor Francis II appears here in idealized form, in the costume of a Roman emperor, a title he no longer held. In 1806 he had renounced the imperial Roman crown, bringing to an end the Holy Roman Empire that had existed for more than 800 years.

The emperor's facial features were conveyed to Canova by making a face mask of the ruler. With the masterful subtlety of his stone carving, the sculptor succeeded in creating a portrait that has vibrant liveliness while at the same time exuding statesmanlike dignity. In every detail down to the delicately folded drapery, Canova demonstrates outstanding control of the chisel, and the bust was enthusiastically praised by his contemporaries.

CKG

Antonio Canova (Possagno, 1757–Venice, 1822)
Venice, c. 1803/5
Carrara marble, H. 87 cm (34¼ in.), W. 68 cm (26¾ in.)
Inv. no. KK 6156

Bibliography and Sources

Inventories and primary literature

'Inventar des Kunstbesitzes der Erzherzogin Margarete von Österreich, Mecheln vom 20.4.1524 mit Nachträgen bis zum 21.3.1530', in *Jahrbuch der kunsthistorischen Sammlungen des Allerhöchsten Kaiserhauses*, vol. 3/2, 1885, reg. no. 2979, pp. XCIII–CXXIII

'Inventar des Kunstbesitzes König Ferdinands I. vom 27. Dezember 1544 mit Nachträgen bis Ende 1547', in *Jahrbuch der kunsthistorischen Sammlungen des Allerhöchsten Kaiserhauses*, vol. 7/2, 1888, reg. no. 4793, pp. XCVI–C

Der Anfang der Museumslehre in Deutschland. Das Traktat 'Inscriptiones vel Tituli Theatri Amplissimi' von Samuel Quiccheberg, Latin and German, edited and with commentary by Harriet Roth, Berlin, 2000

Karl Rudolf, 'Die Kunstbestrebungen Kaiser Maximilians II. im Spannungsfeld zwischen Madrid und Wien. Anhang: Das Kammerinventar Kaiser Maximilians II. (1568) – Der Nachlass Kaiser Ferdinands I. (1568)', in *Jahrbuch der kunsthistorischen Sammlungen in Wien,* vol. 91, 1995, pp. 231–253

'Inventar des Nachlasses Kaiser Maximilians II. (sechs Teillibelle), 10.4. bis 19.6.1578', in *Jahrbuch der kunsthistorischen Sammlungen des Allerhöchsten Kaiserhauses,* vol. 13/2, 1892, reg. no. 9093, pp. XCI–CIV

Barbara Gutfleisch, Joachim Menzhausen, '"How a Kunstkammer Should Be Formed": Gabriel Kaltemarckt's Advice to Christian I of Saxony on the Formation of an Art Collection', 1587, in *Journal of the History of Collections* 1, 1987, pp. 3–32

Die Münchner Kunstkammer (Bayerische Akademie der Wissenschaften, phil.-hist. Klasse, Abhandlungen, NF no. 129), eds. Dorothea Diemer, Peter Diemer, Lorenz Seelig et al., 3 vols., Munich, 2008

'Inventar des Nachlasses Erzherzog Karls II. von Innerösterreich vom 1. November 1590', in *Jahrbuch der kunsthistorischen Sammlungen des Allerhöchsten Kaiserhauses,* vol. 7/2, 1888, reg. no. 4597, pp. XVII–XXXIII

'Inventar des Nachlasses Erzherzog Ferdinands II. von Tirol in Ruelust, Innsbruck und Ambras, vom 30. Mai 1596', in *Jahrbuch der kunsthistorischen Sammlungen des Allerhöchsten Kaiserhauses,* vol. 7/2, 1888, reg. no. 5556, pp. CCXXVI–CCCXII

Jacobus Schrenckhius a Nozingen, *Bildinventar mit lateinischen Viten der porträtierten Waffenbesitzer,* Innsbruck, 1601

Rotraut Bauer, Herbert Haupt (eds.), 'Inventar der Kunstkammer Kaiser Rudolfs II., 1607–1611', in *Jahrbuch der kunsthistorischen Sammlungen in Wien,* NF 36, 1976, pp. 1–140

'Inventar des Nachlasses Kaiser Matthias', nach dem 5. Mai 1619', in *Jahrbuch der kunsthistorischen Sammlungen des Allerhöchsten Kaiserhauses,* vol. 20/2, 1899, reg. no. 17408, pp. XLIX–CXXII

'Inventar der Prager Schatz- und Kunstkammer vom 6. Dezember 1621', in *Jahrbuch der kunsthistorischen Sammlungen des Allerhöchsten Kaiserhauses,* vol. 25/2, 1905, reg. no. 19421, pp. XX–LI

'Inventare der kaiserlichen Schatz- und Kunstkammer in Prag von 1650, 1718, 1737 und 1782', in *Jahrbuch der kunsthistorischen Sammlungen des Allerhöchsten Kaiserhauses,* vol. 10/2, 1889, reg. no. 6231, pp. CXXXI–CXXXII (29 July 1650); reg. no. 6232, pp. CXXXII–XCLI (8 April 1718); reg. no. 6234, pp. XCLII–CLXXI (5 October 1737); reg. no. 6238, pp. CLXXIX–CC (3 January 1782)

'Inventar der Kunstsammlungen des Erzherzog Leopold Wilhelm von Österreich aus dem Jahre 1659', in *Jahrbuch der kunsthistorischen Sammlungen des Allerhöchsten Kaiserhauses,* vol. 1/2, 1883, reg. no. 495, pp. LXXIX–CLXXVII

Marko Deisinger, 'Die Galerie Erzherzog Leopold Wilhelms und die Schatzkammer Kaiser Leopolds I. im Jahre 1659. Die Darstellungen eines italienischen Gesandten am Wiener Kaiserhof' (annotated edition), in *Jahrbuch des Kunsthistorischen Museums Wien,* vol. 10, 2008, pp. 401–409

'Einmal Weimar – Wien und retour. Johann Sebastian Müller und sein Wienbericht aus dem Jahr 1660' (*Veröffentlichungen des Instituts für Österreichische Geschichtsforschung,* vol. 42), eds. Katrin Keller, Martin Scheutz and H. Tersch, Vienna and Munich, 2005

Edward Brown, *Durch Niederland, Teutschland, Hungarn, Serbien, Bulgarien, Macedonien, Thessalien, Oesterreich, Steurmarck, Kärnthen, Carniolen, Friaul etc. gethane gantz sonderbare Reisen [...],* Nuremberg, 1711

Johann Basilius Küchelbecker, *Allerneueste Nachricht vom Römisch-Kayserl. Hofe nebst einer ausführlichen historischen Beschreibung der Kayserlichen Residentz-Stadt Wien, und der umliegenden Oerter,* Hanover, 1730

Arnold Luschin von Ebengreuth, 'Die ältesten Beschreibungen der kaiserlichen Schatzkammer zu Wien', in *Jahrbuch der kunsthistorischen Sammlungen des Allerhöchsten Kaiserhauses,* vol. 20/2, 1899, pp. CXC–CXCVI

'Inventar der kaiserlichen geheimen kleinen Schatzkammer von 1731', in *Jahrbuch der kunsthistorischen Sammlungen des Allerhöchsten Kaiserhauses,* vol. 10/2, 1889, reg. no. 6241, pp. CCIII–CCXLIII

Prodromus oder Vor-Licht des eröffneten Schau- und Wunder-Prachtes aller deren an dem Kaiserl. Hof [...] Carl des Sechsten [...] sich befindlichen Kunst-Schätzen und Kostbarkeiten [...], eds. Francisco de Stampart and Antonio de Brennerns, Vienna, 1735

'Inventar der kaiserlichen Schatzkammer von 1750', in *Jahrbuch der kunsthistorischen Sammlungen des Allerhöchsten Kaiserhauses,* vol. 10, 1889, pp. CCLII–CCCXXIV

'Inventar der in der Schatz- und Kunstkammer der k. k. Burg zu Graz vorgefundenen Effekten vom 21. Mai 1765', in *Jahrbuch der kunsthistorischen Sammlungen des Allerhöchsten Kaiserhauses,* vol. 24/2, 1903, reg. no. 19325 f., pp. XII–XLV

Versuch einer Beschreibung der Kayserlich-Königlichen Schatzkammer zu Wien, Nuremberg, 1771

Johann Primisser, *Kurze Nachricht von dem K. K. Raritätenkabinet zu Ambras in Tyrol mit 158 Lebensbeschreibungen derjenigen Fürsten und Feldherren, deren Rüstungen und Waffen darin aufbehalten werden, für die Neugierde der Liebhaber und Reisenden,* Innsbruck, 1777

Guides to the collections, catalogues of the holdings

Alois Primisser, *Die kaiserlich-königliche Ambraser Sammlung,* Vienna, 1819

Eduard von Sacken, Friedrich Kenner, *Die Sammlungen des k. k. Münz- und Antiken-Cabinets,* Vienna, 1866

Albert Ilg, Wendelin Boeheim, *Führer durch die k. k. Ambraser Sammlung (im Unteren Belvedere),* Vienna, 1882

Albert Ilg, *Kunsthistorische Sammlungen des allerhöchsten Kaiserhauses. Führer durch die Sammlungen der Kunstindustriellen Gegenstände,* Vienna, 1891

Julius von Schlosser, *Kunsthistorische Sammlungen des Allerhöchsten Kaiserhauses. Ausgewählte Gegenstände der kunstindustriellen Sammlung,* Vienna, 1901

Julius von Schlosser, *Werke der Kleinplastik in der Skulpturensammlung des A. H. Kaiserhauses,* vol. I: *Bildwerke in Bronze, Stein und Ton,* Vienna, 1910

Julius von Schlosser, *Werke der Kleinplastik in der Skulpturensammlung des A. H. Kaiserhauses,* vol. II: *Bildwerke aus Holz, Wachs und Elfenbein,* Vienna, 1910

Leo Planiscig, *Die Estensische Kunstsammlung,* vol. 1: *Skulpturen und Plastiken des Mittelalters und der Renaissance,* Vienna, 1919

Leo Planiscig, *Die Bronzeplastiken, Statuetten und Reliefs, Geräte und Plaketten (Publikationen aus den Sammlungen für Plastik und Kunstgewerbe,* vol. IV), Vienna, 1924

Fritz Eichler, Ernst Kris, *Die Kameen im Kunsthistorischen Museum. Beschreibender Katalog (Publikationen aus den Kunsthistorischen Sammlungen in Wien,* vol. II), Vienna, 1927

Ernst Kris, *Goldschmiedearbeiten des Mittelalters, der Renaissance und des Barock,* Part I: *Arbeiten in Gold und Silber. Beschreibender Katalog (Publikationen aus den Kunsthistorischen Sammlungen in Wien,* vol. V), Vienna, 1932

Leo Planiscig, Ernst Kris, *Katalog der Sammlungen für Plastik und Kunstgewerbe,* Vienna, 1935

Katalog der Sammlung für Plastik und Kunstgewerbe, Part I: *Mittelalter (Führer durch das Kunsthistorische Museum,* no. 9), Vienna, 1964

Katalog der Sammlung für Plastik und Kunstgewerbe, Part II: *Renaissance (Führer durch das Kunsthistorische Museum*, no. 11), Vienna, 1966

Elisabeth Scheicher et al., *Kunsthistorisches Museum. Sammlungen Schloss Ambras, Die Kunstkammer (Führer durch das Kunsthistorische Museum*, no. 24), Innsbruck, 1977

Rudolf Distelberger, Manfred Leithe-Jasper, *The Kunsthistorische Museum, Vienna: The Treasury and the Collection of Sculpture and Decorative Arts*, Florence and London, 1982.

Kunsthistorisches Museum Wien. Führer durch die Sammlungen, Vienna, 1988

Bildführer, Weltliche und Geistliche Schatzkammer (Führer durch das Kunsthistorische Museum, no. 35), Vienna and Salzburg, 1987

Rudolf von Strasser, assisted by Sabine Baumgärtner, *Licht und Farbe. Dekoriertes Glas – Renaissance, Barock, Biedermeier. Die Sammlung Rudolf von Strasser (Schriften des Kunsthistorischen Museums*, vol. 7), Vienna, 2002

Hauptwerke der Geistlichen Schatzkammer (Kurzführer durch das Kunsthistorische Museum, ed. Wilfried Seipel, vol. 1), Vienna, 2004

Hauptwerke der Weltlichen Schatzkammer (Kurzführer durch das Kunsthistorische Museum, ed. Wilfried Seipel, vol. 2), Vienna, 2005

Christian Beaufort, Matthias Pfaffenbichler, *Meisterwerke der Hofjagd- und Rüstkammer (Kurzführer durch das Kunsthistorische Museum*, ed. Wilfried Seipel, vol. 3), Vienna, 2005

Cäcilia Bischoff, *Meisterwerke der Gemäldegalerie (Kurzführer durch das Kunsthistorische Museum*, ed. Wilfried Seipel, vol. 5), Vienna, 2006

Sabine Haag, *Meisterwerke der Elfenbeinkunst (Kurzführer durch das Kunsthistorische Museum*, ed. Wilfried Seipel, vol. 8), Vienna, 2007

Rudolf Hopfner, *Meisterwerke der Sammlung alter Musikinstrumente (Kurzführer durch das Kunsthistorische Museum*, ed. Wilfried Seipel, vol. 7), Vienna, 2007

Meisterwerke der Sammlungen Schloss Ambras (Kurzführer durch das Kunsthistorische Museum, ed. Wilfried Seipel, vol. 9), Vienna, 2008

Meisterwerke des Münzkabinetts (Kurzführer durch das Kunsthistorische Museum, ed. Sabine Haag, vol. 10), Vienna, 2009

Meisterwerke der Kunstkammer (Kurzführer durch das Kunsthistorische Museum, ed. Sabine Haag, vol. 12), Vienna, 2010

Exhibition catalogues

Die Künstler der Kaiser. Von Dürer bis Tizian, von Rubens bis Velázquez aus dem Kunsthistorischen Museum in Wien, ed. Götz Adriani, Baden-Baden: Museum Frieder Burda, 2009

Todas las historias del arte. Kunsthistorisches Museum de Viena, ed. Wilfried Seipel, Bilbao: Guggenheim Museum, 2008

Kaiser Karl V. (1500–1558). Macht und Ohnmacht Europas, ed. Wilfried Seipel, Bonn: Kunsthalle; and Vienna: Kunsthistorisches Museum, 2000

Kaiser Rudolf II. zu Gast in Dresden, ed. Anne Veltrup, Dresden: Grünes Gewölbe, 2007

Elfenbein. Barocke Pracht am Wiener Hof, eds. Sabine Haag and Maraike Bückling, Frankfurt am Main: Liebieghaus, 2011

Natur und Kunst. Handschriften und Alben aus der Ambraser Sammlung Erzherzog Ferdinands II. (1529–1595), eds. Alfred Auer and Eva Irblich, Innsbruck: Ambras Castle, 1995

Türkische Kostbarkeiten aus dem Kunsthistorischen Museum, ed. Wilfried Seipel, Innsbruck: Ambras Castle, 1997

Philippine Welser und Anna Caterina Gonzaga – die Gemahlinnen Erzherzog Ferdinands II., ed. Wilfried Seipel, Innsbruck: Ambras Castle 1998

Für Aug' und Ohr. Musik in Kunst- und Wunderkammern, ed. Wilfried Seipel, Innsbruck: Ambras Castle, 1999

Alle Wunder dieser Welt. Die kostbarsten Kunstwerke aus der Sammlung Erzherzog Ferdinands II. (1529–1595), ed. Wilfried Seipel, Innsbruck: Ambras Castle, 2001

Werke für die Ewigkeit. Kaiser Maximilian I. und Erzherzog Ferdinand II., ed. Wilfried Seipel, Innsbruck: Ambras Castle, 2002

Herrlich Wild. Höfische Jagd in Tirol, ed. Wilfried Seipel, Innsbruck: Ambras Castle, 2004

Wir sind Helden. Habsburgische Feste in der Renaissance, ed. Wilfried Seipel, Innsbruck: Ambras Castle, 2005

Die Entdeckung der Natur. Naturalien in den Kunstkammern des 16. und 17. Jahrhunderts, ed. Wilfried Seipel, Innsbruck: Ambras Castle, 2006

Erzherzog Ferdinand Karl. Ein Sonnenkönig in Tirol, ed. Sabine Haag, Innsbruck: Ambras Castle, 2009

All'Antica. Götter & Helden auf Schloss Ambras, ed. Sabine Haag, Innsbruck: Ambras Castle, 2011

Sammeln! Die Kunstkammer des Kaisers in Wien, eds. Sabine Haag and Alfried Wieczorek, Mannheim: Reiss-Engelhorn-Museen, 2012

Women of Distinction. Margaret of York, Margaret of Austria, ed. Dagmar Eichberger, Mechelen, 2005

The Habsburg Cabinets of Arts and Wonders: Magic of Nature and Mechanism of the Universe, Moscow: Collection of Arms and Armour, 2005

Rudolph II and Prague. The Court and the City, ed. Eliška Fučiková, Prague, 1997

Manfred Leithe-Jasper, *Renaissance Master Bronzes from the Collection of the Kunsthistorisches Museum, Vienna*, Washington, DC: National Gallery of Art, 1986

Katja Schmitz-von Ledebur, *Habsburg Treasures: Renaissance Tapestries from the Kunsthistorisches Museum, Vienna*, West Palm Beach, Columbia, Sarasota, 2010

Curiositäten und Inventionen aus Kunst- und Rüstkammer, eds. Ortwin Gamber and Christian Beaufort-Spontin, Vienna: Kunsthistorisches Museum, 1978

Maria Theresia und ihre Zeit. Zur 200. Wiederkehr des Todestages, Vienna: Schönbrunn Palace, 1980

Prag um 1600. Kunst und Kultur am Hofe Kaiser Rudolfs II., Vienna: Kunsthistorisches Museum, 1988

Zu Gast in der Kunstkammer, Vienna: Kunsthistorisches Museum, 1991

Die Portugiesen in Indien. Die Eroberungen Dom João de Castros auf Tapisserien 1538–1548, Vienna: Kunsthistorisches Museum, 1992

Eros und Mythos. Die Kunst am Hofe Rudolfs II. in Prag, Vienna: Kunsthistorisches Museum, 1995

Spielwelten der Kunst. Kunstkammerspiele, ed. Wilfried Seipel, Vienna: Kunsthistorisches Museum, 1998

Exotica. Portugals Entdeckungen im Spiegel fürstlicher Kunst- und Wunderkammern der Renaissance, ed. Wilfried Seipel, Vienna: Kunsthistorisches Museum, 2000

Kaiser Ferdinand I. 1503–1564. Das Werden der Habsburgermonarchie, ed. Wilfried Seipel, Vienna: Kunsthistorisches Museum, 2003

Rudolf Distelberger, *Die Kunst des Steinschnitts. Prunkgefäße, Kameen und Commessi aus der Kunstkammer*, ed. Wilfried Seipel, Vienna: Kunsthistorisches Museum, 2003

Katja Schmitz-von Ledebur, *Szenen aus dem Buch Tobias. Aus der Tapisseriensammlung des Kunsthistorischen Museums*, ed. Wilfried Seipel, Vienna, 2004

Bernstein für Thron und Altar. Das Gold des Meeres in fürstlichen Kunst- und Schatzkammern, ed. Wilfried Seipel, Vienna: Kunsthistorisches Museum, 2005

Giambologna – Triumph des Körpers, ed. Wilfried Seipel, Vienna: Kunsthistorisches Museum, 2006

Arcimboldo. 1526–1593, eds. Wilfried Seipel and Sylvia Ferino-Pagden, Vienna: Kunsthistorisches Museum, 2008

Schätze burgundischer Hofkunst in Wien, eds. Sabine Haag, Franz Kirchweger and Katja Schmitz-von Ledebur, Vienna: Kunsthistorisches Museum, 2009

Paulus Rainer, *Glanz der Macht. Kaiserliche Pretiosen aus der Wiener Kunstkammer*, eds. Sabine Haag, Cornelie Holzach and Katja Schneider, Vienna, 2010

Additional secondary literature

Gabriele Bessler, *Wunderkammern. Weltmodelle von der Renaissance bis zur Kunst der Gegenwart,* 2nd edition, Berlin, 2012

Cäcilia Bischoff, *Kunsthistorische Museum: History, Architecture, Decoration,* ed. Elisabeth Hermann, Vienna, 2010

Horst Bredekamp, *The Lure of Antiquity and the Cult of the Machine: the Kunstkammer and the Evolution of Nature, Art and Technology,* Princeton, NJ, 1995, 2002

Dominik Collet, *Die Welt in der Stube. Begegnungen mit Außereuropa in Kunstkammern der Frühen Neuzeit (Veröffentlichungen des Max-Planck-Instituts für Geschichte,* vol. 232), Göttingen, 2007

Thomas DaCosta Kaufmann, *The Mastery of Nature: Aspects of Art, Science and Humanism in the Renaissance,* Princeton, NJ, 1993

Thomas DaCosta Kaufmann, 'Remarks on the Collection of Rudolf II: The Kunstkammer as a Form of Representation', in *Grasping the World: The Idea of the Museum,* eds. Donald Preziosi and Claire Farago, Aldershot, 2004, pp. 526–37

Dagmar Eichberger, *Leben mit Kunst, Wirken durch Kunst. Sammelwesen und Hofkunst unter Margarete von Österreich, Regentin der Niederlande,* Turnhout, 2002

'Exotica. Portugals Entdeckungen im Spiegel fürstlicher Kunst- und Wunderkammern der Renaissance. Beiträge des am 19. und 20. Mai 2000 veranstalteten Symposiums', in *Jahrbuch des Kunsthistorischen Museums Wien,* vol. 3, eds. Helmut Trnek and Sabine Haag, Vienna, 2001

Die Galerie Kaiser Karls VI. in Wien. Solimenas Widmungsbild und Storffers Inventar (1720–1733), eds. Sabine Haag and Gudrun Swoboda, Vienna, 2010

Géza von Habsburg, *Princely Treasures,* New York, 1997

Herbert Haupt, *Das Kunsthistorische Museum. Die Geschichte des Hauses am Ring. Hundert Jahre im Spiegel historischer Ereignisse,* Vienna, 1991

Herbert Haupt, 'Bemerkungen zur Charakteristik von Schatz-, Silber- und Kunstkammer in der frühen Neuzeit am Beispiel der habsburgischen Sammlungen', in *Silber und Gold. Augsburger Goldschmiedekunst für die Höfe Europas,* eds. Reinhold Baumstark and Helmut Seling, Munich, 1994, pp. 127–34

Franz Kirchweger, 'Die Schatzkammern des Hauses Habsburg im Mittelalter und die Wiener Hofburg', in *Die Wiener Hofburg,* vol. 1: *Mittelalter,* ed. Mario Schwarz; in press

Franz Kirchweger, 'Zwischen Kunst und Natur: Arcimboldo und die Welt der Kunstkammern', in *Arcimboldo. 1526–1593* (exhibition catalogue), eds. Wilfried Seipel and Sylvia Ferino-Pagden, Vienna: Kunsthistorisches Museum, 2008, pp. 189–94

Selma Krasa-Florian, 'Die kaiserlichen Sammlungen. Von der mittelalterlichen Schatzkammer zum Kunsthistorischen Museum', in *Neues Museum,* nos. 2 and 3, 1991, pp. 22–40

Beatrix Kriller, Georg Kugler, *Das Kunsthistorische Museum. Die Architektur und Ausstattung,* Vienna, 1991

Georg Kugler, 'Kunst und Geschichte im Leben Ferdinands I.', in *Kaiser Ferdinand I. 1503–1564. Das Werden der Habsburgermonarchie* (exhibition catalogue), ed. Wilfried Seipel, Vienna: Kunsthistorisches Museum, 2003, pp. 201–13

'100 Jahre Kunsthistorisches Museum. Das Kunsthistorische Museum als Denkmal und Gesamtkunstwerk', in *Jahrbuch der kunsthistorischen Sammlungen in Wien,* vol. 88 [NF 52]), ed. Gabriele Helke, Vienna, 1992

Das Kunsthistorische Museum in Wien, ed. Kunsthistorisches Museum, Vienna and Salzburg, 1978

Collection, Laboratory, Theater: Scenes of Knowledge in the 17th Century, eds. Helmar Schramm, Jan Lazardzig and Lutger Schwarte, Berlin and New York, 2003

Stefan Laube, *Von der Reliquie zum Ding. Heiliger Ort – Wunderkammer – Museum,* Berlin, 2011

Alphons Lhotsky, *Festschrift des Kunsthistorischen Museums in Wien, 1891–1941. Erster Teil: Die Baugeschichte der Museen und der Neuen Burg,* Vienna, 1941; *Zweiter Teil. Die Geschichte der Sammlungen,* 2 vols., Vienna, 1941–45

Arthur MacGregor, *Curiosity and Enlightenment. Collectors and Collections from the Sixteenth to the Nineteenth Century,* London, 2007

Macrocosmos in Microcosmo. Die Welt in der Stube. Zur Geschichte des Sammelns 1450 bis 1800, ed. Andreas Grote, Opladen, 1994

Patrick Mauriès, *Cabinets of Curiosities,* London, 2002

Debora J. Meijers, 'Kunst als Natur. Die Habsburger Gemäldegalerie in Wien um 1780', in *Schriften des Kunsthistorischen Museums,* ed. Wilfried Seipel, vol. 2, Vienna, 1995

Klaus Minges, 'Das Sammlungswesen der frühen Neuzeit. Kriterien der Ordnung und der Spezialisierung', in *Museen – Geschichte und Gegenwart,* vol. 3, Münster, 1998

The Origins of Museums: The Cabinet of Curiosities in Sixteenth- and Seventeenth-Century Europe, eds. Oliver Impey and Arthur MacGregor, Oxford, 1985

Peter W. Parshall, 'The Print Collection of Ferdinand, Archduke of Tyrol', in *Jahrbuch der Kunsthistorischen Sammlungen in Wien,* vol. 78, 1982, pp. 139–184

Friedrich Polleross, '"Pro decore majestatis". Zur Repräsentation Kaiser Leopolds I. in Architektur, Bildender und Angewandter Kunst', in *Jahrbuch des Kunsthistorischen Museums Wien,* vol. 4/5, 2002/2003, pp. 191–295

Prag um 1600. Beiträge zur Kunst und Kultur am Hofe Rudolfs II. (Symposium, Prague, June 1987), Freren, 1988

Karl Rudolf, 'Die Kunstbestrebungen Kaiser Maximilians II. im Spannungsfeld zwischen Madrid und Wien', in *Jahrbuch der kunsthistorischen Sammlungen in Wien,* vol. 91, 1995, pp. 165–256

Veronika Sandbichler, "AMBRAS [...] worinnen eine wunderwürdig, ohnschäzbare Rüst=Kunst und Raritaeten Kammer anzutreffen'. Erzherzog Ferdinand II. und die Sammlungen auf Schloss Ambras', in *Dresden & Ambras. Kunstkammerschätze der Renaissance* (exhibition catalogue), ed. Sabine Haag, Innsbruck: Ambras Castle, 2012, pp. 31–41

Elisabeth Scheicher, *Die Kunst- und Wunderkammern der Habsburger,* Innsbruck and Munich, 1979

Elisabeth Scheicher, 'Zur Ikonologie von Naturalien im Zusammenhang der enzyklopädischen Kunstkammer', in *Anzeiger des Germanischen Nationalmuseums,* 1995, pp. 115–25

Julius von Schlosser, *Die Kunst- und Wunderkammern der Spätrenaissance. Ein Beitrag zur Geschichte des Sammelwesens,* Leipzig, 1908

Renate Schreiber, '"ein galeria nach meinem humor". Erzherzog Leopold Wilhelm', in *Schriften des Kunsthistorischen Museums,* ed. Wilfried Seipel, vol. 8, Vienna, 2004

Ralf Schürer, 'Wenzel Jamnitzers Brunnen für Maximilian II. Überlegungen zu Ikonographie und Zweck', in *Anzeiger des Germanischen Nationalmuseums,* 1986, pp. 55–59

Maria Stieglecker, '"Was ich eingethan und erkhauft, wille ich mit erster gelegenheit überschickhen". Zum Gütertransfer von Spanien an den Kaiserhof, in *Hispania – Austria II. Die Epoche Philipps II. (1556–1598)',* in *Studien zur Geschichte und Kultur der iberischen und iberoamerikanischen Länder,* vol. 5, ed. Friedrich Edelmayer, Vienna and Munich 1999, pp. 225–45

Werner Telesko, 'Das Haus Habsburg zwischen Kunstgeschichte und Naturwissenschaft. Zur Genese der Programmatik des Kunst- und Naturhistorischen Museums in Wien', in *Wiener Geschichtsblätter* 61, 2006, no. 2, pp. 22–45

Alfred Walz, 'Weltenharmonie – Die Kunstkammer und die Ordnung des Wissens', in *Weltenharmonie. Die Kunstkammer und die Ordnung des Wissens* (exhibition catalogue), Braunschweig: Herzog Anton Ulrich-Museum, 2000, pp. 9–21

Index

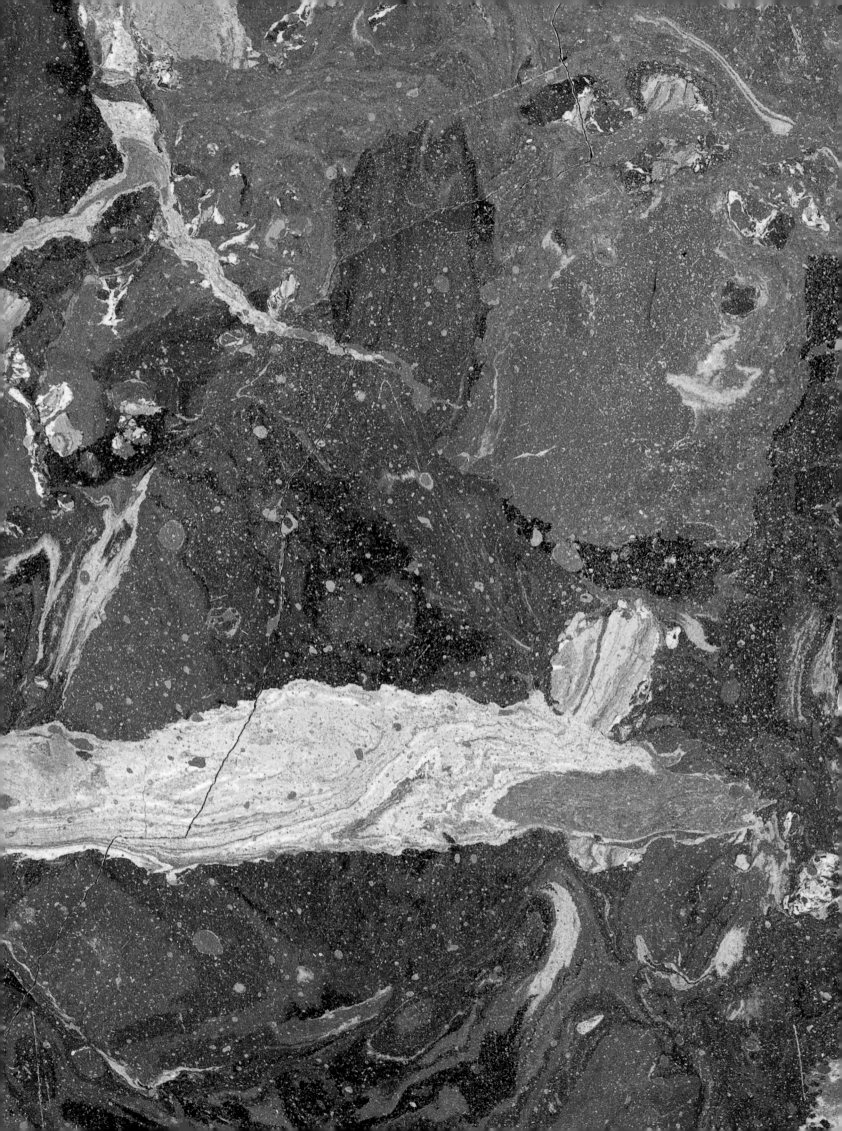

HIMALAYAN
DESERT

HIMALAYAN DESERT

Nina Rao

Lustre Press
·
Roli Books

ISBN: 81-7436-063-8

© **Roli Books Pvt. Ltd. 1999**
Lustre Press Pvt. Ltd.
M 75 Greater Kailash II Market
New Delhi 110 048, INDIA
Ph: (011) 6442271, 6462782
Fax: (011) 6467185

Text
Nina Rao

Design
Shuka Jain

Map
Virender Kumar

Conceived and designed at
Roli CAD Centre

Printed and bound at
Star Standard Industries Pte. Ltd.
Singapore

Right: **Perched high on an overhang is the sixteenth
century Dhankar *gompa*. Once a prison it now
houses over 150 lamas and contains Buddhist
scriptures and murals of healing Buddhas.**
Far right: **A Drok pa or Dard villager from Ladakh.
Originally from the Gilgit area of Jammu and
Kashmir (now in Pakistan), the Drok pa settled
along the Indus valley, adopted Islam and introduced
irrigation in the region.**
Following pages 6-7: **A novice, the younger son of a
family, stands at the door of a monastery in
Mustang, Nepal.**

contents

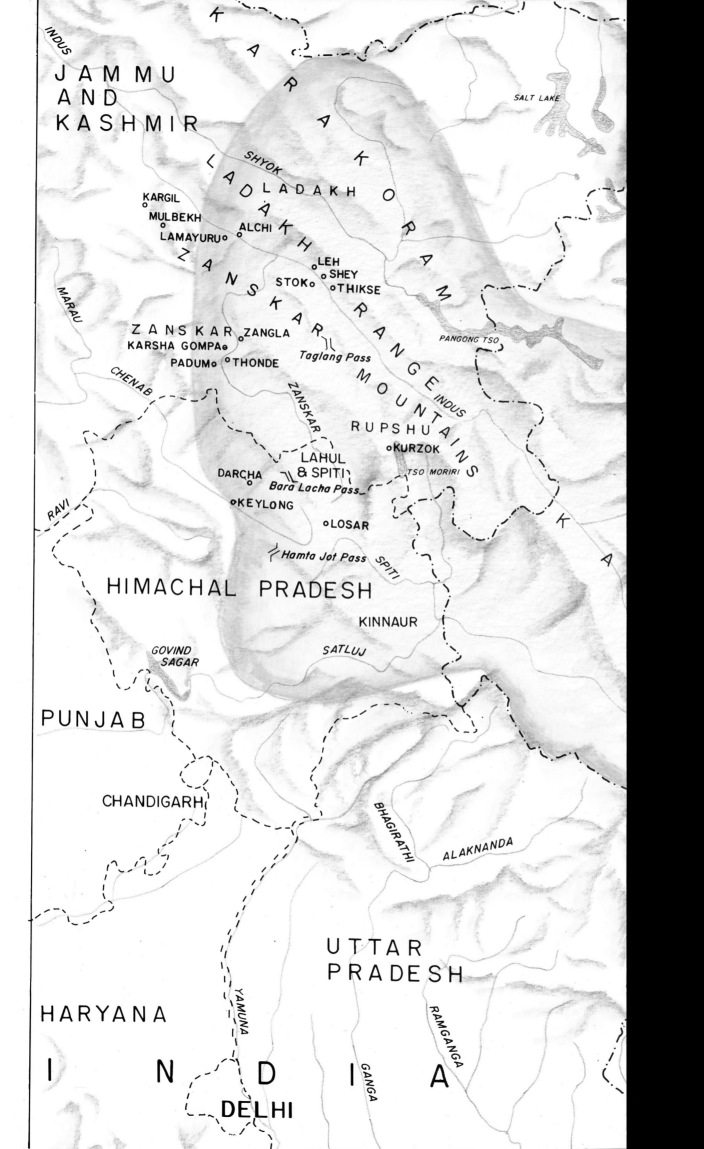

CHINA

T I B E T

K A I L A S H   R A N G E

RAKAS LAKE

MANASAROWAR
LAKE

KALI

SETI

KARNALI

PHOKSUMDO
LAKE

D O L P A

ºDUNAI

MUSTANG

KALI GANDAKI

N E P A L

SARD

LADAKH is situated between the Karakoram and Pangong ranges. The snow-covered Himalayan ranges in their morning glory.

LEH

The ancient **TIBETAN KINGDOM** of Gu-je included Lahul until the seventeenth century. A spectacular view of the mountains in Tholing in Gu-je.

SPITI: Kaza, Tabo and Pin form a triangle which is the core area of interest and habitation. Thangyud *gompa* in Spiti.

11

The Himalaya is a vibrant, personal experience that is recaptured and renewed with every visit. Due to its immense height and massive topography, it creates a rain shadow zone to the west. Called the Great Himalayan Desert, this rain shadow zone extends from the Tibetan plateau and includes the Indian districts of Ladakh, Lahul, Kinnaur and Spiti as well as the enclave of Mustang in western Nepal. This vast desert is made up of barren rock and sand-covered valleys.

Though the Himalaya forms a gigantic east-west arc, dividing the Indian sub-continent from the high plateau of Central Asia, the Himalayan desert was not intended as a barrier between the lands which have given the world some of the greatest civilisations. In fact, its high passes facilitated an exchange of cultural ideas and traditions. Greek aesthetics merged with ideas from the Indian kingdoms and a local school of art developed. Persian, Indian and Greek cultures encountered each other at what today is known as the Karakoram Highway, linking the sub-continent to Kashgar and Khotan, the southern-most market towns on the ancient silk route.

Tossing in the turbulence of this cold and arid land, caught in the current of a powerful and exacting habitat, responding to the tug of time to shape their lives, the people of this desert have lived out their dreams in a sacred agreement with the elements. The mountains for these people are homes of gods and goddesses who possess supernatural powers of defence. They are not to be torn apart, walked over or climbed upon; they are the sacred land where the living and the dead walk hand in hand, not an arena for sport and adventure.

The ecological prudence and restraint shown by the nomadic wanderers in their pattern of transhumance is till today a guide for all those who wish to learn about the great Himalayan desert. They have moved up and down the mountain slopes, conserving resources for the long term, even though such restrictions have made their immediate present difficult. Vegetation has been nurtured by animal dung, pastures have been visited by seasonal rotation, communal resources have been shared justly, taboos have been respected because they

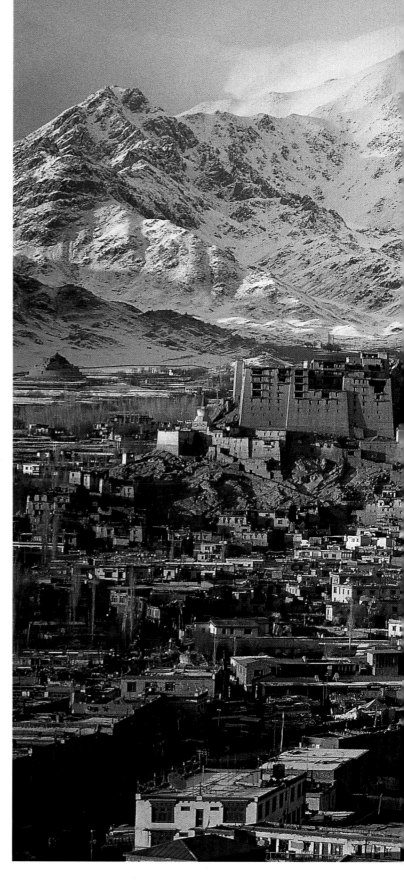

An aerial view of the city of Leh, an historical entrepot and an important market.

represent the wisdom of the elders, and the life-cycle of the animal and human resource-base has been protected to ensure sustainability for future generations.

THE LAND OF
CITADELS AND...

...FORTIFIED MONASTERIES

To an outsider, the Himalayan desert is a wild, desolate and little known region; it is a land of great peaks and deep valleys; of precipitous gorges cut by persistent rivers that rise in the high plateaux of snow and ice; a barren and beautiful land of intense sunlight, clear sparkling air and wonderful colours. Here, both man and mountain seem to have been fashioned from the same earth and seem to share something in common. In a world that is mapped in the minds of the wandering nomads, it is only the hardy races which can cope with the wearisome life that demands hardship and struggle to survive.

Political whirlwinds have often accompanied the sandstorms at these heights. Religion, art and culture have flourished despite the antagonism between the nomadic herdsmen, hunters and agriculturists. Water— the wealth of the desert—has determined the way of life of these people and overshadowed their relationships right up to the recent past.

Popularly known as the crossroads of the world, it is here in the high reaches of the Himalayan desert that the settled people tamed their wild conquerors. These civilised races often had to escape or start afresh in entirely new areas, when their civilisational advantage was not to the taste of the invaders. In times of peace, city-states grew in size and prosperity, embellished with fine mansions, palaces, monasteries, mosques and markets. Artists and craftsmen developed their skills to establish their own canons. Scholars and merchants travelled from court to court enriching the trade routes from east to west. Hospitality to strangers, who were the source of new ideas and influences, became a tradition for a people sophisticated enough to want to increase their knowledge. Merchants were

Facing page: **Tourists trek on the frozen Zanskar river in Ladakh.**

also welcomed as a respite from the ceaseless toil of subsistence farming.

This vast area has individual features that are extremely complex and no single feature can be considered representative of the region. The inordinate complexity of the formational process is indicated by the unnatural order of the various ranges, the flatness of the river beds and the incisive gorges that seek an opening into the plains. These form several divisions based on the drainage areas of the four major river systems: the Indus, known as the *Sing ka bab* (Rising from the Lion's Mouth) in the west, the Bhramaputra or the *Ster-chuk ka bab* (Rising from the Horse's Mouth) in the east, the Ganges, called the *Mab cha ka bab* (Rising from the Peacock's Mouth) in the north and the Sutlej, *Lang-chin ka bab* (Rising from the Mouth of the Elephant) to the south. The tendency to personify rivers and to give them human expressions and emotions was perhaps an attempt by the locals, Tibetans and Hindus, to bring them under control.

The greater part of the 8,000 meter high Himalaya lies above the snow line. This is the home of the snowfields that feed the glaciers and the torrential streams that tumble down steep gradients to the plains below. The rugged landscape and the high peaks are the result of fluvial erosion. The great glaciers include the Siachen (70 km), the Baltoro (60 km), the Biafo (60 km) and the Hispar (62 km). Found in the Karakoram range, they feed the Nubra and Shyok rivers that form the lifeline for these hidden valleys, that are otherwise unconnected by road. In fact, this region saw no intervention from the outside world until the armies of India, China and Pakistan turned Ladakh into the highest battleground in the world. High altitude lakes have also been formed by glacial depressions

and rock falls, for example, the Pangong and Tso Morari in the Rupshu region.

Ladakh, a land of many names, like *Maryul* (Lowland), *Khachanpa* (the Land of Snow) and *Ladwag* (Ladakhi name for the region) is situated between the Karakoram and Pangong ranges. It is India's highest plateau, containing the remains of three peneplains at heights between 5,300 to 5,800 meters that are mostly above the snow line. Its height is one of the reasons for the dry and desert-like conditions. The plateau is dissected into the Lingzi Tang plain, the Lokzhung plain, the Aksai Chin and the Soda, all of them so dry and bare that even nomads do not venture into this terrain. Similarly, the Chandra valley of Lahul is uninhabited, except for nomadic shepherds in search of pastures on the southern slopes.

The Himalaya to the north and its spurs to the north-east constitute two closed sides of a box. The monsoon currents cannot enter this region and the extreme difference in day and night temperatures shatters rocks and creates fissures in the hardest surfaces. Rock and ice falls are common occurrences which threaten existence.

All along this vast region there are remains of flourishing human settlements with irrigation works, forests and evidence of a more moist climate. The continental desiccation has been exacerbated through increasing aridity caused by the deflection of moisture bearing winds along the northern slopes and the disruption of drainage lines along the river basins.

The high plateaux receives only 3 cm of rain annually. Cultivable land is not easy to find. The population is sparse, 2 persons per sq km, and communications are difficult. The presence of armies have brought in roads and technology which have had an impact on these frontier regions in more than one sense. However, language, life-style and the customs of the people vary from one valley to the next. Stock breeding, particularly of the hardy yaks, goral sheep and goats, has been the primary resource of these mountain communities, supplemented by trade in the winter when there are no pastures to seek.

Travellers in this desert have described the illusory sounds and mirages that have lured the unwary to death. These are usually the tramp and hum of the caravans and at other times, the sound of a variety of musical instruments, particularly the drum. The shepherds, porters and traders have described these as the work of evil spirits or the voices of their ancestors calling to them.

The resource base of the Himalayan desert is highly diverse and heterogeneous, added to which are spatial discontinuities caused by altitude, slope and relief. Historical, cultural and ethnic specificities have introduced further dimensions to the naturally determined constraints of the mountains. Indigenous institutions, knowledge systems and traditional survival strategies are a part of the mountain perspective that are not valued adequately in the march towards modernisation. Just as the Moravian missions replaced Tibetan medicine and lamaism with allopathy and western education, the same modernising intervention through development in these marginalised regions has created conflicts with the environment and amongst the communities.

Caravans through history have only skirted the edges of this fabled land. Although the area is vast, few roads pass through it and life has revolved around a few settlements that are nurtured by natural water courses, wherever they exist. The north-south movement is restricted to a few icy passes which have their own grim tales for the traveller. Dangerously narrow, at a height of over 5,000 meters with precipitous drops into deep ravines, they are the most difficult to cross.

While Buddhism survives along the intricate network of rivers that feed the Indus, the Sutlej and

Above: **Cold and forbidding yet attractive because it is rarely visited, the North Rimo glacier in Ladakh.** *Previous pages 16-17:* **Precariously balanced at the edge of a cliff is the Phugtal monastery in Zanskar. This eleventh century *gompa* has been carved out of the mountain and is home to some fifty monks.**

the Chenab, the trading importance of Ladakh and its environs has been replaced by its strategic importance. It is clear that despite its isolation, this region has had a turbulent history reflected in its mixed racial stock: Chinese, Tibetan, Kashmiri and Indo-Iranian (Dardic). In the first century AD, the extent of the Kushan empire—a Buddhist people descended from the Yueh-Chih, a Mongolian tribe—created a stable and prosperous basis for long distance trade. To their west, the Parthians were not so free

and open, being middlemen in the trade with Rome. To the east lay China, across the Taklamakan desert. Some oasis kingdoms of the Tarim Basin like Khotan, Yarkhand and Kashgar were more friendly with the Kushans than with the Chinese. The Kushans converted their neighbours to Buddhism instead of exacting tribute. Shrines and temples became the mainstay of the traders on the silk route and later for the pilgrims. When Fa-hsien visited Khotan in the fourth century, he found a world at peace, with richly

Above: **The spectacular silt formations on the peaks in Ladakh.**
Previous pages 20-21: **It is hard to believe that these strangely contoured, craggy outcrops are actually badlands near Lamayuru monastery in Ladakh.**

decorated monasteries and no sign of devastation by the Mongolian hordes. Hsuang-tsang describes the now vanished Sogdians as the guardians of the trade routes. They were peaceable and industrious and divided their time between farming and trade. They were also noted artisans renowned for wood carving, glass making, carpet weaving and metal works, crafts which are still practised in the high desert.

The history of Spiti has been closely linked to that of Ladakh until it was brought under the administration of Kullu by the British to access the shawl wool trade of the Chang Thang plateau. Lahul continued to be a part of the kingdom of Gu-je until the seventeenth century when it was transferred to Chamba, and subsequently to the Sikh kingdom that took over Chamba. The nomadic life (*chang pa*) is a remnant of the old lifestyle of the Ladakhi and Spiti people, similar to the Chiangs who used to roam the pastures of Central Asia. Till today, the farmers and dairy producers continue

The Zangla *gompa* stands alone and remote in Zangla, one of the most forbidding areas in the Himalaya.

their barter economy. This division is climatic and so ingrained that neither Buddhism nor feudalism has interrupted the chain of production in the region.

Between the seventh and ninth centuries, Islam made inroads into the Himalayan desert through an alliance between the Western Turks and Tibetans against the Chinese. Invasions from Baltistan, (now in the northern frontier region of Pakistan) converted the populations of Kashmir and Nubra. The Arabs were to prove implacable enemies of Buddhism and the Tibetan way of life. Twentieth century archaeologists have found that the dry desert sands have preserved deserted Buddhist

23

The Karakoram range sweeps across the northern border of Ladakh.

centres almost intact on the silk route between India and China.

The accommodation between Islam and Buddhism continued till recent times; Ladakhi kings often took Balti princesses as wives or themselves converted to Islam. Marriage between Buddhist women and Muslim men was not questioned and the mixed community of Argun families was an interesting feature in the land of the lamas. In the wake of militancy in the Kashmir valley, the two communities have once again begun to view each other with hostility. The mistrust could partly be due to the control of tourism by the Kashmiris as well as their domination of Ladakhi administration. Kashmir is considered an alien power. The movement for an autonomous hill council, which was successfully established in 1993, has helped to a limited extent to overcome the schism.

In the thirteenth century, the Mongols began to migrate from Manchuria and brought in new racial characteristics. They had round heads, pale skins, slanted eyes and high cheek-bones. They were not hirsute and had so much value for water that they were known to be malodorous, not bathing for days together. These characteristics are shared by the desert people even today.

Genghis Khan, Kublai Khan and Tamurlane established the military as well as the cultural excellence of the extensive Mongolian empire, with Samarkhand as the greatest city of the fifteenth century. Babur, a descendent of Genghis Khan, conquered India in the sixteenth century after he was ousted from Ferghana and founded the Mughal dynasty. As Russia and China expanded, the freedom of the nomads was curtailed and they were confined to the high valleys of the Himalaya. By the nineteenth century, India was under the control of the British East India Company and the great game of spying

24

between Russia and Britain brought many travellers to the desert domain.

What had once been the preserve of monks, merchants, peasants, and shepherds was now mapped by members of geographical societies, scientists, botanists and tea traders, all of whom carried surveying material. Native 'pundits' were sent by the Survey of India disguised as holy men and pilgrims because of the local people's hostility to white men. These early explorers made headlines in their home countries, and travellers were attracted to explore the Himalayan desert for themselves. However, many of the treasures of the lost cities and monasteries that were excavated in the twentieth century were carried away to Europe. Ladakh has suffered in the same way ever since it was opened to tourism in 1974.

Even after the Independence of India in 1947, the Himalayan desert has remained a battleground. No longer do caravans trace their lengthy routes across the high passes as various tribesmen fight over territory and resources.

Today, regular air services link Ladakh with the rest of the country. Helicopter services access the remotest areas of the districts above the snow line.

The Border Roads Organisation maintains the roads and the army has established an all-season road via Manali, which has proved to be a popular entry point for tourists. Regular bus services connect all the districts to the capital of Himachal Pradesh, Shimla. Satellite communication has brought television and telephone to the major settlements, integrating them into the mainstream of Indian social and political life. Projects like the Igufey canal and social forestry have helped to push the desert further away from the settlements. The presence of the army and civil works by the administration have undermined the control of the feudal families. These families had supported the monasteries (*gompas*), not only in terms of land and money, but also by sponsoring novice lamas.

These changes have brought about a transformation in terms of language, manners, values and attire. The younger generation is no longer enthusiastic about monasticism. It prefers employment in the army, contracting for development projects or providing services and facilities for tourists. The era of independence and self-sufficiency of Ladakh and its neighbouring areas has come to a close. Traditional ties which fertilised the religion, art and culture of the region have been abruptly arrested by boundaries

Willows and poplars bring the beauty of autumn colours to the bare Ladakhi landscape.

Above: **The Ridzong *gompa* appears suddenly at the end of a winding walk through the valley on the road to Ladakh.**
Facing page: **The giant fifteen meter high image of the Maitreya Buddha dominates the Thikse monastery outside Leh.**

Previous pages 26-27: **Lamayuru, on the Leh-Srinagar road, is Ladakh's oldest living monastery. It is also a region that has the most interesting morain formations that are typical of the Himalayan desert. In the foreground are the *chortens*. The village straggles down the slope, reflecting the position of the monastery in the social hierarchy.**

which are contested till today. A fiercely independent people have been declared tribal and have become dependent on the developmental agencies of the central government as they try to enter the mainstream of modern Indian life.

Yet, the desert retains its character. It remains remote, sparsely populated, close to its religious traditions. With outside influences beginning to undermine its society and culture, documentation of people's art and architectural heritage, oral, literary and folk traditions is being given importance. Ecology and environment are being protected by several non-governmental organisations, many of which are headed and controlled by local people. Traditional beliefs and practices, so closely linked to Buddhism, are also being protected and revived.

The recent changes have not transformed the basic simplicity of life in the Himalayan desert. Changes have come, but the classical life-style has proved successful beyond doubt. It has maintained its chronological seam in relating to nature, reality and daily life and the vehicle to communicate it to others. This is what conveys to the visitor a sense of its pride, self-sufficiency and its rock solid foundation. The weaknesses and transgressions are a part of the desert's charm. It creates in us the modest desire to share in the people's dreams, to be a part of their longings, to respond to their imagination, not in the form of amicable condescension but as an enabling participant in the cross-current of life.

The main range or the Great Himalaya—known in ancient literature as Himgiri—rises like a massive screen south of the 5,000 meter high plateau of Tibet. This is the region known as the Trans Himalaya, an ill-defined mountain tract covering an area of 1,000 km. There are no deep river gorges here, but it is home to some of the highest passes and the sources of the Bhramaputra, Indus and Sutlej rivers, as well as the Kailash Range. This is also the land of fluttering prayer flags invoking the favour of the lord of compassion. The famous *kumbum* (a stupa containing thousands of images and multiple chapels) at Gyantse represents the importance of Buddhism in giving courage to the faithful as they perform the *parikrama* (ritual circumambulation) of the stupa.

The other mountain range in Tibet is the great Karakoram, known in Sanskrit literature as Krishnagiri, and as the Black Gravel mountains to the travellers on the silk route. It lies north of the Indus, in a steppe-like, semi-desert landscape. The Great Asian Desert, with the Thar in the south and the Taklamakan in the north, incorporates the Himalayan rain shadow zone.

The Tibetan plateau, the unique site of a sophisticated medieval culture, is reached after great physical hardship, crossing wide valleys, undulating sand dunes and small villages. The esoteric world of lamas has remained isolated and closed, as much due to the geographical and climatic conditions as due to the desire to remain true to its religious beliefs.

Tibet and the Tarim Basin are the most desolate reminders of an on-going historical process, to which human intervention and pressures are adding their own stress. As rivers have disappeared into the growing volumes of sand or when precipitation was low due to climatic changes, the desert spread itself.

The landscape of the Tibetan plateau is barren as patches of vegetation and settlements grow further apart. Since the Chinese takeover, there is a new route to Tibet across the Lakpa and Tsu passes. This takes one to Zhigatse, the old capital of Tibet and the home of the Tashilumpo monastery, founded by the first Panchen Lama (teacher of the Dalai Lama) in 1477. Built on a sacred burial site, it has the tallest gilded copper image of the Buddha Maitreya. The monastery

The monks and lamas conduct the festival at Derge Gonchen monastery in Tibet. This recently renovated *gompa* is the seat of the Sakya Trizin, head of the Sakya-pa school.

is testimony to the fact that Zhigatse was the gateway to the later Buddhist kingdoms.

TRANS HIMALAYA:
THE TIBETAN EMPIRE

Buddhism transformed the various tribes and autonomous clans into centralised kingdoms, thus encouraging the development of feudalism in the Himalayan region bordering Tibet. The role that the Buddhist kings played in subduing the tribes, collectively called the followers of the Bon religion, can be seen in the history of Tibet. The expansion of the Kingdom of Lhasa corresponded to the spread of Buddhism. The western Tibetan kingdom of Gu-je (which included parts of Ladakh, Lahul, Spiti and

organisations that provided defence and administration along with spiritual guidance.

The Bhotias, an ethnic Tibetan community who migrated from the inhospitable plateau, are found in the border lands of India and Nepal. As they moved, they carried with them the prayer flag, the prayer wheel and the *chorten* (reliquary object), a vital part of daily life in the deserts, thus spreading the religion.

After the death of the Buddha, three schools of Buddhism emerged: Mahayana, Hinayana and

Above: **A Bon-po monastery in the western Tibetan kingdom of Gu-je.**
Previous pages 32-33: **The high desert near Tholing, the capital of the ancient kingdom of Gu-je. With its spectacular views, Tholing gives one a real sense of Tibet as the roof of the world. This place is near Tsaparang.**

Kinnaur) covered the area from Tholing to the borders of Kashmir, the forts and monasteries being evidence of its imperial control. The subjugation of the clans was violent and force was the basis of territorial control. The concept of the fortress-monastery was a product of this time: realising the need of the people, the monasteries emerged as politico-religious

Vajrayana. It was the Mahayana form that triumphed in Tibet and its surrounding areas since it was a socially more relevant philosophy. Apart from caring for its monks and novices, Mahayana Buddhism established effective contact with the community. Also, since the new sect wanted to gather adherents, it adopted a doctrine which allowed space for secular life.

During the reign of the Kushan king, Kanishka, the Mahayana school turned militant; the emperor took the title of Dharmapala, the defender of faith. In Tibet, this militancy led to the splitting of the Buddhists into four major sects: Nying-ma-pa (the elders), Ka-dam-pa (black hat), Drug-pa (red hat) and Ge-lug-pa (yellow hat), a process in which monks fought each other. Kye monastery in Spiti has a fine collection of weapons used by the monks at the time.

Despite the political and religious turmoil,

to last several months had to be carried for both man and beast. Besides, there were the vagaries of weather, unfriendly lands and people, strange languages, and the eternal fear of failure or death. The dangers of thirst, cold, sandstorm, snow blizzard and animal attack were constant. But there were compensations: the invigoration of ascent and the arrival at the threshold of a high valley; the clear water of a mountain stream; the flight of water birds or the sudden appearance of a herd of

A young monk rotating the prayer wheel.

travelogues show that traffic through this torturous land was fairly routine. Guidebooks listed the kind of goods that were desired, market towns where stopovers could be made and supplies replenished and the best areas to pick up new ideas, products and technologies. Travellers were attracted by the sheer pleasure and the adventures that the Himalayan highway offered.

A journey through the great Tibetan desert was one of great length and hardship. Food and water

wild asses; the welcome sight of a nomadic camp or a fortified town with its guardian *gompa*. The simple comforts of these monasteries were like undreamed of luxuries. Even when sea routes were discovered by adventurers, the overland route was not forgotten. It continued to be a busy thoroughfare for the towns established by conquerors, nourished by colonists and refugees, enriched by traders, edified by lamas and pilgrims.

Above: **The image of the Maitreya is in the centre of the temple to allow two rows of monks to recite the scriptures. The canonical library is situated behind the image in the *Du Khang*.**
Previous pages 36-37: **Nomads in eastern Tibet handling herbal aphrodisiacs.**

They continued to grow even as the sands claimed some of them in the course of time.

As Freya Stark has written, 'no mere river of water can be compared to this perennial stream of caravans, that has carried a half of human history, from stage to stage, from wasteland to wasteland and climate to climate, on the puny strength of men.' (*Rome on the Euphrates: the Story of a Frontier.*)

The most sacred Buddhist shrine in the Tibetan plateau is the Jokhang temple at Lhasa. It is a part of the legacy of strong cultural links between Vajrayana Buddhism of Tibet, faithful to its Indian inspiration, and the institution of the *gompa* which was basic to its

Kham or eastern Tibet contains some of the most rugged mountains and deep gorges. This fertile land, the most populated region in Tibet, is now a part of Chinese territory.

growth. Songsen Gampo of Tibet was the first king to exploit the power of Buddhism in the seventh century when his Nepalese queen, Bhrikuti, built the temple on a site divined by his Chinese wife, Wengcheng, as the power centre of Tibet. She herself built the Ramoche temple at a site that she, as a clairvoyant, said was the location of the subterranean crystal palace of the Nagas (gods of the nether world). Mahayana Buddhism crossed over the bridge to Central Asia, Tibet and China on the strength of the vast number of *sutras* and *tantras*, canonical works that needed to be housed, indexed and referred to. Thus, the monastery became the centre of scholarship. Once the mission of spreading the word had been accomplished, Buddhism became a powerful contemplative force.

adakh is for the most part a desert of bare crags and granite dust, with arid table-lands, no forests and few pastures. But braving this cold and inhospitable nature are settlements at an elevation of 12,000 to 16,000 ft. Ladakhi texts testify to the slow emergence of the Ladakhi plateau from the sea in the pre-Cambrian period and the consequent desiccation of the area as the Himalaya continued to grow. Early records substantiate the difficulties of travel, the major movement being those of Kashmiri merchants and local traders who monopolised the emporium trade.

Ladakh's historical records go back to 400 BC when Sargyal established the kingdoms of Ladakh and Tibet. *Gyalpo* or hereditary kingship was established in 333 AD, replacing the earlier feudal clans. The Lha-chen dynasty ruled Ladakh until the coming of the Mughals. It was in this period that the famous Buddhist text, the *Kanjur,* was written. Gyalpo Rinchin of this dynasty became the ruler of Kashmir (1324-27 AD) and was influenced by the Sufi saints who converted him to Islam. In 1531, Ladakh was invaded by Mirza Haidar Daulat, an adventurer from Central Asia.

In 1541, the Mirza was invited by Kashmiri nobles to attack Kashmir again. Mirza Daulat provided the route to the conquest of Ladakh, but the severe cold of Tibet defeated him as it defeated others like Zorawar Singh, the general of the Dogras, who ruled Kashmir between the sixteenth and twentieth centuries. Ladakh thus was a stepping stone to the conquest of Kashmir and Tibet. Its prosperity was related to its role as a provision station between Khotan and Kashmir. Adventurers knew that the monasteries were repositories of treasures collected over the years. At Hemis, one can see the strong room where the gold and silver are still stored. The room is built into the rock and difficult to identify.

The Namgyal dynasty was established in the sixteenth century, with its capital at Leh. Sovang Namgyal extended this kingdom to the outskirts of Lhasa in the east and Shigar, Kharko and Baltistan in the north, forcing the rulers of these states to become his vassals. Sovang was a great builder too; he built a great palace on Tsemo Hill which has now perished.

***Mane* walls and *chortens* in Zanskar inspire trekkers and traders to reach their destination.**

But the temple decorated with Buddhist images still survives and is worth a visit as it has a panoramic view of the valley. One can almost share the feeling

of the temple guardians as they look down upon the town. Sovang Namgyal also built roads and bridges across the rivers of Ladakh. He was succeeded by his brother Jamyang who was defeated by the chief of Skardu (in present Pakistan), Raja Ali Sher. Jamyang

LADAKH, LAHUL...

Lahul is a popular trekking destination because of the numerous snow-covered peaks that appear and disappear in the clouds.

Traders winding up their camp as they return home.

and Ali Sher made a matrimonial alliance by marriage with each other's daughters. The Skardu princess Argiyal Khatun gave birth to two sons, Singe and Norbu.

Singe (lion) Namgyal ascended the throne in 1610. He subdued Purang, Zanskar and Spiti and defeated the Raja of Baltistan who attempted to reconquer Ladakh. He tried to annex Tibet, but was unsuccessful. He was subdued by the Mughal army which came from Kashmir. Like all Ladakhi *gyalpos*, Singe's primary concern was to somehow buy peace with Kashmir and China so that Ladakh could prosper. Singe was also a devout Buddhist and he established the *gompas* or monasteries of Hemis, Chimre, Hanle and Timosgang. His campaigns across the valleys of Ladakh have enriched them with *mane* walls (stone walls on which travellers and pilgrims inscribe the Buddhist *mantra* or chant *Om Mani Padma Om*).

Singe's son Delden was a benevolent and popular ruler. The Rengmo *mane* wall leading to Leh was built by him. He also built the Shey palace and monastery which are still a major attraction for visitors. Once the Ladakhi army was defeated at Bodh Kharbu near Kargil and the Mughals invaded Ladakh, Delden submitted to the mighty Muslim power. He built the famous mosque in Leh bazaar where he agreed to get the *khutba* recited in honour of the Mughal emperor Jahangir. In the reign of his son Delek, Tibet invaded Ladakh. He retreated to Bazgo fort, and since the governor of Kashmir came to his aid, Delek took the name Aqbat Mehmood Khan and established a trade link between Kashmir and Tibet.

Once peace was established, the next king, Nyima became a great patron of art and letters. He established a paper mill and introduced hand-printing. Sacred Buddhist texts were edited and printed extensively during his reign. Many well-known foreigners visited his court at Leh and his palace at Nubra is still worth a visit. After his death in 1750, the subsequent Ladakhi kings were weak and ineffectual. Zorawar Singh, commander of the Dogra army, took advantage of the disorder to invade Ladakh in 1833. He entered over the Botkol pass between Kargil and Kishtwar, and defeated the Ladakhi army at Suru. However, a large Ladakhi army awaited the

...SPITI AND KINNAUR

Dogras at Mulbekh, so Zorawar made a strategic retreat to his fortress at Suru. After four months of skirmishes, the Ladakhi king appealed for peace and paid a large sum in exchange. Zorawar then proceeded to Lamayuru and subdued Zanskar. He built a fort at Leh which can be visited today, but in place of Zorawar Singh's garrison, we now have the Indian army. The mud fort is an attractive remnant of Ladakh's turbulent past. It is also a sad reminder of the end of the independent Kingdom of Ladakh, since it became a part of the state of Jammu and Kashmir by the treaty of Amritsar, signed by the British and the Dogras. Zorawar Singh invaded Baltistan and elated with his success, marched on to Tibet. He defeated the Tibetan outpost at Rudok, but perished at the legendary battle of Kardamkhar.

Tibetan interest in Ladakh dates from the seventh century AD. It was at this time that Lalitaditya Muktapada, the king of Kashmir and a great patron of Buddhism, defeated the Dards, of Indo-Iranian stock similar to the Kashmiris and Tibetans. In the tenth and eleventh centuries, with the establishment of the kingdom of Gu-je, Ladakh began to integrate with Tibetan culture. Lahul was also a part of the kingdom of Gu-je and continued to pay tribute to Ladakh until it was annexed by the Sikhs, a martial community from the plains of Punjab, in 1840. It was invaded by the Tibetans in 1055, and by Kublai Khan's troops in 1262 . By the seventeenth century, Spiti had come under the rule of Ladakh. The Balti penetration into Ladakh in 1740 extended to Spiti as did Zorawar Singh's invasion a century later. Spiti was coveted by the British for its access to Chang Thang, where the Pashmina herds were located. They traded Spiti with Kashmir and brought it under the administration of Kullu.

Coming back to Ladakh, though it is divided into three administrative divisions of Kargil, Zanskar

Above: Marsh marigolds (*Colta palustris*) heralding the beginning of spring in Ladakh.
Facing page: Pin valley, Spiti: It is the women who work in the fields in the high desert, the men being away trading or pasturing the animals.

and Leh, the geographical divisions are more important for the understanding of Ladakhi culture. Central Ladakh covers the villages along the Indus and the streams and rivers that form its tributaries. This includes the extraordinarily fertile and picturesque region between Lamayuru and Leh, which forms the primary tourist circuit of Ladakh. In the early days, visitors who came along this road were amazed not only by the wealth of culture and hospitality of the people but also by the splendour of the Indus river which adds life and colour to the dun-coloured landscape. The winter route was via Kullu, since guides and porters refused to brave the passes on the road from Kashmir for fear of whirlwinds in the moraines. Even today, 80 ft high walls of ice and deep glacial depressions make the road difficult and dangerous. Army convoys have added to the delay through a gate system which controls up and down traffic. However, there is a sense of achievement as one drives over the Fotu-la pass on the Kashmir side or the Baralacha pass on the Kullu side. *Mane* walls and towers stand as reminders of those who managed to reach their destination safely, and give courage to those who come after them.

Exchanging wool for grain, the traffic between Ladakh and Lahul has been undeterred by the difficult terrain. The hardy, well-trained ponies and sheep which are used by the local communities for carrying goods have ensured that trade between these remote valleys has remained alive. Protected by amulets blessed by the lamas, these wandering communities have maintained their oral traditions, even though the fortified strongholds of the past have now been exchanged for peaceable commerce and interaction.

The old road to Ladakh can be seen from Darch across beds of snow, small patches of herbage and narrow streams escaping from beneath the snow fields. The path lies over slips of rock hemmed in by barren and high mountains which darken the narrow valley, with no villages or signs of life. At the Baralacha-la, *mane* stones and streamers maintain a lonely vigil over a plain which marks the remains of a mighty mountain destroyed in all probability by an earthquake. Crossing

the pass, many have felt the effects of exposure and fatigue. The sun can be intensely hot while the piercing winds extremely cold. Sunburn and headaches are common discomforts. The plains below are barren, when not covered with sandstone rocks which are tinted yellow due to their iron content. Snow melt runs off rapidly at this height leaving the area dry. This is the Ling-ti plain that divides Lahul from Zanskar.

As the road zig-zags towards Zanskar, the mountains resembling towers, columns and spires—with caverns of great depth housing trickling streams of fine sand—are often mistaken for temples or monasteries. The black and slate coloured rocks make the area forbidding and it is a relief to reach the Rup-shu plateau and meet the

caravans of traders, and perhaps catch a glimpse of wild sheep.

On crossing the Tung-lung, granite peaks pierce the skies once again. Here, one can see the snow clouds advance and retreat between the crests of the high summits. The shepherd station and the monastery at Giah must have given refuge to many a weary traveller.

At Giah, one can see the close relationship between administrative and religious power: the traditional feudal chief is attended by the *Kah lun* or headman and the two in turn accept the supremacy of the lama or Kushok. This is a pattern repeated all over the region, although feudal titles have been removed in the modern state. Lamas are not mere spiritual guides but serve as chief municipal officers

Above: **Clouds descending on the sacred peaks of Kinnaur, renowned for the Kinner Kailash Yatra.**
Facing page: **The oracle (La-ba) at Matho monastery in Ladakh cutting his tongue. Every year, during the annual festival in March, the oracles are said to be possessed by spirits when they perform dramatic feats and also foretell the future of the people and the region.**

of the towns. They have represented the Ladakh region in the Parliament as well as on the Minorities Commission. Some of them have even served as Indian ambassadors to Buddhist countries.

Coming back to Giah's geography, poplar plantations are the only sign of vegetation near the township. The river is bordered by rock walls studded with quartz and crystals. The road weaves back and forth across the river. At Upshi, the Giah river falls into the Yuma, the main branch of the Indus. This is a small township of stone houses, golden fields and the recently set up Pashmina goat station, where research is being conducted to improve the quality and output of the famed Pashmina shawls. Ladakhi Pashmina is usually grey or brown and the animal husbandry department is attempting to create more of the white wool which is far superior and more expensive.

The road between Upshi and Leh lies through an uncultivated plain, now disturbed by the civil works for the Stakna project and road building activity. Snow-covered mountains enclose the plain as the road crosses and recesses between the the banks of the river. The poplar parks and fields closer to Leh are representative of the benefits of irrigation for the villages that lie near the river bed. Here it is possible to taste gur gur tea, a salted mix of Tibetan tea and butter churned in beautifully carved containers and served in equally beautiful samovars. Pinkish in colour, it tastes like weak broth and is extremely refreshing in the dry climate and replenishes energy at high altitudes. The Chemrye monastery is a short distance away and well worth a stop. Stakna, Mahto and Thikse are other monasteries that beckon the visitor off the road.

The extensive Chu-shot valley is a pastoral dream of houses and farms. The flat roofs covered with firewood and fodder, the walls washed white and studded with pretty balconies, are in sharp relief to the rugged landscape. The industry of women is evident in the fields, whilst the men lend a hand in threshing if they are not away on a trade mission. A typical meal of salted tea, wheat cakes, Tibetan

biscuits, Ladakhi apricots and Kashmiri grapes gives one a flavour of the past when Leh was an entrepot on the old silk route. It was common to see Chabba traders from Lhasa arrive on yaks laden with tea, caravans from Yarkhand carrying wool, felts and silk as well as sturdy horses with deep chests and strong forelegs which were prized in Punjab, a frontier region of India. Today, the exotic has given way to a Tibetan market where smuggled goods from Nepal and China sell alongside the produce of Punjab and Kashmir.

The road to Leh is a sandy ascent completely devoid of vegetation. *Mane* walls lead to a large *chorten,* embellished with copper, gold and silk, that stands guard at the entrance to the town. The south-east and north-west axis of the Indus valley where Leh stands continues to Dras and the frontiers of the Kashmir valley. To the north-east, at an elevation of 11,000 ft, lies the Nubra valley, 2,000 ft higher than Leh. The Rudok valley is another major watershed for the Shyok river, the winter road for Balti traders before the occupation of Kashmir by Pakistan.

The Zanskar joins the Indus river from the south at Nyemo. This is the great drain through which the snows from the lofty Tibetan plateau come down to fertilise the plains of Punjab. The speed and force of the rivers is due to the strong current and not due to their depth. This region is now being exploited for white-water rafting, a popular tourist activity in the Himalaya.

Given the broken surface of Ladakh, cultivation is possible at levels that border the streams and on

Above: **A vendor weighing dried tomatoes at the Leh market, Ladakh.**
Facing page: **A nun cooking potatoes in Karsha monastery in Zanskar, Ladakh.**
Following pages 50-51: **Snow-covered *chortens* in Leh, Ladakh.**

the lower slopes of the hills. The soil consists almost entirely of pulverised rocks; the mountains being primitive, the decomposition of granite clothes the fields with a coating of clay, sand, gravel and pebbles. The peasants therefore have to work extremely hard. But the interesting feature of this soil is that it yields abundant crops year after year, without any crop rotation or the need to leave land fallow. When fields are cleared for cultivation, the large rocks are left undisturbed, whilst the shards are collected to enclose the fields within the characteristic stone walls, to create

terraces which are then linked to streams or springs on higher ground for irrigation. Terraces on higher slopes are formed by catching debris from melting snows and leaving it for nature to act upon for future generations. This practice has helped to expand the inhabited area in these otherwise sterile valleys.

The general appearance of Ladakh is one of extreme barrenness: inhabited by poplars and furze or a few tufts of wormwood, dog rose and other desert plants. The rocks seem to enhance the barrenness of the soil. The climate is equally uncompromising. Frost, snow and sleet commence in September and continue till May, with extremely low temperatures between December and February. Ice coats the surface of the streams even in May and June. Between July and August, the summer sun is intensely hot and temperatures can reach 40⁰C. This heat rapidly matures the crops, and barley, the staple in

Left: **Traders return to Spiti, their yaks loaded with supplies.**
Below: **A herd of goats skid downhill as they return from the high pastures.**

these high altitudes, ripens for harvesting within two months of sowing.

Wheat, known as *to*, is a common crop and the Tibetan variety known as *to karma* is very hardy and productive. It gives very little straw, unlike the *hasora* variety grown to the west. The straw is often plaited by the women to make caps decorative items for the hair which are still used by the Drok-pas or the Dards who live north of the Suru valley. The six-variety naked barley, known as *sherokh*, is extremely suitable for the cold climate. It is alternated with buck wheat for a second crop in the intense summer. Since Ladakhi cuisine is flour-based, as is the popular beverage *chang*, a kind of barley beer brewed in every house, grain is the major agricultural produce. For harvesting, the plant is either pulled up from the roots just before maturity or cut with a sickle so designed that the hand of the peasant does not get scraped by the gravelly soil. Fodder is supplemented with lucerne, called *olh* or *champu*, which is stored on the roof of every Ladakhi house.

Onions, carrots, turnips and cabbage form the vegetable store and are dried for winter use. Rhubarb is another valuable vegetable found mainly in the Chang Thang plateau. Earlier, it was imported from China for its medicinal value and for dyeing. Apricots and apples are the only fruit grown but there are at least ten varieties of apricots which long ago were dried and carried by the traders along with *sattu* (barley flour) on the long marches out of Leh. Apricot seeds also yield sweet almonds. Saspul, on the banks of the Indus, is a beautiful village with its apricot orchards. The sarsinh tree yields a fragrant flower which is a prized form of perfume for the local people. Its fruit which resembles an olive or a *ber* (an Indian berry) is considered a delicacy since it is not found very commonly. When dried, the powder is used to make sherbet. Its fermented form gives a brandy which is popular in Yarkhand. Balti pears were popular as were the melons of Yarkhand. Now fruit is brought in from the south of the Himalaya, since the borders are closed.

All Ladakhi villages had willow or poplar plantations since fuel was required for the long winter. This practice has not been kept up since coal is replacing wood, despite the fact that it comes to Ladakh at a much higher price. The yaks of Ladakh are not as impressive as those from Chang Thang, but they are extremely docile. Similarly, the Purik sheep, kept for shawl wool and homespun cloth, are much smaller than the Chang Thang breeds. This domesticated sheep pastures in the mountains in the summer but in the winter is like a pet dog looking for table scraps.

The Chang Thang goat whose fleece provides the famous Pashmina for the Kashmiri shawl is now a protected species. The hair of the Pashmina goat is used for ropes, sacks and blankets for home consumption. Wild animals include the ibex whose horns adorn homes and mountain shrines (*nazars*) as charms to ward off the evil eye. There is the blue sheep and the highly elusive *kiang*. Hare and marmots, lynx, foxes and snow leopards can be glimpsed in the mountains. Road works have disturbed the traditional burrows and in summer it is possible to see these animals near the roads. A high altitude national park has been established to protect the snow leopard, an extremely shy animal. The Stok Nallah is a good spot to view some of the wildlife near Leh. It is a comfortable trek and a popular camping area. Ravens, chakhors, sparrows, linnets and robins are visible during harvest time, whilst the crested skylark and the snowlark are found in the higher mountains. Visitors have often mistaken their songs for human voices. Water birds and fish abound in the lakes but the Buddhists do not touch them.

The mineral wealth of Nubra and Chang Thang is well known, particularly the rich deposits of sulphur and gold. But none of this is being excavated as lamas have declared that it will lead to a bad harvest.

Leh stands on the northern boundary of the Indus plain. Once a walled town, much of its fortifications have now fallen apart. Only a few conical and square towers stand guard over the summits. The city is approached by a double line of sacred walls or *manes*. Earlier outlying houses had no walls and the doors were never locked or bolted. Now mud brick walls protect them. In the old town, which forms a heritage zone, the streets form a labyrinth with houses

running into each other, so that from the outside it is difficult to estimate the size of the mansion.

Generally two to three storeys high, with walls of unburnt bricks, houses are sometimes white washed on the outside but retain their mud plaster on the inside. Light wooden balconies on the upper floors add to their charm. The roofs are flat, formed by small poplar trunks, with a covering of willow shoots and a coating of straw. Although State-sponsored PWD architecture and modern city designs can be seen in plenty, Leh still retains its original flavour. In the traditional homes, rooms are large with low ceilings. In the houses of the rich, the ceilings are made of wood, often in a lozenge pattern, and varnished. Pillars holding up painted and varnished columns and capitals are replaced by capitals of straw and wheat in peasant homes.

The most remarkable building in Leh is the seven-storeyed Palace below which the old town straggles down to the riverine plain. Most of its wooden capitals and columns had been vandalised for fuel and weathering has washed away the murals. But the Palace has been acquired from the late king's widow by the archaeological survey department and is being reconstructed. The Palace is the prototype of the Po-tala palace in Tibet. Its 250 ft is broken by slit windows which are a source of light and protect against the cold. The courtyard near the *gompa* is used for theatre performances by the North Zone Cultural Centre, since the rocks form a natural amphitheatre.

The monasteries are built in the same way as the mansions, since they form a part of the civil and military administration. Each monastery controls a number of villages and combines the functions of a landlord with those of money-lending, trade and barter. Through the conversion of tribal customs and practices into Buddhist rituals, and in the transformation of the totemic Bon culture, the monasteries became more formal and institutionalised, and the infrastructure was consolidated with the increasing wealth accumulated through their growing

power. They also became the focus of cultural activities providing skills in literacy, medicine, fine art, philosophy and astrology. The monasteries' maintenance, repair and ornamentation have improved since tourists began to visit Ladakh in large numbers. they are raising money by holding festivals in the summer when tourists buy tickets to see the traditional Cham dances.

On the eastern frontier of Leh is the sandy plateau of Chang Thang, spotted with salt-lakes and pastures. The Rudokh fort and Pangong lake dominate the sparsely populated Chusul valley. Most of its people are shepherds who subsist on the sale of wool to Leh merchants. The road north of Rudokh leads to Khotan and to the south lie Sumgiel and Tholing, bordering Spiti and Kinnaur. Garo is the main connecting link on the Indus towards Ladakh. Market stops and shepherd stations make one feel that time has stood still on the road to Gartokh. This region still has strong links with Tibet although its lamas are no longer sent by the Dalai Lama, who is now in India. Formerly there was extensive trade between Khotan and Ladakh, but political changes have all but destroyed it.

The route to Nubra valley now goes over the high pass, the Khardong-la, but previously, it passed through the royal village of Sabu, a more pleasant and fertile region than Leh. The ascent on both routes is extremely steep and fatiguing and the difficulty in breathing is acute. Not just men but even horses and yaks are known to pass out at this great height. The road is a tumbled mess of sand, gravel and rock, the sun is powerful and the vista an impregnable wall of mountains.

The local people wear a plait of yak's hair across the forehead to protect their eyes from the sun. Digar, Lok-jum and Tagar, villages that emerge magically from the sand and rubble of the mountain, have red stone pillars outside every house to ward off evil. Here, sand ridges are formed and reformed by the high velocity winds that howl through the plain. Some distance away, at Tarsha, we come upon the hot springs which flow out of the mountain ridge. The openings are small and the water flows gently, in a clear stream. Simple baths

Double-humped Bactrian camels in Nubra, Ladakh.

Wild asses are a rare sight in the uninhabited desert.

made of stone walls collect the water and crusts of soda called *phul* are used as soap.

South-east of the Rupshu plain lies the old road to Spiti. Here, the soil is made of loose clay or micaceous sand scattered over with stones. Thin patches of furze provide pasturage for the flocks of sheep and goats. The *mane* walls are the only imprint of human passage. Whirlwinds are common on this plain: sand rises in a column to a great height whilst all around it the air is calm and still. The road passes the Tso Morari lake, deeper than Pangong but less clear. There is no sign of life here and although water courses fill the lake, its level seems to be maintained purely by evaporation.

The nomads of Spiti and Rupshu meet at Parang-la for their barter trade. The women are adorned in the traditional Chang Thang fashion with a *perak*, a head-dress shaped like a cobra-hood and studded with turquoise. The men wear caps trimmed with fur. The

Parang-la pass is one of the narrowest and the most difficult to cross, but it leads into a fertile valley. The Losar and Pin rivers create a broad valley which terminates at the steep slopes of the Dhankar fortress. The Key Gompa lies a day's journey from here. These heights have been the battleground for the rulers of Leh, Chamba and Kullu, since each one wanted control of the shawl wool trade.

Kaza, Tabo and Pin form a triangle which is the core area of interest and habitation in Spiti. A few landholding families control the political and economic power of the region. In recent times, development in the form of tourism and anti-desertification programmes have brought in changes that have undermined the barter economy. Family, culture and traditional forms of socialisation have given way under the pressure of modernisation. However, the Spiti tourism authority has taken up the challenge of the new situation and hopes to realise the benefits of modernisation through monitoring and controlling the pace of change.

The boundary between Kinnaur and Spiti is formed by the Spiti and Pare rivers near the Indo-Tibetan border. Upper Kinnaur is in the arid Trans Himalayan region. Three roughly parallel ranges run in Kinnaur: the Zanskar, the Great Himalayan Range and the Dhauladhar. The legendary Pandavas of the *Mahabharata* (world's longest epic in which the five Pandava brothers fought their cousins, the Kauravas, to regain the kingdom of Hastinapur) are said to have built many mud forts in the Baspa valley during the period of their exile. Hereditary oracles recount the oral history of Kinnaur, known as *chironings*, where myth and reality are hard to distinguish. For instance, the legendary king Banasur is said to have brought the Sutlej river to the plains from Lake Mansarovar; the topography seems to suggest the forcing of the river through the wall of a rock.

Kinnaur lies in the valley of the Trans Himalayan river Sutlej and its tributary, the Baspa. It is renowned for the Kinner Kailash Yatra, a four-day trek that is undertaken by both the Buddhists and the Hindus. The northeast-southwest orientation of the Baspa valley follows the Himalayan drift. The north-east is arid, whilst the south-west is a veritable garden. Entering the valley at Chit-kul, we can observe millions of butterflies and alpine flowers. Here, the Ge-lug-pa sect has a monastery; the mane walls and *chortens* leading to the rotating prayer wheels which travellers visit before climbing to the higher ranges. Legend has it that the Baspa was a pre-historic lake, and a hydro-electric project is set to make the legend come true.

Heaven and earth seem to meet at the Tso Morari lake in northern Ladakh, home to the bar-headed geese.

Kye monastery, the largest in Spiti, is a typical example of the fortress monastery. Its basement contains a rare collection of arms, a reminder of its turbulent past.

The Hangrang valley, which borders Tibet, is extremely rugged and barren in contrast.

Nomadic shepherds inhabit the small villages here. Kinnaur was renowned for the town of Nichar, accessed by the Indo-Tibet border road, which still provides rest and refreshment to the travellers. Kalpa offers incredible views of the snow and being less dry than the core desert, is surrounded by dry pine and chilgoza (fruit pine) forests. Pooh is a small town located in the core desert zone and receives 40 cm of rain and snow in a year. Barren mountains and large scree slopes give Pooh its characteristic lunar landscape. Moorang is another small settlement in the cold desert zone, although its lower elevation makes it slightly warmer. Traditionally, in each settlement, lamas were responsible for the care of travellers whilst the nuns carried on the tasks of chanting prayers, printing sacred texts and performing the daily tasks. Lamas continue to direct the welfare of the people regardless of their religion, whether it is the starting of the agricultural season, fixing the date of a marriage, the leave-taking of the nomadic shepherds, the birth of a child or the death of an old resident.

The life of the nomads, so frequently encountered here, is hard. They are simple, superstitious people who live in tents made from rough blankets. The tents are simply furnished with goat and sheep skin which are roughly stitched together to make winter coats. A few iron cooking pots complete their possessions. Goat-skin bags hold cream and butter for the salted tea that is an essential requirement at the heights which they go in search of pasture. Their clothes are made of homespun woolen cloth, woven in long narrow strips, one end of the loom tied to the waist of the weaver and the other attached to a stone.

Since cultivable land was scarce, polyandry was practised in most of the region so that the holdings were not fragmented. Myth links this practice to the Pandava brothers who married Draupadi, but the basis of polyandry is clearly economic. However, monogamy has become the norm amongst the urban communities today and is also influencing rural patterns of marriage and family tradition.

The mountains are all of blue slate, steep and naked to the top. Their barrenness and decay is frightful. The road follows the bed of the river and is passable only in the winter. In summer, the steep

Above: **At a height of 18,380 feet, Khardung-la pass is the highest motorable road in the world.**
Facing page: **Dressed in their finery, Ladakhi women in traditional home-spun brocade shawls and dresses and with *peraks* or hats make a colourful group.**
Previous pages 60-61: **The 17,200 feet high Nyertse-la pass south of Lamayuru in Ladakh.**

gradient makes the passes accessible only to the most experienced. The red hat sect of Buddhists predominates here; the people are extremely superstitious and each house has a charm in the form of a yak's tail or a flag painted with *mantras*. Stalks of barley hang upside down on every door. The *mane* walls which indicate that a passage is possible, are always crossed from the right side so that the *mantra Om Mane Padma Om* is not read backwards. Prayer wheels when not turned by pilgrims are moved by the wind.

Snow melt is scanty and therefore vegetation is of the dwarf variety. Clouds flit over the peaks as misty vapour and roll down the slopes, dispersing into invisibility. Brilliant minerals arrest the eye of the

traveller, as does the steep incline of the granite cliffs. Lamas have maintained the rope bridges and some temples have pagoda-like forms that indicate the Chinese influence in Kinnaur before it was handed over to Bushar. These are quite different from the flat roofs in the rest of the region.

Visitors are fascinated by the impregnable massif of the Himalaya because travellers have narrated, documented and added to the metaphysical attraction of the high mountains, their ridges interrupted by passes. Buddhism has endured along with the merchant and the conqueror, and created a spiritual aura that personifies the peaks and creates an interaction between the valleys. The dependence on barter economy, has created a sharing of information, ideas, technology and festivals that strengthen the ties between people who have braved the cold deserts, to live in the valleys protected by gods.

In the political and cultural cross-currents that buffeted the Western Himalaya, it was not just geography or climate that determined the regional identity of the people. The deepest impact was inspired by the spread of Buddhism. The lama and the *raja* made an alliance that survived the ups and downs of history. By imposing the law of Dharma, the peasant and the trader were made to support the monastic order. The wealth husbanded by the monastery brought about social stability as

An oracle inflicting wounds on himself during the annual oracle festival at Matho monastery.

well as the development of art and architecture through out the region.

Buddhism has had a tenacious hold on the people of these hill regions because the outsider is a temporary visitor. It is religion which has sustained the local people through the violent upheavals and the bitter cold, which determined the daily routine, the seasonal activity and the rites of passage. Even today, oil lamps are lit in the family temple, scriptures recited and *Om Mane Padma Om* chanted with devotion and fervour.

Buddhism developed in the Western Himalaya in two phases. The first phase was its introduction and propagation by Indian monks and visits by Tibetan scholars to the *mahaviharas* (universities) of Nalanda, Odantapura and Vikramsila. The establishment of the Sam-ya monastery in Tibet in 722 AD is credited to the Indian monk Padmasambhava, regarded as the second Buddha due to his role in the propogation of Buddhism. The second phase was what the Tibetans call the Second Advancement. This process was centred on the central Tibetan kingdom of Gu-je, which included the kingdoms of Lahul and Spiti and parts of Kinnaur.

However, it should not to be assumed that Buddhism spread through peaceful missionary activity. Between the fifth and the tenth centuries, it established itself and emerged as a pan-Asian religion through guile, conversion and the elevation of clan chiefs to kingship. Songsen Gampo, the first Buddhist king of Tibet, used his marriage alliance with the princesses of Nepal and China to beat his rival clansmen to the throne. It were these princesses who brought the political and religious features of Buddhism to Tibet. In time, Tibet became a Buddhist theocracy, with the Dalai Lama as the temporal and spiritual leader.

BUDDHISM: THE CREATOR AND...

...PRESERVER OF THE HIMALAYAN KINGDOMS

Ladakh is often called Little Tibet because the form of Buddhism here is closely linked to that of Tibet; both Leh and Tabo recently celebrated thousand years' of ties with Tibet. Though the Dalai Lama now resides in India, the Tibetan teachers have adhered faithfully to the teachings of the Buddha enshrined in the sacred Indian texts that pilgrims and monks carried with them far and wide.

The commentaries on the tenets of basic Buddhism as they were handed down from generation to generation, have been termed Nikaya, Mahayana and Tantric forms of Buddhism. Mahayana or the Great Wheel, which believes in the possibility of salvation for all, spread to Tibet in the seventh and eighth centuries. When Tibetan influence increased in the eleventh century, this form of Buddhism adapted to the Tibetan schools.

The appeal of Mahayana was that it allowed salvation through *bhakti* (devotion) and the vow of religious discipline, while living the life of a lay man. From this concept emerged the *Bodhisattva*, the being who held back his salvation so that he may help others seek the path of enlightenment. Once the Buddha became the Saviour, a pantheon of deities developed. This brought about a change in the representation of the Buddha as well as the social role of the monastery.

The hierarchy of deities, each approached by the recitation of a specific *mantra* (ritual speech), led to a personified form of representation as against the symbolic form practised earlier. Stories from the life and times of the Buddha also found expression in literature and the oral tradition of knowledge was replaced by written texts. The *Tanjur* (1,108 texts)

Facing page: **The elaborately ornamented and imposing image of Chhamba (Maitreya Buddha) at the Thikse monastery.**

and the *Kanjur* (3,461 texts) came into being which can be found in the libraries of the monasteries at Phiyang and Shashur. Knowledge of these scriptures was most important for the monks. The Chinese traveller Hsuan-tsang noted: 'He who can explain one class of these books is exempted from the control of Karmadana. If he can explain two classes, he receives the assignment of an upper seat. He who can explain four classes has lay followers. He who can explain five classes is allowed an escort... If one of the assembly distinguishes himself by refined language, subtle investigation, deep penetration and severe logic, then he is mounted on an elephant and conducted in procession through the gates of the monastery. If one of the members breaks down in argument, or uses poor and inelegant language, his face is disfigured with red and white and his body covered with dust and he is carried off to some deserted spot and thrown into a ditch.'

One is reminded of these words as young novices recite the texts under the vigilant eye of the abbot who walks between the rows of chanting lamas brandishing a horsewhip. The rigours of teaching brought to Tibet by the Indian *acharyas* (teachers) Padmasambhava and Atisa, and later introduced to Ladakh by Rin-chen Zang-po, continue in the monasteries of the region even today.

The core of Buddhism was the Sangha, the order, which centred itself on the *vihara* or monastery and the *mahavihara* or the university. This was the concept of the Triple Gem that the Buddha required of every disciple. The Sangha became an extremely sophisticated organisation by the time the large monasteries of Tibet like Tashilumpo Ganden and Dera were established. Modelled on the *bhiku* or almsman, the Sangha evolved from the haphazard, independent existence of the *bhiku* into an organised collective with common aims and discipline.

The *vinaya* or monastic way of life evolved from the institution of *vassavasa* or rain retreat which gave the wandering *bhikus* an opportunity to meet other monks and experience a communal life. From a temporary resting place away from the laity, there emerged the *avasa* or rural retreat and the *arama*, the urban retreat. The former required the monks to be self-sufficient whereas in the latter they could accept patronage of the local community. The *arama* was founded on land donated by the patron and had a boundary wall which enclosed the dwellings. This evolved into the *sangharama* where the patron could be invited to take part in

As the *sangharama* transformed into the *lena*, there was increasing formalisation of the monastic order. Apart from the teaching and care of monks and novices, contact with the community also had to be established.

As Buddhism matured, the teachings of the Buddha came to be interpreted variously which led to sectarianism. Buddhist texts were written in Sanskrit and required translation. King Songsen Gampo developed the practice of inviting monks and scholars from India to translate these works and also teach them to his people. Padmasambhava, who is represented in many icons in the monasteries of the region, came to Tibet in the eighth century. His followers are known as the Nying-ma pa or the ancient ones. Milrepa, a teacher of the eleventh century founded the Ka-gyud pa sect, known as the profound ones. In the fourteenth century, there emerged in Tibet a reformist sect known as the Ge-lugs pa

Left: **Founded in 996 AD, Tabo *gompa* in Spiti is the oldest living monastery. Only a part of the old structure remains today, since much of it was destroyed in a massive earthquake that struck the region in 1975.**
Facing page: **A Bonpo monk in dark retreat in Lubrok, Mustang.**

discussions relating to the teachings of the Buddha. The boundary walls soon enclosed assembly halls, temples and spaces for *parikrama* rituals. As links with the merchant-patron grew, monastic art and architecture reached great sophistication because of the resources that were made available to give permanence to these institutions. Construction which had followed the Indian prototype developed from wood and brick to rock and stone. Even today, the foundation is of stone with wooden beams, stone columns and mud walls.

or the virtuous ones. The first monk of this sect, Tsong-kha pa is renowned for his teachings and the sect is famous as the yellow hat sect. The Dalai Lama belongs to this sect. In Ladakh, a sub-sect of the Ka-gyud pa called the Duk-pa, along with the Ge-lugs pa, gained prominence. Hemis, which is the premier monastery of the Duk-pa order, controls several smaller monasteries in the Indus valley and Zanskar. Spituk, Thikse and Likir, the most historic monasteries of the region, belong to the Ge-lugs pa sect. Alchi, perhaps the most extraordinary Buddhist

Above: **Trekkers negotiating the steep descent to the frozen Zanskar river in Ladakh.**
Previous pages 70-71: **A Buddhist monastery in Mustang, Nepal.**

gompa in the Indus valley and justly renowned for its murals, belonged to an obsolete order, Ka-dam pa, which was prominent in the eleventh century.

Ladakhis are, however, not sectarian. They revere the teachings of the Buddha regardless of the sect, and villages have adherents of all prominent beliefs. The *Lha-khang* or sacred shrine in the family home is a constant reminder to the people to tread the noble path. Lamas come once a month to offer special prayers for the family. No event is complete without the presence of the lamas and all major decisions are taken with their advice and consent. The spiritual presence of the monastery and monks in the heart of the community is a representation of the spirit of Buddhism that dominates our consciousness when we are in the region.

The multifunctional Odantapura was the model for the earliest Tibetan monastery Sam-ya, which then became the prototype for all the monasteries constructed in the Himalaya. The central temple rooms were only a small part of the complex. Teaching blocks and residential apartments were enclosed by a wall that had four gates at the cardinal points. The *chaityas* (large arched openings) on the walls were covered with inscriptions. To the left of the main chapel door was a large painting of the wheel of life. The complex was built on the *mandala* plan (geometric diagram representing the universe) oriented towards the cardinal points. The central temple was three-tiered, conforming to the style prevalent in India, China and Tibet. In an adjacent enclosure, the demons had a space to devour humans who were not protected. Despite the destruction unleashed by King Lang Dar Ma in the ninth century to revive the Bon religion, it is claimed that he could not destroy the sacred images which had magical powers.

72

According to Tibetan texts, a goat-herd named Kar gyal, inspired by a Naga, began preaching a strange religion (a form of Bonism) which was opposed to Buddhism. Rin-chen Zang-po overcame him and also suppressed some of the *tantriks* (religious men with occult powers) who under the garb of religion were committing obscenities. By purifying the sacred religion Rin-chen gained the confidence of the people and Buddhism survived.

Most of the temples in the Second Advancement period were constructed in Kinnaur, Spiti and western Gu-je. In the year 990 AD, King Ye-she-od became a monk and built the monastery at Tholing. Rin-chen Zang-po was the first abbot of this monastery which was modelled on Sam-ya. In 996 AD, the duo founded Tabo. In 1010 AD, the two brothers of the king who were also monks, invited the Indian *acharya* Atisa to Tibet. They restored Tabo and set up the Mangang

gompa. These are the only evidences of Indo-Tibetan architectural heritage in the Himalaya. This period also saw the penetration of artistic and cultural influences from the Buddhist kingdom of Kashmir, from which we can trace the West Asian influences that are evident in the Western Himalaya and western Tibet.

The later complexes built in the fourteenth and fifteenth centuries by the Ge-lugs pa are however different. The multifunctional monastery complexes had by now become centres of rival political power, a manifestation of sectarianism. The fortified monasteries are a product of this period. These were perched on hill tops, hidden in gullies or carved into rocks or sandy plains so that access became difficult. A comparison of Alchi or Tabo monastery with Hemis or Phiyang makes this difference clear. Lamayuru monastery towers above Senge-sgang, where the boundary wall acts as a

A monk closing the doors in Ladakh's Alchi monastery, founded in the eleventh century by the 'Great Translator', Rin-chen Zang-po. This exquisitely painted and carved monastery is one of the most important centres of Buddhist art in Ladakh.

symbolic barrier circumscribed by a band of flames, lotus petals and a belt of diamonds.

The early temples were dedicated to the Vairocana (white) Buddha, always found in the centre with the five *tathagathas* (future Buddhas): Akshobhya (blue) to the east, Ratnasambhava (yellow) to the south, Amitabha (red) to the west and Amoghasiddha (green) to the north. The cult of Vairocana was rare in Tibet. The Vairocana *mandala* has 37 divinities including the *tathagathas*, the four *shaktis* (female divinities) of whom the Tara of the north-east is the most famous, eight subsidiary goddesses (*vajras*), sixteen *bodhisattvas* belonging to the Vajra, Ratna, Padma and Visvavajra families and the four guardians covering the cardinal points. Many of the decorative *mandala* motifs are influenced by Byzantine-Syrian art.

The Lha-lun temple near Dhankar in Spiti is well preserved and one can see the features of the early period reflected in its east-west orientation and layout. As the hegemony of the Ge-lugs pa strengthened, the socio-cultural links with India were weakened and the lamas reoriented themselves to Lhasa. Later monasteries were closely linked to the programme of territorial expansion. The defeat of the tribal chiefs was achieved by superior arms and tactics learnt through Buddhist cultural links forged with both India and China. Thus, the fort and the monastery became the military and administrative units and began to be combined.

The civil function of the *gompa* was discharged through the land ownership system, where a number of villages were under the administrative control of the monasteries. Monasteries owned land in the villages which they leased out on a crop-sharing basis. This surplus was converted into silver, gold and art treasures. The monastery extended its control to bartering, money-lending, trade and mortgaging. Tribal customs and festivals were transformed into *gompa* festivals. Tribal beliefs and knowledge were also appropriated and given a basis in Buddhist theology, not ridiculed as mere superstition. The system of primogeniture helped to keep the monastery system alive as every family in the village provided a novice. Thikse, Phiyang, Likir, Basgo, Lamayuru, Karsha, Kye, Tanjur and Dhankar all follow this pattern.

Above: **Monks blowing trumpet horns at the annual festival in Spituk monastery.**
Facing page: **The exquisitely carved image of Maitreya, the Buddha yet to come.**

The image of Padmasambhava at the Hemis _gompa_ in Ladakh.

social and economic links are thus strengthened.

Buddhist architecture has now moved away from the four-way orientation of Samya to the one-way orientation of the early monasteries facing the altar. There is a physical division here between the temple complex and the secular structures. The newer _gompas_ are built around a court with the temple placed in the centre. In Ladakh and Spiti, one sees a fourth type of complex with individual buildings spread across the top and sides of a hillock with no symmetrical axis or arrangement. This style was created more for defence than for symbolic representation. Spituk is a good example of this type of structure. Ridzong, Kye and Dhankar monasteries were reconstructed according to the new concept once they were taken over. Shankar in Leh and others in Nubra and Chang Thang also follow this pattern.

The new style is recognisable by the temple at the highest elevation, identified by the flags and umbrella on its roof. The walls are white and sloping, with slit windows framed in black and timber balconies at upper levels. The courtyard through which the temple is entered is the space for _cham_ dances and other festivals. The _parikrama_ is performed in a covered passage which surrounds the temple. This

In the newer monasteries, the _Du-khang_ or assembly room is the largest and central to the complex, since the Ge-lugs pa follow the Mahayana tradition. However, the rigid adherence to canonical laws of the _mandala_ system are now replaced by a haphazard arrangement of deities on the walls and the altar. The features of the icons are much more Mongoloid and decorative. Aspects like clouds, flowers and landscapes recall the Chinese influence. The interesting feature of these monasteries is that each household maintains a cell in the residential quarters, for those who join as novices, and the householder provides for their sustenance. The

tradition is linked to _stupa_ architecture. The corridor or space around the temple often has a row of prayer wheels at elbow level and it is customary to turn the wheel once, thrice or one hundred and eight times. There is a portico that symbolically separates the temple from the world beyond. The gateway is protected by the four guardians: Dhritarashtra (white, with a stringed instrument) on the east, Virudhaka (blue or green, with a sword) on the south, Virupaksha (red with a _chorten_, a serpent or a jewel) on west and Kuvera (yellow and carrying a banner in the right hand and a mongoose in the left) on the north.

Cham or masked dancers at the Matho monastery festival in Ladakh.

In addition, the eight glorious signs are painted in the porch. These are two gold fish, an umbrella, a conch shell, a symbolic diagram, banner, vase, lotus and the wheel of law. The *Du-khang* has images on the short wall opposite the entrance so that two rows of monks can be accommodated before the head lama who always sits to the right of the image, on a raised platform. Some monasteries have large images which recall the tradition of the cave temples at Bamian. The *Gon-khang* houses the malevolènt deities and has protective devices on the door. The *Gon-khangs* at Phiyang and Thikse have murals of monks of the old Ka-gyu pa sect and the terrifying Lah-mo forms of gods. The monks' cells, large kitchens and *chortens* make up the rest of the complex. These have eight forms: unity in diversity, magical power, descent from heaven, emanation of happiness, victory, nirvana, enlightenment and a bunch/mound of lotuses. Of these, the divine manifestation and enlightenment forms are the most common. The *Lha-khang* houses the *Kanjur* and the *Tanjur.*

Lahul is primarily controlled by the Druk-pa sect. The most interesting temple here is that of Guru Ghantal situated above the confluence of the Chandra and Bhaga rivers at Tandi. The monks officiating here come from Stakna in Ladakh. Its pyramidal roof is distinctly decorated with a *mandala* pattern and is older than the slate roof from Kangra. There is a sealed room which today contains only rocks. The dormer door is decorated with Celtic, Byzantine and Hellenistic designs, perhaps created by the craftsmen brought from different parts of the world by king Lalita Muktapada.

Monastery records, all of which have not been plundered or lost, have to be documented and translated if we are to have more than a cursory knowledge of the history of the region and its monastic institutions. They are bound to have a detailed history of the area which would enrich our knowledge of the region's heritage. At present, our source of information is the oral history of the local religious and social elite. International scholars have generally ignored the wealth of art and culture of the Western Himalaya because of their fascination with Central Asia.

The Kesar Saga, a richly detailed narrative of the life and times of the Ladakhi hero Gyapo Kesar, has been passed down in the tradition of story telling from one generation to the next. While keeping to the spirit of the epic, many new tales have been added which tell us a great deal about the changes that have come about in the cultural history of the high desert areas.

Ladakh does not need to transform to modern systems which are very difficult to maintain at such heights. However, no culture can remain isolated. As changes occur, the people of these valleys continue to absorb all new inputs into their social and spiritual framework. Where change has been of doubtful value, as in Spiti and Mustang, it has been due to unrestricted tourism. Mountain people have survived because they were capable of healthy adaptability, since they could control outsiders by limiting their entry. Tourism, however, is now penetrating into the private sphere and threatening the very *dharma* of their lives.

Today, the Ladakhis have shifted to the extended family system. They no longer follow the tradition of the *Khang bu*, where the elder couple move to a hermitage to allow the younger ones to stand on their feet. This change is a result of the increasing wealth of the land-owning families and of Muslim culture, which does not follow the noble path of the rites-of-passage. Changes have also occurred in the self-sufficiency of the household which used to produce all its needs. Today, the domestic market sells products made all over India and there is much more dependence on it than in earlier times.

What remains unchanged is the rhythm of the seasons. Spring and summer are the months of agricultural activity. Autumn is the time for collecting fuel for the long winter. Here again, tourism has intervened. The monastery festivals which gave people the opportunity to replenish their winter stocks have been shifted to the summer, so that monasteries can earn an income since they no longer control trade. Now families spend their time making ropes, weaving carpets and baskets and of course, running the civil administration which has been taken over by the

The Ladakhis have an incredible capacity to assimilate and change with the times. Primitive mud stoves have been replaced by copper or iron ones.

secular state. The *Kahlon* has been superseded by the district collector.

THE KARMA AND
DHARMA...

Mountains dominate the life cycle. The village that has a mountain in the rear is fortunate, because the snow melt provides the water of life to it. The June heat brings a steady stream of water in a happy, gurgling race down the slopes to the well ploughed fields below. Earlier, each village was divided into sections with its appointed *go-pa* who ensured proper sharing of water. Now the district administration has replaced the traditional system and the *scurrim-ba* or water festival which celebrates the first snow melt, is often the scene of conflict between farmers and hoteliers who are opening for the tourist season.

Where towns are distant, bartering willow for grain still continues. Barley from the uplands is also bartered for wheat from the valley, used for *tagi* (a form of bread) which is a necessary food at high altitudes. Families provide labour to each other on a rotational basis. Teams are established for sowing and harvesting and the rich and poor alike share in this communal labour.

Every village has its own artists and craftsmen. So important is their work that the status of villages is determined by the quality of work of its masons, carpenters, metal workers and painters. These products are not for the market, the souvenir trade is supplied from the government crafts shop. Tibetan carpets, *Chog-tse* tables (low Tibetan tables) and samovars and Kashmiri handicrafts can be bought in Leh or Kargil. Woolen textiles, particularly Pashmina shawls and tweeds, are also available. Chilling is renowned for its metal craft workers who were originally settlers from Nepal.

In July and August, villagers herd their cattle to the *phu* or high pastures. This is also the time for churning butter, making fuel cakes of animal dung and fermenting *tara*, a popular drink. After harvest,

Muslim women in Nubra bake *nans* or wheat bread. Though a small community, Nubra Muslims are a prosperous and influential lot.

...OF DAILY LIFE

Ladakhi roadworkers refresh themselves with a cup of hot salted butter tea.

At first light on a winter morning, large copper trumpets can be heard on the roof top of the monastery, announcing the annual festival. In the courtyard below, the ritual articles are laid out, while monks dress themselves in robes and masks to participate in the *cham* or masked dances. The large *thang-ka* (religious painting) is unfurled at the entrance. Hemis has an exquisite Chinese *thang-ka*, which is displayed every 12 years. Incense is offered to the *thang-ka* as the music gets louder, reaching a crescendo. The excitement is muted but the anticipation of the main event is palpable. Villagers are free to roam the monastery on festival days offering butter, oil, incense and money to the deities. Merchants set up stalls to tempt villagers and makeshift restaurants provide refreshments.

To the accompaniment of ritual music and chants, the Rimpoche (the head lama who is sometimes a *tulku,* a reincarnate monk) enters the courtyard dressed in his ritual robes. This is a rare sight for many since the Rimpoche is normally busy in meditation and prayers. Villagers who have taken a vow or promised a gift to the monastery on fulfillment of a wish contribute in cash and kind towards holding the festival. The beneficiaries stand before the good and evil spirits, as they perform their ritual battle.

Karsha is an important *gompa* in Zanskar and maintains the classic features of Tibetan feudalism. It holds a substantial part of the land which is tilled by the villagers who bring grain and butter to the monks. Butter is the ultimate gift in this dry and cold land

the dzos are taken up to the pasture again, time and weather permitting.

Winter is the time to sit around kitchen fires spinning yarn from raw wool and attending to the animals stabled on the ground floor. These days, families crowd around television sets, since satellite communication has brought modern entertainment to the towns. The carpet loom becomes busy as does the needle stitching new *gonchas* or *jubas*, long gowns favoured by men and women either in rough hand-woven wool or in Chinese velvet.

These days, families are warming their homes with a *shel-khang*, a glass room for passive solar heating, or trombe walls developed by environmentalists from traditional designs using the principle of vacuum heating. Fuel saving is an important cultural practice in the dry desert areas. The *kangri* (a basket with live coal inside a container) from Kashmir is also used to keep oneself warm though it is more fuel intensive.

and is the most valuable item in the barter trade. Rangdom is another important *gompa*. It was attacked for its riches by the Bakerwals from Kishtwar in Kashmir at the time of the partition of India.

Each monastery calls its festival by a different name. The festivals of Taktak and Chimrey are known as Anchuk while that of Shey is called Shrulpa. The most famous however are the Chheshu at Hemis monastery and the Dasmochhe at Likir.

The other important festival in the Himalayan region is Losar or the Buddhist New Year which is celebrated at the Palace. King Jamyang advanced the date of Losar as he wanted to invade Skardu on the day of the festival. It is now celebrated on the last two days of the tenth Bodhi month, which falls in December. Houses are illuminated and torchlight processions are taken out through the village. Tampe Chonga, celebrated on the fifteenth day of the first Bodhi month, commemorates Buddha's entry into his mother's womb. Prayers are held at the *gompa* and at home. Jipe Chonga, the fifteenth day of the fourth Bodhi month, is said to be the Buddha's birth anniversary. Devotees fast on this day, offer special prayers and illuminate their homes.

The 'house' is a symbol of family space amongst traditional Buddhists. Earlier, while the father moved out to a shack on the outskirts of the village, the younger son was ordained as a monk and the undivided property was inherited by the eldest son. Since agriculture was dependent on irrigation by small streams, this system worked. The maintenance of the younger brother in the monastery was the responsibility of the elder brother. The family built only one house which anchored all its members and did not put a strain on the environment.

Polygamy was common since a significant proportion of young males were ordained monks. The elder brother often married all the daughters of a particular family while the rest of the women became nuns.

Even today houses reflect the status of the family. The aristocrats have three-storeyed homes with several wings, each opening on to its own courtyard. Every wing has a prayer room, hall, sitting room, bedroom, dressing room, toilet and a servant's room. On the second floor are the guest rooms and the assembly hall which has a picture of a deity or a Buddhist *acharya*. All festivals and family events are celebrated here. The ground floor houses animals, fodder and the *chang* (strong drink from fermented barley) room. All houses in Tibet face south to catch the sun and this is the general orientation wherever possible.

Many rich families have country estates following the same pattern. Landed families build three-storied houses, the bottom three or four feet of stone, the rest of mud brick, each of which is fairly long. The roofs are flat because of shortage of timber, and covered with willow twigs. This is sufficient protection in the dry climate. Houses do not have chimneys since the heat is required to keep warm in winters. The smoke rises to colour the ceiling with tar. Chrome yellow and red ochre bands are painted below the roof for decoration and poles are put up in the front courtyard, with a yak's tail at the top to ward off the evil eye.

In the Western Himalaya, animals form an important aspect of the family's assets. Self-sufficiency in milk and milk products is essential for survival. The poorer families rely on nomads to provide butter as they can only afford to keep sheep and goats. Fodder is not plentiful and the animals have to be housed in the winter. Animal heat from the lower floor (the *Tang-ra*) warms the upper floor where the family lives. The winter kitchen (*chensa*) is sometimes located on the leeward side of the lower floor. The summer rooms on the upper floors are much more open and airy. On starry summer nights, youngsters go up to the roof to dream sweet dreams. In winter, the stock of fuel wood is left on the roof which is also used for catching the sun on cold winter mornings.

Today, families have a smokeless *chula*, introduced by the Moravian missionaries. The tin flue helps to clear the room of smoke and the *chensa* is often used as the family room. All houses have a toilet inside and one outside for the use of visitors.

Lahul houses are larger because the extended family system is prevalent here. Younger sons also remain at home and do not join the monastery. While the family house retains its traditional appearance, 'typical' construction favoured by the government in Shimla and Srinagar is changing the face of Kaza,

A vividly painted mural covering a wall of Likir *gompa* in Ladakh.

Kyelong and Leh. Houses are located on stilts in the midst of fields greened by mountain streams, or in the labyrinthine town. Atop the hill, facing the village is generally a small votive structure which protects the village from the evil eye.

The Khosias of Kinnaur are Buddhists and live in the areas adjoining Spiti. Polyandry is common amongst the villagers, all the brothers being husbands of the bride. Marriages are restricted to *khandans* or clans which form economic units and are believed to be the regulation of the local deity. Buddhism

dominates the Kalpa and Pooh districts. Tibetan deities, Tungma and Milayung, are worshipped along with Mahasu Devta and his demonic relations. These are village gods which are approached by the oracle, who determines every decision in the life of the villagers. The village god travels in a palanquin covered with yak's tail. The *yatra* (pilgrimage) around the Kinner Kailash is an important event for these simple and devout people.

Lamaism is practised in Kinnaur. The *gyo-lang* are celibate monks who shave their heads while the *durpus* can marry. *Jamos* or nuns are also seen in large numbers. They do not have any restrictions on marriage but spend their time reciting the scriptures. Kinners believe that mountain tops, caves and passes are inhabited by supernatural beings, including evil spirits called *khunkch* which are passed on by the sale of animals. *Ban chir*, the ghost of the blue pine, locals say, can assume any shape and cause great damage. Homes are adorned with the horns of domestic animals to ward off these evil spirits.

Pooh and Moorang are alive with festivals throughout the year. Dakhraini, Flaich, Fulaunchi, Sazo and Suskar are celebrated with drinking and merrymaking, although their origins are lost in myth and legend. Dances like Kayang and Bonyungabu are also performed. Wine is offered to the gods and goats are sacrificed as a part of the ritual. Being tribal areas, brewing is a legal activity and the locals make delicious beer from apricots, apples and grapes.

The Lahulas closely resemble the Tibetan and Ladakhi people. Their dialect is also similar. The family forms the basic unit of kinship and as a result of the system of polyandry, the Lahulas follow the system of the extended family. The head is the patriarch, who is the most competent amongst the senior members of the family. He is called the *yundo* and his wife the *yundamo*. Lahulas revere their elders. Families are part of clans or *rhus*. These clans divide the village into units, which then live and work closely. Marriage within the clan is not permitted. However, the mother's family is outside the clan, and this cross-cousin marriage is favoured. The Lahulas are egalitarian and do not discriminate on the basis of caste. They restrict themselves to their own valley. Polyandry has survived into modern times because of the socio-economic poverty of the region and the harsh physical conditions. It has also helped check population pressure on small landholdings. Women are given equal status in society. Divorce is not common but when it occurs, the husband has to pay compensation to the woman if she does not remarry.

Hinduism and Buddhism are closely linked in Lahul. At the temple of Trilokinath in Tandi, the same image is worshipped by the Hindus as Shiva and by the Buddhists as Avilokateshwara. Pilgrims from Spiti and Ladakh also come to worship here. Halda or Losar is a popular festival. Celebrated in January, it is akin to Diwali, the Hindu festival of lamps. Siskar Apa, the goddess of wealth in the Buddhist pantheon, is worshipped like Lakshmi, her Hindu counterpart.

The metal workers of Chilling have handed down their craft from generation to generation.

The Leh bazaar is where women sell vegetables, gossip and refresh themselves with *chang* or barley beer (see the white bottle).

Torchlight processions are taken out through towns and villages and all the people meet at a spot determined by the lamas, where a bonfire is lit. Drinking, feasting and dancing are the secular part of the ritual.

Spiti is a Buddhist stronghold. The monasteries control daily life and some of the most important monasteries are located here. In 1996, Tabo monastery celebrated its 1,000th anniversary. People from all over the country came to worship, led by the Dalai Lama. Said to be one of the 108 monasteries constructed by the great translator, Rinchin-Tsang-po in his propagation of the Buddhist faith in the Himalaya, Tabo is renowned all through the world. It is not on the crown of a hill and its mud-plastered walls merge into the countryside. Inside, in the dark halls, life-size images mounted on high platforms surround the visitors. Miniature panels, including the famous 1,000 Buddhas, can be seen on the walls.

Bumkhor is another important festival when religious books are carried around the fields. The procession is lead by a lama who chants *mantras* to ensure a plentiful harvest. The villagers gather around to offer prayers, food and *chang*.

The Ladarch and Pori fairs are well-attended by the farming community as well as the nomads. People dress in the particular style of their valley and the dances also reflect the costumes and masks of the region. The Chandra, the Bhaga and the Chenab valleys have their own fairs and festivals, since each area has subsisted through these interlinks. However, the mobility of the people has had cross-cultural influences in all the valleys.

The Muslim and Christian communities that have become a part of the Buddhist world celebrate their own festivals like Id and Christmas, but the folk form of celebration gathers all the communities together in a bond of fun and frolic.

To our city-bred, 'scientific' minds, the common fears of the people and their popular imagination, their traditional medical systems (the inspiration for *ayurveda*), rituals and taboos may seem quaint, archaic, exotic or simply out-of-date. However, Buddhism has an integral spirituality, a holistic world within which it seems plausible to live one's life according to the wisdom of the lamas and the regulations of the ancestors, who have created a sustainable world where others have feared to tread.

The Kali Gandhak valley is perhaps the most dramatic region in the Himalaya. The river pierces the Dhaulagiri and Annapurna ranges and one can actually see evidence of the great thrust fault that is said to have given such immense height to the Himalaya. As one climbs the valley, the humid and sub-tropical weather gives way to the cold and the arid. Along with the climatic change, there is also a transformation in the cultural and agricultural practices.

The dry cold winds that blow from the Tibetan plateau rush through this valley whose walls rise to over 5,000 meters. Jomosom, the entrance to the Mustang valley, is thus subjected to swirling, blustery dust storms made more intense due to the surface conditions. In the bygone days, this was the traditional route to Tibet. As one travels from Jomosom to Thanti, the valley widens out and one can see Tukche set in the dusty, arid landscape, like a speck of sand below an azure sky; the land mass pushing into the heart of Asia. Amonite fragments and fossils in the rock add a black outline to the sun-dazed eyes. This region is known as Thak Khola, after the Thakals who have peopled this natural corridor to give economic and cultural access to the landlocked Tibetan plateau.

This corridor is a path for pilgrims as well as for nature-lovers. The Tibeto-Nepalese tribes who have made their home here are mainly Sherpas and Thakals. They speak a Tibetan dialect and follow the lamaist tradition of Buddhism. Their two-storeyed houses, *chang* and *tsampa* meals and their art of story-telling are reminiscent of the simplicity of the old way of life. Khamba tribes from Tibet have also settled in the Mustang valley, after the flight of the Dalai Lama from Tibet.

From Muktinath, where the temple of Jwala Mai has a natural flame burning constantly, pilgrims take the route to the Kali Gandhak valley. Called the Black River, the Krishna Gandaki rises in a lake on the Tibetan plateau and flows down to the Ganges. This is an important trade route in the Himalaya. Thakal traders control this trade link, their pack animals loaded with salt. They survive on *rakshi*, a strong brew of rice and millet. This route is, however, misused by the Khambas for smuggling rare and valuable artifacts from Tibet.

The windswept plain of Mustang at an incredible height of 12,400 feet.

Tukche is the main resting point between the two mountain ranges. The valley floor is flat with incredibly steep walls of rock rising on all sides. The

MUSTANG:
THE LAND OF...

dust bowl of the Himalaya lies just beyond this insignificant outpost. At night, as the light flickers in the cold wind, stories of Yeti are common around camp fires. A mythical beast, the Yeti is either an ape or a bear which lost its natural habitat when the Himalaya rose. The locals believe that whoever sees it will be possessed by evil spirits. Yeti lore goes beyond mere footprints, it includes the stealing of yak and kidnapping of young girls.

The pass at Nisango-la is a 15,000 ft wall of red earth beyond which the desert flourishes. Virtually treeless, the villagers in this region have a hard life.

They trek for days looking for fuel wood. The winter is so bitterly cold that it is difficult to keep warm.

Mustang is a remote enclave of western Nepal. Its capital, Lo Manthang lies at a height of 12,400 ft on a windswept plain, far from any road leading to the modern world. Its small community of herdsmen leave their white-washed homes early to reach the pastures. Some who own land go past the walls of the town to the terraced fields. The rest of the region is a desert of scree and dirt, an expanse of gorges and cliffs, where every drop of water is treasured. Till recently, Mustang was closed to outsiders because it became a launching pad for Tibetan resistance. Closure led to the severance of its traditional ties with Tibet. The monks from the monasteries in Mustang now study in Nepal or India but this has diluted the rural culture of the people.

As in the rest of the Himalaya, in Mustang too, the traditional power of the king has been undermined by the police, bureaucrats and teachers of the government. The 600 year old tradition of Mustang is best illustrated by its Tiji festival, a spring rite. The copper horns herald the beginning of the festival as the abbot, dressed in ceremonial robes, emerges from the gate of the walled capital town. Five monks follow behind, carrying bowls of water containing evil spirits. The spirits are believed have been captured in the three days of dancing and singing that preceded the beginning of the

Tibetans at the Marpha Tibetan Refugee Camp in Kali Gandaki. Even in camp, these Tibetans recreate their traditional kitchen, with the tea urn and kettle, knitting and stitching.

...PEACE
AND FRUGALITY

cleansing rites. The king, adorned in a golden robe with a turquoise ear-ring—that symbolises membership to the court of the Dalai Lamas—fires his gun in the air. The joyous crowds from distant villages watch the bowls being dashed to the ground one by one, symbolising the destruction of the forces of fire, flood, drought, famine and earthquake. As the crowds return to the village, they jump over the ceremonial fire lit at the gate so that the bad spirits do not re-enter the village.

The abbot of the monastery, a lama since he was eleven years old, explains that the Tiji is a rite of peace that encompasses all faiths. Tourism has undermined its sacred significance and most people view it as a spectacle, a touch of local colour or a remnant of the past. As the *thang-ka* of the Vairocana Buddha is unfurled, the entertainment value overshadows the ancient rite of asking for blessings. Today, an airstrip has been constructed at Jomosom, but it is still a nine-day trek to Lo Manthang at the top of the valley, located between the ancient monasteries of Luri to the south and Chudzong to the north. Village houses are adorned with 'spirit catchers'.

Prayer flags fluttering over the Yangsha Tibetan Refugee Camp. The red structure on the far left is the Yangsha *gompa*.

DOLPA in the western region of Nepal has been rarely visited because it adjoins areas which have been designated as restricted. However, its scenic beauty and historical importance are as rich as the Kathmandu or Pokhra valleys. Bordering Tibet, this valley is enclosed by a ring of massive mountains which kept it culturally and environmentally secure. Dolpa become a part of Nepal 200 years ago when the Gorkhas gained control. But its cultural life remains closely linked to Tibetan Buddhism even today.

Shey and Ban-Thang are the principal valleys where the sparse population of Rangbar, the 'valley farmers' and the Drok, nomadic herdsmen, eke out a living at elevations beyond 4,000 meters. Air services are available to Jamla, the fourteenth century capital of the Khasa Mallas who controlled the area from Taklakhar in western Tibet to the Terai. The town has several fine temples which are proof of its golden past. However, the flights are not very frequent and food and accommodation is extremely basic.

Dolpa closely resembles Ladakh and Spiti with high winds swirling around the village before noon.

Above: **A Dolpa girl peeping out of her window.**
Below: **Hemmed in by steep mountains lies the Dolpa valley in western Nepal.**
Facing page: **The Phoksumdo Lake in Dolpa valley, Nepal.**

North of the valley is the Shey Phoksumdo National Park. Established in 1981, it is Nepal's biggest national park and straddles the Dolpa and Mugu districts and extends across the Kanji Roba Himal to the Tibetan border. This region has peaks over 6,000 meters in height and a variety of environments ranging from

that of the lower Himalaya to the arid vastness of the southern Tibetan plateau. Animals which have adapted to the high cold desert climate like the gazelle and the wild yak thrive here. But the pride of the region is of course the snow leopard, an endangered species found commonly at high attitudes in the mountain ranges that surround Central Asia. The main attractions of the park are the lake and the 1,000 year old Shey *gompa* which attract pilgrims from all over the Dolpa district. Its principal festival takes place on the Purnima (full moon) day in August every year when pilgrims circumambulate the Shey mountain on three consecutive days. From Phoksumdo, we follow the river to the village of Pungmi and towards the lush meadows to view the spectacular Kajmera peaks.

These relatively isolated villages are peopled by a variety of ethnic groups who have evolved a distinct culture. Their dances are extremely liberal and include the Ghatu which is performed by young virgins on Buddha Purnima day (the Buddha's birthday). This dance is influenced by Tantricism as the dancers fall into a trance during the performance. Village houses painted in yellow indicate the wealth of the monks while those washed in white belong to the lay population. This region is extremely difficult to enter since there are no roads and much of the trekking is over 3,000 meters high.

Above: **The fearsome tantric image of Mahakala in Mustang, Nepal. *Previous pages 92-93:* The Indus flows towards the fortified town of Leh. The old watch towers that top the mountains are now in ruins as sand and scree covered slopes bring the desert to the outskirts of the township.**

excitement of watching Indian movies on the video and carrying back posters to decorate their mud walls. The four-storey high palace approached by a wooden staircase and guarded by a prayer wheel is an impressive structure. Hierarchy still survives in Mustang. No one can sit on a platform higher than that of the king, the descendent of Ame Pal who united the warring tribes in 1380. There is also a caste system. Butchers and blacksmiths are considered unclean and therefore forbidden entry into the house. The poverty of the people and intrusion of the central government in civic affairs have undermined the culture. The ecological and cultural fragility of Mustang is further endangered by the entry of tourists. Two decades have brought greater changes than the hundreds of years that have gone by.

At its peak, the rulers of Mustang patronised art and scholarship that all Buddhist kingdoms in the Western Himalaya are known for. The 40 ft high gilded statue of the Maitreya Buddha in the Jampa temple at Lo Manthang is a living reminder of the cultural heights that the artists of Mustang had achieved. *Mane* walls and *chortens* guard the walls of the villages in the valley. Ornately-bound scriptural texts are found in the wayside monasteries. Temples and *gompas* hum with the sound of Buddhist chanting. However, the independent kingdom

The ancient trade of grain and salt has been replaced by trading sweaters from Punjab and Assam. This has helped those who have remained behind to buy articles of daily use from the market. The attractions of the southern valleys include the

of Mustang ceased to exist when it was incorporated into the Kingdom of Nepal in the eighteenth century. Since then, the Buddhist heritage is in decay, people have neither the time nor the money for its survival.

Villages cluster near the river, forming an oasis. The ochre walls indicate the monastery.

Agricultural practices remain traditional. In the post-summer harvest, wheat is winnowed with cries to the wind to take away the chaff. A good harvest is the resullt of not only the hard work of the farmer and his yak, but the successful driving away of demons during Tiji. The grain is stored in sacks made from yaks' hair; and dung is collected in baskets to make cakes for the winter ahead.

As one leaves the village, the parting rite is performed. Lung-ta Tang-en involves lighting a fire with juniper wood and incense. As the fire burns, scraps of cloth on which prayers have been written are thrown to the wind that howls through the gorge. As in other parts of the Himalaya, the prayers express the hope that the visitor may return home safely.

As stubborn as the yak which can survive the thin air and on meagre forage, the farmers of Mustang are a hardy lot. Their barter system includes dried yak dung exchanged for the farmer's grain. Herdsmen come down from their tented world, their goatskin bags full of yak butter. With this money, they shop in the market or buy household utensils on the trade route. The sight of the terraced fields greened by narrow irrigation channels must be welcome after the long trek through frost-hardened mountains. Milking closely bunched goats and bringing to life fields of grain, the herders and farmers tend their resources with great care. How long this caution will last, with the new trends from the plains coming in, remains to be seen. At the moment Mustang remains a hidden corner, a lost world, a caravan *serai*.

As our journey through the Himalayan Desert comes to an end, the universal spirit of love and compassion that permeates the high valleys, the mud-walled villages and the meditative peace of the *gompas* lives on.

PHOTO CREDITS